CONTEMPORARY
Black
Biography

ISSN-1058-1316

CONTEMPORARY

*B*lack
*B*iography

Profiles from the International Black Community

Volume 52

THOMSON

GALE

Detroit • New York • San Francisco • San Diego • New Haven, Conn. • Waterville, Maine • London • Munich

Contemporary Black Biography, Volume 52

Sara and Tom Pendergast

Project Editor
Pamela M. Kalte

Image Research and Acquisitions
Robyn V. Young

Editorial Support Services
Nataliya Mikheyeva

Rights and Permissions
Margie Abendroth, Jackie Jones, Tim Sisler

Manufacturing
Dorothy Maki, Rhonda Dover

Composition and Prepress
Mary Beth Trimper, Gary Leach

Imaging
Lezlie Light, Mike Logusz

ISBN 0-7876-7924-0
ISSN 1058-1316

Printed in the United States of America
10 9 8 7 6 5 4 3 2 1

Advisory Board

Contents

Introduction

Contemporary Black Biography provides informative biographical profiles of the important and influential persons of African heritage who form the international black community: men and women who have changed today's world and are shaping tomorrow's. *Contemporary Black Biography* covers persons of various nationalities in a wide variety of fields, including architecture, art, business, dance, education, fashion, film, industry, journalism, law, literature, medicine, music, politics and government, publishing, religion, science and technology, social issues, sports, television, theater, and others. In addition to in-depth coverage of names found in today's headlines, *Contemporary Black Biography* provides coverage of selected individuals from earlier in this century whose influence continues to impact on contemporary life. *Contemporary Black Biography* also provides coverage of important and influential persons who are not yet household names and are therefore likely to be ignored by other biographical reference series. Each volume also includes listee updates on names previously appearing in *CBB*.

Designed for Quick Research and Interesting Reading

- **Attractive page design** incorporates textual subheads, making it easy to find the information you're looking for.

- **Easy-to-locate data sections** provide quick access to vital personal statistics, career information, major awards, and mailing addresses, when available.

- **Informative biographical essays** trace the subject's personal and professional life with the kind of in-depth analysis you need.

- **To further enhance your appreciation** of the subject, most entries include photographic portraits.

- **Sources for additional information** direct the user to selected books, magazines, and newspapers where more information on the individuals can be obtained.

Helpful Indexes Make It Easy to Find the Information You Need

Contemporary Black Biography includes cumulative Nationality, Occupation, Subject, and Name indexes that make it easy to locate entries in a variety of useful ways.

Available in Electronic Formats

Diskette/Magnetic Tape. Contemporary Black Biography is available for licensing on magnetic tape or diskette in a fielded format. Either the complete database or a custom selection of entries may be ordered. The database is available for internal data processing and nonpublishing purposes only. For more information, call (800) 877-GALE.

On-line. Contemporary Black Biography is available on-line through Mead Data Central's NEXIS Service in the NEXIS, PEOPLE and SPORTS Libraries in the GALBIO file and Gale's Biography Resource Center.

Disclaimer

Contemporary Black Biography uses and lists websites as sources and these websites may become obsolete.

We Welcome Your Suggestions

The editors welcome your comments and suggestions for enhancing and improving *Contemporary Black Biography*. If you would like to suggest persons for inclusion in the series, please submit these names to the editors. Mail comments or suggestions to:

The Editor

Contemporary Black Biography

Thomson Gale

27500 Drake Rd.

Farmington Hills, MI 48331-3535

Phone: (800) 347-4253

Hana Yasmeen Ali

1976—

Author

Ali, Hana Yasmeen, photograph. Peter Kramer/Getty Images

Hana Yasmeen Ali, the daughter of boxing great Muhammad Ali, helped her father write *The Soul of a Butterfly, Reflections on Life's Journey*. Published in 2004, the tome is less a recap of the three-time world heavyweight champion's dramatic career than a collection of inspirational anecdotes, spiritual reflections, and even poems that seem to illustrate why the elder Ali is one of the world's most admired and beloved athletes. "There are already so many books written about him," Ali told Vicky Allan of Glasgow's *Sunday Herald*. "And they're pretty much all the same…they're just recapping his life. Only, my father was more than just a boxer, you know? He has aspirations and many, many stories; he has virtues and morals that he lives by."

Ali was born when her father was one of the world's richest athletes, a major celebrity and boxing legend who was also one of the first African Americans to achieve such superstar status in the twentieth century. She was born in March of 1976 to the woman who would become her father's third wife, Veronica Porche. At the time, her famous father was 34 years old, a Kentucky native born Cassius Clay who first attained fame as a gold-medal finisher at the 1960 Rome Olympics. After turning professional, he converted to Islam and changed his name to reflect his newfound faith. He won boxing's world heavyweight title in 1965, but was stripped of it two years later when he refused to obey a military draft order that could have sent him to fight in the Vietnam War. He made a spectacular comeback in the early 1970s, and his legendary, hugely hyped fights—against Joe Frazier in 1971 at Madison Square Garden, with George Foreman in Zaire in October of 1974, and the 1975 "Thrilla in Manila," against Frazier again—entered the annals of sports history as some of the most notable events of the decade.

Devastated by Parents' Split

Ali never saw her father fight, but she does remember him training for his last two bouts in the early 1980s. Her parents divorced when she was nine years old, and Ali was told of the impending split by a child psychologist who "wasn't supposed to tell me," Ali recalled in an interview with *Birmingham Post* writer Hannah Stephenson. "She said to me, 'How do you feel about

At a Glance . . .

Born on March 27, 1976; daughter of Muhammad Ali (a boxer) and Veronica Porche Anderson (a model). *Education:* Two years of college.

Career: Taught school in Los Angeles, late 1990s; author and poet.

Addresses: *Office*—c/o The Muhammad Ali Center, One Riverfront Plaza, Suite 1702, Louisville, KY 40202. *Home*—Berrien Springs, Michigan.

your parents getting divorced?' I just remember blacking out. I don't remember my mum picking me up or going home. I think I blocked it out. My next memory after that moment was living in our new house long after they were divorced."

Ali's father was by then showing signs of so-called Pugilistic Parkinson's disease, a debilitating condition that left him shaky and his speech slurred. Officially retired from the ring, he sought to spend as much time as possible with Ali and her younger sister Laila. The girls, raised in the Muslim faith, lived in Los Angeles with their mother, but spent a great deal of time with their famous father. Ali admitted to inheriting a bit of her father's legendary confidence, when he would trash-talk his opponent to the press in rhyming quatrains, but both parents discouraged such superior attitudes. "I remember bragging a lot about him. I'd say, 'I can do whatever I want; my dad is Muhammad Ali,'" she confessed to the *Guardian*'s Emma Brockes. "That sort of thing. But at the same time, I was humble too, because it was instilled in me from a young age that I shouldn't flaunt things that other kids might not have."

Ali recalled that her father would often help out the homeless or destitute, even to the extent of paying for a place for them to live. He also provided well for his own children, who would number nine in all, including Ali: in addition to her sister Laila, there was a son, a daughter, and set of twins born to the boxer's second wife, Belinda, and several children born out of wedlock; two were nearly the same age as Ali and Laila. All of them spent summers at a western Michigan ranch where the retired champ lived with his fourth wife, Lonnie, and their son. Ali has noted that though marital infidelity was her father's weakness, he was determined to see that none of his children suffered because of it. "He made sure we all loved each other," she told Allan in the *Sunday Herald*. "It was good because it wasn't some secret to discover later in life."

Book Began as Father's Day Project

As a young woman, Ali spent two years at a Boston college and watched her sister Laila emerge as a talented boxer, despite their father's objections to seeing his own daughter in the ring. Ali taught school for a time in Los Angeles—where she and Kenisha Norton, daughter of heavyweight boxer Ken Norton, were roommates—and wrote poetry. She decided to write something for her father for Father's Day. "It's really hard to give him stuff because he doesn't need anything," she told Deborah Caldwell in an interview on the *Beliefnet* Web site. "The things that make him the happiest are books or things you make. So I tried to create a memoir. I was going to go to Kinko's and copy it, but my mom thought it was so good that she called a friend who is now my agent and had her look at it. And it got published."

That book, *More Than a Hero: Muhammad Ali's Life Lessons Presented Through His Daughter's Eyes,* was issued by Pocket Books in 2000. In it, she recalled her father's countless acts of generosity to others over the years, both large and small. "Yes, my father is a hero," she wrote in the introduction. "The world knows it, and I know it. However, I get the privilege of witnessing the little things, which in the end are really where true heroism lies. For example, I once asked my father how he finds the strength to do all that he does. He gracefully replied, 'Service to others is the rent we pay for our room here on earth.'"

That book spurred Ali to begin helping her father with his autobiography, which took over two years. "My dad has always wanted to write a book, but he never does anything about it," she explained to Caldwell. "He still likes to read his fan mail and a lot of people have a lot of questions and there's a lot of things he feels that he would want to share with the world." *The Soul of a Butterfly*'s title was adapted from one of the boxer's most famous utterances about his prowess over his hapless opponents: "Float like a butterfly/Sting like a bee/Your hands can't hit/What your eyes can't see." Its chapters offered anecdotes from his life, reflections on fame and fortune, and the profound lessons he has learned from his Muslim faith. "I conquered the world and it didn't bring me true happiness," the champ writes. "The only true happiness comes from honoring God and treating people right."

Ali's father is still active in many charitable causes, including the Special Olympics, and even traveled to Afghanistan in 2002 as a United Nations "messenger of peace." Ali even moved to Berrien Springs, Michigan, to be closer to her father, where she discovered an immense cache of tape recordings made over the years. "With all of the prizes, trophies, awards, and treasures that my father has received and given away," she wrote near the close of the book, "his greatness lay in the way he kept the recordings of his children's voices protected in a small safe."

Selected writings

More Than a Hero: Muhammad Ali's Life Lessons Presented Through His Daughter's Eyes, Pocket Books, 2000.

(With Muhammad Ali) *The Soul of a Butterfly, Reflections on Life's Journey,* Simon & Schuster, 2004.

Sources

Books

(With Muhammad Ali) *The Soul of a Butterfly, Reflections on Life's Journey,* Simon & Schuster, 2004.

Periodicals

Birmingham Post, September 30, 2000, p. 52.
Booklist, October 15, 2004, p. 362.
Ebony, November 2004, p. 29.
Guardian (London, England), September 20, 2000, p. 16.
Knight-Ridder/Tribune News Service, December 9, 2004.
Library Journal, December 1, 2004, p. 129.
Mail on Sunday (London, England), December 9, 2001, p. 42.
Sunday Herald (Glasgow, Scotland), December 12, 2004, p. 5.
Sunday Times (London, England), August 27, 2000, p. 4.
Times (London, England), November 13, 2004, p. 11.

On-line

"Muhammad Ali's New Spiritual Quest," *Beliefnet,* www.beliefnet.com/story/160/story_16045_1.html (March 28, 2005).

—Carol Brennan

Muhammad Ali

1942—

Boxer

Three-time world heavyweight boxing champion Muhammad Ali, known for his lyrical charm and boasts as much as for his powerful fists, has moved far beyond the boxing ring in both influence and purpose. Ali won an Olympic gold medal in 1960 and later tossed it into a river because he was disgusted by racism in America. As a young man he was recruited by Malcolm X to join the Nation of Islam. He refused to serve in Vietnam—a professional fighter willing to serve time in jail for his pacifist ideals. He has contributed to countless, diverse charities and causes. And his later years have found him interested in world politics as he has battled to keep Parkinson's disease at bay.

Born to Box

Muhammad Ali was born Cassius Marcellus Clay, Jr., on January 17, 1942, and was raised in a clapboard house at 3302 Grand Avenue in middle-class Louisville, Kentucky. He began boxing at the age of 12. A white Louisville patrolman named Joe Martin, who had an early television show called "Tomorrow's Champions," started Ali working out in Louisville's Columbia Gym, but it was a black trainer named Fred Stoner who taught Ali the science of boxing. Stoner taught him to move with the grace of a dancer, and impressed upon him the subtle skills necessary to move beyond good and into the realm of great.

After winning an Olympic gold medal at 18, Ali signed the most lucrative contract—a 50-50 split—negotiated by a beginning professional in the history of boxing, with a 12-member group of millionaires called the Louisville Sponsoring Group. Later, he worked his way into contention for the coveted heavyweight title shot by boasting and creating media interest at a time when, by his own admission, he was only ranked number nine on the list of contenders. Even from the beginning, it was clear that Ali was his own man—quick, strong-willed, original, and witty. In 1961 he told *Sports Illustrated*'s Gilbert Rogin, "Boxing is dying because everybody's so quiet.... What boxing needs is more...Clays." Ali knew that his rhymes and press-grabbing claims would infuse more interest and more money into the sport of boxing, and he was his own best public relations man. In February of 1964 he told readers of *Sports Illustrated*, "If I were like a lot of...heavyweight boxers...you wouldn't be reading this story right now. If you wonder what the difference between them and me is, I'll break the news: you never heard of them. I'm not saying they're not good boxers. Most of them...can fight almost as good as I can. I'm just saying you never heard of them. And the reason for that is because they cannot throw the jive. Cassius Clay is a boxer who can throw the jive better than anybody."

The following month Ali—then still known by the name Cassius Clay—fought Sonny Liston in a match of classic contenders for the heavyweight championship of the world. The Miami fight almost single-handedly restored intelligence and balance to boxing. Cassius Clay had been chanting the war cry "Float like a butterfly, sting like a bee" for weeks; he beat Liston in a display of beautiful, controlled boxing. Liston could hit with deadly power, but Ali utilized his skills and courage with forethought and aplomb. He won the

At a Glance . . .

Born Cassius Marcellus Clay, Jr. on January, 17, 1942, in Louisville, KY; name changed to Muhammad Ali, 1963; son of Cassius (a piano player) and Odessa Clay; first wife, Sonji Roy; second wife, Belinda Boyd; third wife, Veronica Porche; married fourth wife, Yolanda "Lonnie" Williams, 1986; children: seven daughters, two sons.

Career: Boxer, 1960-81; humanitarian. Began professional boxing career, 1960; first became heavyweight champ, 1964; boxing record: 56 wins, 5 losses, with 37 knockouts.

Awards: Olympic Gold Medal in boxing, 1960; six Kentucky Golden Gloves titles; National Golden Gloves titles, 1959-60; World Heavyweight Championship, 1964-67, 1974-78, 1978-79; U.S. Olympic Hall of Fame, inductee, 1983; named the greatest heavyweight champion of all time, Ring Magazine, 1987; International Boxing Hall of Fame, inductee, 1990; Jim Thorpe Pro Sports Award, Lifetime Achievement, 1992; Muhammad Ali Museum, Louisville Galleria, opened 1995; Essence Award, 1997; Arthur Ashe Award for Courage to All, ESPN (Espy) Award, 1997; Service to America Leadership Award, National Association of Broadcasters Foundation, 2001.

Addresses: *Office*—c/o The Muhammad Ali Center, One Riverfront Plaza, Suite 1702, Louisville, KY 40202.

fight to become heavyweight champion of the world. At the tender age of 22 Ali knew that he was something above and beyond a great boxer: He had marketing sense, political finesse, and a feeling of noble purpose.

Committed to Political Ideals

Throughout his career and life, Ali has always professed to want to help other black Americans—and he has, time and time again. When he returned from Italy, having just won an Olympic gold medal, he was so proud of his trophy that he wore it day and night and showed it to everyone, whether they wanted to see it or not. In the *Philadelphia Inquirer* Ali's first wife remembered him saying "I was young, black Cassius Marcellus Clay, who had won a gold medal for his country. I went to downtown Louisville to a five-and-

dime store that had a soda fountain. I sat down at the counter to order a burger and soda pop. The waitress looked at me…. 'Sorry, we don't serve coloreds,' she said. I was furious. I went all the way to Italy to represent my country, won a gold medal, and now I come back to America and can't even get served at a five-and-dime store. I went to a bridge, tore the medal off my neck and threw it into the river. That gold medal didn't mean a thing to me if my black brothers and sisters were treated wrong in a country I was supposed to represent."

While in Miami, at the age of 21, Ali was inspired by human rights activist Malcolm X to become a member of the Muslim faith. The following year Malcolm X said of Ali, as was quoted by Houston Horn in *Sports Illustrated*, "[He] will mean more to his people than any athlete before him. He is more than [first black major-league baseball player] Jackie Robinson was, because Robinson is the white man's hero. But Cassius is the black man's hero. Do you know why? Because the white press wanted him to lose [his heavyweight championship bout]…because he is a Muslim. You notice nobody cares about the religion of other athletes. But their prejudice against Clay blinded them to his ability." Twelve years later, on *Face The Nation*, Ali said "We don't have Black Muslims, that's a press word. We have white brothers, we have brown, red, and yellow, all colors can be Muslims…. I'm looking for peace one day with all people." Cassius Clay, Jr., was given the name Muhammad Ali by Muslim patriarch Elijah Muhammad; it was not just a name, but a title meaning "beloved of Allah," deity of the Muslim faith.

Ali retained his world heavyweight champion title in June of 1965 by again knocking out Sonny Liston, this time with a stunning right-hand punch to the side of the head. The knock-out blow was thrown with the astounding speed that separated Ali from other heavyweights; it had sufficient force to lift Liston's left foot—upon which most of his weight was resting—clear off the canvas.

As a Muslim and thus a conscientious objector, Muhammad Ali refused to even consider going to Vietnam when he was drafted in 1966. His refusal brought a tremendous public outcry against him. According to Jack Olsen in *Sports Illustrated*, "The governor of Illinois found Clay 'disgusting,' and the governor of Maine said Clay 'should be held in utter contempt by every patriotic American.' An American Legion post in Miami asked people to 'join in condemnation of this unpatriotic, loudmouthed, bombastic individual.' The *Chicago Tribune* waged a choleric campaign against holding the next Clay fight in Chicago…. The noise became a din, the drumbeats of a holy war. TV and radio commentators, little old ladies…bookmakers, and parish priests, armchair strategists at the Pentagon and politicians all over the place joined in a crescendo of get-Cassius clamor."

Although Ali had not been charged or arrested for violating the Selective Service Act—much less convicted—the New York State Athletic Commission and World Boxing Association suspended his boxing license and stripped him of his heavyweight title in May of 1967, minutes after he officially announced that he would not submit to induction. Ali said to *Sports Illustrated* contributor Edwin Shrake, "I'm giving up my title, my wealth, maybe my future. Many great men have been tested for their religious beliefs. If I pass this test, I'll come out stronger than ever." Eventually Ali was sentenced to five years in prison, released on appeal, and his conviction overturned three years later.

Became the Greatest

In November of 1970 Ali fought Jerry Quarry in Atlanta. His victory was a symbol of release and freedom to the 5,000 people watching the fight; Ali had personally survived his vilification by much of the American public, but more, he had reclaimed his professional reputation and prominence. Four months later Ali had the world as his audience when he went up against Joe Frazier in the Philippines city of Manila. There he fell from invincibility; suddenly Frazier reigned as heavyweight champ. "Man, I hit him with punches that'd bring down the walls of a city," Frazier said to Mark Kram in *Sports Illustrated*. Ali responded, "It was like death. Closest thing to dyin' that I know of." On September 10, 1973, Frazier won a rematch with Ken Norton and continued to reign as heavyweight champion. Returning with a vengeance, however, Ali fought Frazier again in 1974, won the match, and replaced his competitor as the world heavyweight champion. Ali fought Frazier once again in October of 1975, won that match, and secured his title. Taking time to reflect on the tumult of his fifteen-year boxing career, Ali co-wrote his autobiography—characteristically titled *The Greatest: My Own Story*—in 1975.

In 1982 Dr. Dennis Cope, director of the Medical Ambulatory Care Center at the University of California, Los Angeles, began treating Ali for Parkinson's syndrome. Cope and colleague Dr. Stanley Fahn later theorized in the *Chicago Tribune* that Ali was suffering, more precisely, from Pugilistic Parkinsonism, brought on by repetitive trauma to the head—and that only an autopsy could confirm their suspicions. After losing a 1980 title bout to Larry Holmes, Ali had exhibited sluggishness and was misdiagnosed as having a thyroid condition; he was given a thyroid hormone. When Dr. Cope made the connection between Ali's decreasing motor skills and Parkinson's disease, he prescribed Sinemet (L-dopa). Ali was shortly restored to his previous level of energy and awareness; as long as he took his medication regularly, he was able to keep the disease in check. In 1988 Ali told *New York Times Magazine* contributor Peter Tauber: "I've got Parkinson's syndrome. I'm in no pain.... If I was in perfect health—if I had won my last two fights—if I had no problem, people would be afraid of me. Now they feel sorry for me. They thought I was Superman. Now they

can say 'He's human, like us. He has problems.'"

In 1984 another of Ali's medical confidantes, Dr. Martin D. Ecker, ventured in the *Boston Globe* that Ali should have quit boxing long before he finally did—for the second and final time—in 1981 after losing to Trevor Berbick. His bout with Berbick was his 61st and final fight. By then Ali had been showing signs of neurological damage for over a year. Ali's former doctor, Dr. Ferdie Pacheco, told the fighter to quit in 1977 when he first saw signs of Ali's reflexes slowing down. Seven years later, Pacheco, a consultant and boxing commentator for NBC-TV, explained to Betsy Lehman in the *Boston Globe* why he feels Ali didn't quit boxing in 1977: "The most virulent infection in the human race is the standing ovation. Once you've seen that, you can't get off the stage. Once you feel that recognition...the roar of 50,000 people, you just don't want to give it up." When Ali initially surrendered his title in 1979, he was paid $250,000 to quit, but he eventually returned to his sport, perhaps as Pacheco suggested, because the recognition had become habit-forming.

Elder Statesman of Boxing

Toward the end of Ali's boxing career, and afterward, his ambitions took a decided turn toward statesmanship. In 1980 he cast his lot with the Democratic Party, supporting then-Presidential candidate Jimmy Carter. In August of that year, while in intense training for the Holmes fight, he found time to work the floor of the Democratic National Convention in New York City. He also functioned as something of a diplomat in February of 1985 when he attempted to secure the release of four kidnapped Americans in Lebanon; unfortunately, he and his three advisers were not successful.

During his career in the ring Ali made more than $50 million, two thirds of which went to managerial expenses and taxes. He said to *New York Times Magazine* contributor Tauber in 1988, "I never talk about boxing. It just served its purpose. I was only about 11 or 12 years old when I said 'I'm gonna get famous so I can help my people.'" Indicating his continuing desire to help people, in 1990 Ali visited Our Children's Foundation, Inc., on Manhattan's 125th Street. According to Bill Gallo in the *New York Daily News*, he addressed the children there, saying, "The sun has a purpose. The moon has a purpose. The snow has a purpose. Cows have a purpose. You were born for a purpose. You have to find your purpose. Go to school. Learn to read and write.... What is your purpose, your occupation? Find your purpose.... What do you have to find?" "Purpose!," they shouted gleefully in unison. True to form, one of Ali's favored inscriptions when signing autographs is "Love is the net where hearts are caught like fish."

Although Parkinson's syndrome has slowed Ali down, he still remains active—raising money for the Muhammad Ali Foundation and frequently appearing at sports tributes and fund-raisers. Muhammad's wife Lonnie believes "Muhammad knows he has this illness for a reason. It's not by chance. Parkinson's disease has made him a more spiritual person. Muhammad believes God gave it to him to bring him to another level, to create another destiny," she stated in *People*.

During the 1996 Olympic Games in Atlanta, 3.5 billion people watched on television as three-time heavyweight champion Muhammad Ali slowly ascended the stadium steps with trembling hands to ignite the Olympic Flame. Everyone was deeply touched, though no one more so than Ali himself. "He kept turning it [the torch] in his hands and looking at it. He knows now that people won't slight his message because of his impairment." said his wife Lonnie in *People*.

Ali has been blessed to meet with important dignitaries over the years, including with President Clinton, Queen Elizabeth II, Nelson Mandela, and the late Pope John Paul II. His travels are his main source of income, as he charges as much as $200,000 for appearances. He usually travels 275 days out of the year. Although he enjoys his missionary work and public appearances, Ali's greatest pleasure is when he is at home in Berrien Springs, Michigan, with his family—wife Yolanda and his adopted son Asaad Amin.

In Berrien Springs, he lives a modest life in a house at the end of the road on an old farm. He has a pool and a pond and a security gate with an intercom. According to Kim Forburger, Ali's assistant, "He's the only man I know where the kids come to the gate and say 'Can Muhammad come out and play?'" When asked if he has any regrets, Ali responds, "My children, I never got to raise them because I was always boxing and because of divorce," he said in *People*. When asked whether he is sorry he ever got into the ring, he responded, "If I wasn't a boxer, I wouldn't be famous. If I wasn't famous, I wouldn't be able to do what I'm doing now."

Even into the 2000s, Ali's legacy lives on in a number of ways. In November, 2005, after years of preparation, the Muhammad Ali Center was opened in Louisville, Kentucky. The MAC is both a museum celebrating Ali's life and career and—at Ali's request—a forum for sharing his ideals and beliefs, and for promoting respect, hope, and understanding. Ali has been the subject of numerous books and film tributes over the years, including the 1997 documentary *When We Were Kings,* but none were more spectacular than the 2003 publication *GOAT: A Tribute to Muhammad Ali,* a giant (20-inches square, weighing 75 pounds, and costing $3,000) tribute to Ali's entire career; the title GOAT stands for "Greatest of All Time." The work that is closest to Ali's own heart is his memoir *The Soul of a Butterfly: Reflection's on Life's Journey,* which he wrote with the help of his daughter, Hana Yasmeen Ali.

Selected works

Books

(With Richard Durham) *The Greatest: My Own Story*, Random House, 1975.
Ali! Ali! The Words of Muhammad Ali, edited by Sultan Karim, Harcourt Brace Jovanovich, 1979.
(With Thomas Hauser) *Healing,* Collins Publishers San Francisco, 1996.
I Am the Greatest: The Best Quotations from Muhammed Ali, Andrews McMeel, 2002.
(With Hana Yasmeen Ali) *Soul of a Butterfly: Reflections on Life's Journey,* Simon & Schuster, 2004.

Films

The Greatest, 1977.

Sources

Books

Early, Gerald, ed., *The Muhammad Ali Reader,* Ecco Press, 1998.
GOAT: A Tribute to Muhammad Ali, Taschen, 2003.
Kram, Mark, *Ghosts of Manila: The Fateful Blood Feud between Muhammad Ali and Joe Frazier,* HarperCollins, 2001.
Miller, Davis, *The Tao of Muhammad Ali,* Warner Books, 1996.
Muhammad Ali (photographs), Harry N. Abrams, 2004.
Myers, Walter Dean, *The Greatest: Muhammad Ali,* Scholastic, 2001.
Pacheco, Ferdie, *Muhammad Ali: A View from the Corner,* Birch Lane Press, 1992.
Remnick, David, *King of the World: Muhammad Ali and the Rise of an American Hero,* Random House, 1998.

Periodicals

Atlanta Journal and Constitution, December 13, 1988.
Boston Globe, October 1, 1984.
Chicago Tribune, October 9, 1984.
Ebony, April 1969.
Face the Nation (transcript of CBS-TV program), May 2, 1976.
Interview, February 1, 2004.
Jet, July 2, 2001.
Newsweek, June 22, 1987.
New York Daily News, February 2, 1989.
New York Post, July 14, 1987.
New York Times Magazine, July 17, 1988.
People, Jan 13, 1997, p. 40.
Philadelphia Inquirer, August 12, 1990.
Spin, October 1991.

Sports Illustrated, December 20, 1976; April 25, 1988.
Time, December 13, 2004.
Washington Post, June 9, 1991.

On-line

GOAT, www.taschen-goat.com/index1.html (June 8, 2005).
Muhammad Ali, www.ali.com (June 8, 2005).
Muhammad Ali Center, www.alicenter.org/heart/index.shtml (June 8, 2005).
Muhammad Ali: The Making of a Champ, www.courier-journal.com/ali/ (June 8, 2005).

Other

Ali (film), 2001.
When We Were Kings (documentary film), 1997.

—By B. Kimberly Taylor and Tom Pendergast

Amerie

1980—

Singer

Amerie, photograph. Wenn/Landov.

Amerie (pronounced A-Marie) burst onto the music scene at the age of 22 with her chart-topping debut album *All I Have*. A dedicated singer and student of dance since childhood, she graduated from Georgetown University before launching herself into a music career. "It sounds like a cliché," she said in the biography on *Amerie Online,* her fan-run Web site, "but I always knew I was going to sing. I always knew that music was what I was going to do."

Her mother is a singer and classical pianist, and inspired in her daughter a love of music. Amerie also drew inspiration from her father's record collection, starting with the 1960s Motown soul hits that would eventually shape the sound of her own music. "The most influential artists in my life have been Sam Cooke, Marvin Gaye, Whitney Houston, Michael Jackson, Mariah Carey, and Mary J. Blige," Amerie said in an interview with *The People's Urban Beat* Web site. "During *Thriller*, *Bad*, and the *Off The Wall* period...Michael was my favorite."

Moved from Military Bases to Center Stage

Amerie Rogers was born January 12, 1980, in Fitchburg, Massachusetts, to a Korean mother and African-American father. Her father's military career meant that her early years were spent on the move, living on army bases all over the United States and Europe. Rather than leaving her feeling isolated, Amerie says that her childhood experiences have helped her adjust to life in the music business. "When you are constantly moving around," she told the *World Asia* Web site, "you learn how to deal with new people and new surroundings."

Amerie began studying dance and entering talent competitions at a very young age. When she was 12 years old she attended a concert by female rapper MC Lyte and was invited onstage to sing. "They were a rough crowd 'cause they were throwing things, but I was jumping up and down," Amerie told an interviewer from *Soul Train*. "The bodyguard found me and lifted me up and put me onto the stage, and I just grabbed the mic, turned around, and I just started singing. And I wasn't afraid until I stopped singing!"

At a Glance . . .

Born Amerie Rogers on January 12, 1980, in Fitchburg, MA. *Education:* Georgetown University, BA, English and fine arts, early 2000s.

Career: Singer, Columbia Records, 2002–.

Awards: Soul Train Music Awards, Best New Artist, R&B/Soul or Rap, 2003.

Addresses: *Record company*—Sony Urban Music, 550 Madison Ave., Floor 21, New York, NY, 10022.

Earned Degree before Recording a Demo

Amerie's family moved to Washington, D.C., after she graduated high school, and she began to think seriously about making a career in the entertainment business. While developing her vocal talents and working on songs, she also started taking classes at Georgetown University, eventually graduating with a degree in English and Fine Arts. "A lot of people are surprised that I graduated from a good university," she told *Hip Online*. "It makes me feel good to have the degree and I think life is all about options and I think you can get further if you have more options. I also think that college helped me grow a lot. I think college is a really important time."

Her big break in the music industry came when Amerie met Rich Harrison, a Grammy-winning songwriter and producer who had previously worked with hip-hop diva Mary J. Blige. "We met in McDonald's, but it was actually our predetermined meeting spot because we spoke on the phone," Amerie told the Australian Web site *Groove On*. "I knew he was a producer, but I didn't know this guy, so I really didn't wanna go to his house, and I didn't want him to know where I lived, just in case he was a weirdo or something, so I was like, 'Well, let's meet at McDonald's,' and we met at a popular McDonald's." The pair clicked immediately. Amerie later told MTV, "We're each other's musical soulmates." After their first meeting, Harrison produced Amerie's first demo tape.

When executives at Columbia Records heard the demo, they wasted no time signing Amerie to a contract. While recording her debut album *All I Have*, she also sang on tracks by other Columbia stars such as Nas and Royce da 5'9". Though music critics were lukewarm in their reviews of her first album, a great deal of radio play ahead of its release sent *All I Have* straight to number two on the R&B charts, and to number nine on the Top 200. Produced by Harrison, the album smacked strongly of Mary J. Blige. *People Weekly* wrote, "Although Amerie's vibrant vocals are strong throughout *All I Have*, she still needs to develop her own artistic voice." Nonetheless, the single "Why Don't We Fall in Love" earned Amerie a 2003 Soul Train award for best new artist.

Found Sudden Fame and Furious Schedule

The album's success sent Amerie catapulting to fame. Her exotic beauty assured her extensive coverage in magazines and on television. Performing to sell-out arenas with hip-hop superstars like Nelly and Usher assured her a widespread audience. The sudden success took Amerie by surprise. "I find it weird to see myself on the cover of magazines," she told *Hip Online*. "I see myself as plain old Amerie and I'm wondering, 'What am I doing on there?'" She also found the workload disorienting. "You work so much where you feel like you are going through a time warp," she continued in her interview with *Hip Online*.

Despite a grueling schedule of performances, recording, and publicity appearances, Amerie found time to branch out into film work. She initially kept to singing, recording a couple of tracks for *Honey* and *Maid in Manhattan*. In 2004 she made the leap to acting when she landed a co-starring role opposite Katie Holmes in *First Daughter*, directed by actor Forrest Whittaker. "I want to do a lot of things," she told *The Crusade* Web site. "I really want to make my mark as an artist not only for singing, but also for writing songs for other artists. I've been writing songs since high school and I've been doing a lot of writing recently. For myself and also collaborations with other artists. I also want to write fiction. I fell in love with writing stories before I fell in love with singing." She flexed her writing muscles in 2003, co-writing and hosting a daily television for Black Entertainment Television (BET). The program, *The Center,* dealt with issues facing modern teens.

Amerie's second album, *Touch*, was due for release in the spring of 2005. The first single, "1 Thing," co-written by Amerie and Harrison, was featured on the soundtrack for the Will Smith film *Hitch*. The song garnered early praise. "What grabs you first is the monumental funk drum break that the track is built on," wrote a reviewer for the BBC. "... then Amerie lets loose with a song so 'up' and so full of life that I find it impossible to sit still whilst listening to it." True to her multi-talented nature, Amerie co-directed the video for the song. With the album's release, Amerie's life was set to do anything but slow down. Rather than be daunted, Amerie was thrilled. "I think I would say [my career is] more than what I thought it was going to be because I enjoy it more than I thought I would," she told *Soul Train*. "I didn't think I would enjoy the traveling. I didn't think I'd love to perform because at the beginning, I had such tremendous stage fright that I dreaded every show and I was just like, 'Why, why can't I just stay in the studio and just do pictures and videos?' But it's great, and I actually love life on the road too."

Selected discography

Albums

All I Have, Rise/Columbia, 2002.
Touch, Sony Urban Music/Columbia, 2005.

Sources

Periodicals

People Weekly, August 19, 2002.

On-line

"A Little Time with Amerie," *Hip Online,* www.hip online.com/artist/music/a/amerie/interview/1003 55.html (March 1, 2005).

"Amerie," *The Crusade,* http://thecrusade.net/peo ple/cgi-bin/archives/00000033.shtml (March 1, 2005).

"Amerie," *Groove On,* www.grooveon.com.au/fea03. cfm?article=1283 (March 1, 2005).

"Amerie Growing Up But Keeping Her Clothes On, Thank You," *MTV,* www.mtv.com/news/articles/ 1496565/02032005/amerie.jhtml (March 1, 2005).

"Amerie, On the Rise," *The People's Urban Beat,* www.thepubreport.com/amerie.htm (March 1, 2005).

"Amerie, One Thing," *BBC,* www.bbc.co.uk/dna/col lective/A3650267 (March 1, 2005).

Amerie Online, www.amerieonline.net.

"Backstage Interview with Amerie," *Soul Train,* www. soultrain.com/st3/amerie1026.html (March 1, 2005).

"Talkin' to Amerie," *World Asia,* www.worldasia.com/ music/music/people/int_amerie (March 1, 2005).

—Candace LaBalle

Ron Artest

1979—

Professional basketball player

Artest, Ron, photograph. AP/Wide world Photos.

One November night in 2004, forward Ron Artest of the National Basketball Association's Indiana Pacers went into the stands at the Palace of Auburn Hills outside Detroit. He started throwing punches after being hit in the chest by a drink cup a Detroit Pistons fan had thrown. The incident, replayed on television screens around the world, turned into a general melee and resulted in a season-long suspension for Artest. *People* called the fracas "one of the ugliest scenes in NBA history," and it surprised no one who had followed Artest's career closely; he seemed to be, in the words of *Sports Illustrated*'s Chris Ballard, "basketball's version of the Incredible Hulk, morphing into a destructive alter ego and then having no memory of the transformation afterward."

Yet many people knew a very different Ron Artest—one who went broke despite his multimillion-dollar salary because he was so insistent about supporting his family, friends, and community, one who donated his time to wheelchair basketball competitions, one who had developed into one of the top young defensive players in the NBA through a combination of enthusiasm and fierce competitiveness. Born on November 13, 1979, in New York City, Ron Artest grew up in the

Queensbridge housing project, the largest public housing complex in the United States with its 96 buildings. And it was in that concrete environment that the contradictions in his character began to take shape.

Took Up Basketball at Counselor's Suggestion

Artest was one of nine children of Ron Artest Sr., a former boxer who worked at a variety of jobs, and Sarah Artest, a bank teller. Various other relatives lived in the family's five-bedroom apartment, which often served as a home for 15 or 16 people at a time. Artest, who grew to six-feet, seven-inches tall and 245 pounds, took to the project's basketball courts when he was eight, at the suggestion of a school counselor concerned about his angry behavior following his parents' separation. Soon he could be found on the court almost every day, summer or winter. Often he played against his father in tough, physical, all-out one-on-one contests. "We were so competitive," Artest recalled to Mike McGraw of the Arlington Heights, Illinois, *Daily Herald*. "I wanted to beat my dad so badly. Once I was 15, he couldn't beat

At a Glance . . .

Born on November 13, 1979 in Queens, NY; son of Ron Artest Sr. (a former boxer) and Sarah Artest (a bank teller); married Kimesha Hatfield: children: four. *Education:* Attended St. John's University, New York.

Career: Chicago Bulls, professional basketball player; 1999-2002; Indiana Pacers, professional basketball player, 2002–. TruWarier Records and clothing line, founder and CEO, 2003–.

Awards: National Basketball League, defensive player of the year, 2003-04, All-Star team, 2004.

Addresses: *Office*—Indiana Pacers, Market St. Arena, 300 E. Market St., Indianapolis, IN 46204-2603; *Record Label*—TruWarier Records, Suite 1, 500 Newfield Ave., Stamford, CT 06905.

me again." Pickup basketball games in the neighborhood often escalated from hard fouls to fistfights.

At the LaSalle Academy in Manhattan, Artest became a top high school player in a city dense with basketball talent. But he never his competitive drive never blurred his commitment to his community. At one point he turned down a trip to Paris, France, in order to keep a prior commitment he had made to a wheelchair basketball benefit. Scouts from top basketball schools noticed Artest's intensity, and he enrolled at St. John's University in New York. His competitive drive was apparent to the St. John's coaching staff. "He has this fear of failure," head coach Fran Fraschilla told Nicholas J. Cotsonika of the *Detroit Free Press.* "I think it is born out of not wanting to have to go back to Queensbridge without having any status. It's a pride and competitive thing."

Artest played for one year at St. John's. After deciding to turn professional, he was picked by the Chicago Bulls in the first round of the 1999 draft. Even over the course of a single year, however, his teammates got a good taste of his mercurial personality. He could often be kind and generous, chatting with homeless people, giving encouraging talks to school groups, and impulsively making large donations of cash. His bad temper, on the other hand, was well known; he shouted at his teammates and got into fights on the court. Yet again, he showed a crazy streak, wearing a court jester hat during team road trips.

Applied for Appliance-Store Job

Things continued in the same vein over Artest's three seasons with the Bulls. By the end of the 2001-02 season, Artest was both an offensive and a defensive threat, averaging around 15 points per game and stealing the ball from opponents consistently. (He explained his stealing prowess to reporters by referring to his experience as a shoplifter back home in Queens.) Artest became a well-liked figure among basketball writers, who warmed to his unusual perspectives and activities; he recorded a country song with an elderly woman neighbor at one point, and during his rookie year he filled out a job application at a Circuit City store so that he could get an employee discount on the latest electronic gear.

Yet his intensity on the court spilled out beyond appropriate boundaries; playing against the legendary Bulls star Michael Jordan in a pickup game, he broke two of Jordan's ribs. And his inner anger continued to show itself as, in one of several notorious incidents, he picked up and threw a 150-pound stretching machine, leaving a gouge in the floor of the Bulls' practice court. After Artest's girlfriend Jennifer Palma and the mother of one of his children, filed assault charges against him in May of 2002, he was ordered to attend anger management classes. Artest later married Kimesha Hatfield, with whom he had three more children.

Late in the 2001-02 season, Bulls administrators worried about Artest's outbursts traded him to the Indiana Pacers. Honing his skills on the court and working on aggression issues under the care of a team psychologist, Artest seemed to hit his stride as a player, The duo of Artest and Jermaine O'Neal evolved into perhaps the NBA's most-feared pair of forwards, and at the end of the 2003-04 season Artest was named an NBA All-Star and won the league's Defensive Player of the Year award. He held the players against whom he was matched defensively to impressively low averages of 9.4 shots and 8.1 points a game, and he became an offensive threat with a points-per-game average of 8.3.

Smashed $100,000 Monitor

Artest's temper continued to show itself, however; in 2003, at New York's Madison Square Garden, he smashed a video monitor valued at $100,000. He drew six suspensions in the 2002-03 season and two in the 2003-04 campaign. Early in the 2004-05 season, basketball fans wondered whether Artest was beginning to show signs of stress once again. He changed his jersey number from 23 to 91—the number of longtime NBA problem child Dennis Rodman—and he requested time off in order to promote an album he planned to release on the new music label he had formed, TruWarier Records. No one, however, could have predicted what would happen as the Pacers took the court against the Detroit Pistons on November 19, 2004.

The trouble started when Artest fouled Pistons player Ben Wallace in the final minute of the game. Wallace responded with a two-handed shove that sent Artest stumbling backward toward the scorer's table. That might have been the end of it; Artest leaned backward against the table and playfully donned a headset belonging to a radio broadcaster. But then a fan threw a full drink cup at Artest, hitting him near the neck. He instantly leapt several rows into the stands, trading punches with fans along the way, and he was joined by O'Neal and teammate Stephen Jackson. Pistons fans responded with a shower of debris that included a chair, and many present, including Pacers coach Rick Carlisle, feared for their physical safety. Police and guards finally restored order as Artest was dragged from the court.

The resulting suspension Artest drew from NBA commissioner David Stern sidelined him for the rest of the season and cost him $5 million in salary. Artest expressed regret over the incident although he told *Jet* that "I respect David Stern, but I don't think that he has been fair with me in this situation." Advertising appearances for "The Roc," a music and clothing line devised by entrepreneur and Artest friend Damon Dash, helped pay the bills in 2005. Artest's future remained a question mark despite his tremendous talent. "Deep down there's a heart and somebody who cares," sportswriter Jay Mariotti told *People*'s Pam Lambert, "but he can't control himself on the court, and that's tragic. If he had his head together, he could be a Hall of Fame player." In the summer of 2005, Artest faced a charge of misdemeanor assault and battery, with a maximum penalty of three months in jail and a $500 fine, as a result of the Auburn Hills, Michigan, brawl.

Sources

Periodicals

Daily Herald (Arlington Heights, IL), November 16, 1999, p. 1; December 20, 2002, p. 1.
Detroit Free Press, December 26, 2004.
Jet, May 10, 2004, p. 47; December 13, 2004, p. 50.
People, December 6, 2004, p. 103.
PR Newswire, February 4, 2005.
Sporting News, November 29, 2004, p. 10.
Sports Illustrated, February 11, 2002, p. 74; October 28, 2002, p. 98; February 9, 2004, p. 54; November 29, 2004, p. 50.

—James M. Manheim

Leonard Blackshear

1943—

Organization executive, entrepreneur

As founder and president of Annapolis, Maryland's Kunta Kinte-Alex Haley Foundation, Leonard Blackshear shepherded the creation and development of one of the most distinctive monuments of African-American history in the United States. The Kunta Kinte-Alex Haley Memorial, visited annually by crowds estimated to be in excess of one million people, both marks the spot where Gambian slave Kunta Kinte arrived in America aboard the slave ship *Lord Ligonier* on September 29, 1767, and honors his descendant Alex Haley, who told Kinte's story in his pioneering historical novel, *Roots.* The memorial was just one of several important imprints Blackshear left on the Annapolis community, where he had lived since young adulthood.

Born June 29, 1943, in Savannah, Georgia, Blackshear moved with his family of six to New York City when he was six months old. His father was an electronics worker who hoped to become an educator. Blackshear told Dionne Walker of the Annapolis *Capital* that his father "was determined to pursue the career of his choosing and Georgia, at that time, was inclined not to let him." Blackshear's father eventually became a teacher, and Blackshear himself graduated from John Adams High School in 1959 and went on to New York's Hunter College. Outside of the classroom, he was an avid chess lover who played the game competitively on a high school team and later organized chess tournaments.

Enrolled in electrical engineering courses at Hunter, Blackshear became involved with Harlem Youth Opportunities Unlimited, a community-service organization. Idealism and volunteer work squeezed studying out of his schedule, and soon he had dropped out and taken a job at a clothing shop. A union member, he was picked by his co-workers to represent them at the great March on Washington civil rights demonstration in 1963.

Worked for IBM

The following year, Blackshear was drafted and joined the U.S. Air Force. After technician training in Colorado, he was sent to Germany. He finished his tour of duty in 1968 and landed in Maryland, moving in with a family member and taking classes at the University of Maryland. He graduated with a physics degree in 1970 and got a job as an operations supervisor at an IBM corporation office in Baltimore. An early admirer was his wife Patsy, whom he had met while they were both students at Maryland. "It's sort of like living with Don Quixote," she told Walker. "[He] has this real vision out there and is able to connect the dots before other people are able to even see dots." They moved to Annapolis after marrying in order to split the commute between her home base in Alexandria, Virginia, and his job in Baltimore.

Blackshear was a young star at IBM, developing a marketing database system that was eventually implemented company-wide. He worked toward an MBA degree at American University in Washington, D.C., completing that program in 1975. But then, seemingly headed toward a high-flying corporate career, Blackshear found himself steered by more idealistic impulses

At a Glance . . .

Born June 29, 1943, in Savannah, Georgia; father an electronics worker and later a teacher; moved to New York City with family at age six; married, wife's name Patsy. *Education:* Attended Hunter College, New York; University of Maryland, BS, physics, 1970; American University, Washington, DC, MBA, 1975. *Military service:* U.S. Air Force, 1964-68.

Career: IBM, Baltimore, MD, operations supervisor, 1970-73; worked for Anne Arundel County, MD, Economic Opportunity Commission, 1973-78; TeleSonic corporation, founder and president, 1978-2000; Kunta Kinte Celebrations, founder and president, 1985–; Kunta Kinte-Alex Haley Foundation, founder and president, 1992–; organized Annapolis stop (first U.S. stop) of Reconciliation Walk event, 2004.

Selected memberships: Rotary Club Books for International Goodwill project; Annapolis and Anne Arundel County Conference and Visitors Bureau, board member.

Selected awards: Martin Luther King Jr. Awards Committee, Dream Keepers award, 2001; Respect award, 2004.

Addresses: *Office*—Kunta Kinte-Alex Haley Foundation Inc., 31 Old Solomons Island Road, Suite 102, Annapolis, Maryland 21401; *Web*—www.kintehaley. org.

TeleSonic products included a captioned radio for the hearing-impaired and a county cancer-awareness telephone system.

While launching his new company, Blackshear continued his involvement in community service work. Such work was a lifetime commitment for Blackshear; he served on state boards including those of the Maryland Health and Welfare Council and the Small Business Council of the state's Chamber of Commerce, and he became a board member of the Anne Arundel Medical Center. Local Rotary Club projects in Annapolis, such as the Books for International Goodwill book drive, could count on Blackshear's involvement.

Raised Funds for Plaque

But Blackshear reserved his strongest efforts for *Roots* and its Annapolis connections. He learned about the landing of the 17-year-old slave Kunta Kinte from Haley's 1976 book and from its hugely successful television dramatization that aired the following year. Sensing the special significance of the story for Annapolis, he began raising funds for a plaque to mark the spot where Kinte arrived and was sold into slavery. At first, he relied on connections he made within a group called the Strategic Communications Network for African Americans.

By 1978 the group had made a proposal to the Annapolis City Council, requesting permission to place a commemorative plaque on the city's waterfront. They were turned down at first, as city officials argued that Kinte, who was sold into slavery in Virginia, had not been an Annapolis resident. The plaque was finally installed in 1981 after a new mayor, Richard Hillman, was elected. Two days after its unveiling, it was stolen by still-unknown thieves who left a card claiming affiliation with the Ku Klux Klan. The theft, Blackshear told the *Baltimore Sun,* "consecrated" the memorial, which was soon rebuilt and was left undisturbed.

Blackshear built on this successful beginning, organizing an annual event called the Kunta Kinte Celebrations (later the Kunta Kinte Heritage Festival) held on the steps of the Maryland Hall for the Creative Arts. By 1985 the event had spawned an organizational entity, Kunta Kinte Celebrations, of which Blackshear served as president. The festival grew and was moved to nearby St. John's College, adding concerts and educational components and attracting vendors of African products and foods. By 2002 the Kunta Kinte Heritage Festival was drawing upwards of 20,000 visitors a year from all over the metropolitan Baltimore and Washington areas. "Everybody knows that it's fine to go to an Italian festival and enjoy an Italian sausage, or a Greek festival to enjoy Greek food," Blackshear observed to Eileen Rivers of the *Washington Post.* "But somehow European Americans have felt that they need permission to go to an African festival. But this is a festival that all people can appreciate."

once again. He worked for several years with a community development agency in Maryland's Anne Arundel County, taking a leave of absence from IBM. Finally, in 1978, the company insisted that he either return or leave for good, and he chose the latter course.

"I never looked back," Blackshear told Johnathon E. Briggs of the *Baltimore Sun.* He started his own company, TeleSonic, which specialized in computer voice recognition technology. Among the company's products was a software system called TICAL, or TTY Information and Communication Access for Libraries, that merged computer technology with traditional text telephones to allow hearing-impaired patrons to communicate with librarians throughout an entire branch system, rather than having to rely on a single phone number. The TICAL system was installed in the library system of Maryland's Anne Arundel County. Other

The next step in Blackshear's campaign to bring a consciousness of black history to Annapolis was to expand the Kunta Kinte plaque to a full-fledged memorial, said to be the only one in the United States that commemorates the arrival of an individual African-born slave. In 1992 Blackshear founded the Kunta Kinte-Alex Haley Foundation and won approval for a three-part installation centered on the Annapolis City Dock. The centerpiece was a sculpture of Alex Haley, shown reading to a trio of children of different races, was finished in 1999. The memorial also encompassed a "story wall" along nearby Compromise Street, interpreting a sequence of ten quotations from *Roots,* and a large compass built into the ground that enables visitors to orient themselves toward the homelands of their ancestors.

Faced Cancer Diagnosis

In the midst of the busy rush toward the memorial's completion, Blackshear was diagnosed with blood cell cancer in the year 2000. At one point he was given six months to live, but then his condition improved. "It was what you might call a life-altering experience that I think has certainly given me a stronger commitment to help," Blackshear told Walker. "Somebody has some work for me that is not yet done." The Kunta Kinte-Alex Haley Memorial was completed and dedicated in 2002.

That further work included a unique symbolic observance called the Reconciliation Walk, which began in England around the year 2000 and which Blackshear and his foundation brought to Annapolis for its first American enactment in 2004. During a Reconciliation Walk, white participants donned yokes and chains as symbols of repentance for having enslaved Africans, while black walkers affirmed their forgiveness of the injustices of slavery by joining the procession. "The goal of the walk," Blackshear wrote in the *Annapolis Capital,* "is to show that Europeans, Africans, and European and African Americans can walk in harmony, learn about the past, and resolve to take positive steps toward commitments for penitence and forgiveness."

The Reconciliation Walk attracted marchers from Europe and Africa as well as the United States, and it drew its share of controversy. A white supremacist organization from West Virginia distributed racist flyers around Annapolis in advance of the event. But the walk, held on September 29, 2004, went off without incident and featured a handshake between Haley and Orlando Ridout, a descendant of the family that had originally enslaved Kunta Kinte.

Blackshear planned to follow up the Reconciliation Walk with a series of Reconciliation Study Circles, interracial meetings designed to explore the effects of racism in the community. "The circles will lead to action," Blackshear wrote in the *Capital.* "We will then be on the road to Annapolis becoming the first city of healing in America." Honored with several Annapolis community awards in the early 2000s, Blackshear continued to look toward opportunities for service. "If you look back and you haven't helped anyone," he asked Walker, "what was your life about?"

Sources

Periodicals

Afro-American Red Star (Washington, DC), June 8, 2002, p. A1.
Baltimore Sun, January 15, 2001; July 17, 2003.
Capital (Annapolis, MD), August 29, 2004, p. A11; November 8, 2004, p. A1.
Maryland Gazette (Glen Burnie, MD), October 2, 2004, p. A1.
Washington Post, August 12, 1999, p. M1; June 6, 2002, p. T3; August 8, 2002, p. T10; August 26, 2004, p. T2.

On-line

"Leonard Blackshear," *The History Makers,* www. thehistorymakers.com/biography/biography.asp?bi oindex=815&category=civicMakers (April 25, 2005).

—James M. Manheim

Robert D. Blackwell, Sr.

1937—

Executive

Robert D. (Bob) Blackwell, Sr. could very well have settled into an early retirement at the end of his first career. As a consulting director at computer giant IBM, Blackwell was one of the highest ranking African Americans in the information technology (IT) business. Born into a family of domestics barely a generation out of slavery, Blackwell had excelled beyond all expectations, including his own. "People ask about careers, but I thought I needed a job," he told *Crain's Chicago Business* of his corporate beginnings. "It was after I got to IBM and saw it that I became ambitious." In 1992, that ambition caused him to walk away from his cushy corporate job to found Blackwell Consulting Services. In just over a dozen years, Blackwell has built his company into an IT consultancy powerhouse with nearly 500 employees. A generous leader, Blackwell has credited much of his firm's success to those employees. "'We get the work done' is our common attitude," he told the *TeQnology* Web site. "Our ideal type of employee will subordinate to the needs of the client. They need to care about what they do and have passion!"

Rose from Service Class to Computer Sales

On July 28, 1937, Robert D. Blackwell was delivered by a midwife at his grandparents home in Eastville, Virginia. Shortly thereafter, his family moved to the wealthy suburb of Bryn Mawr, Pennsylvania, just outside of Philadelphia. "Black people only represented about 2 percent of the population and represented the service class…. mine was no exception," Blackwell told *TeQnology*. While his father worked as a janitor, Blackwell excelled in football, basketball, and baseball at Radnor High School. "I was also, at the insistence of my parents, a good student," Blackwell told *TeQnology*.

After graduating high school in 1955, Blackwell earned a football scholarship to Wichita State University in Kansas. When an injury forced him to hang up his cleats, Blackwell turned his attention to psychology and earned a bachelor's degree in 1966. He toyed with the idea of pursuing a master's in the field, but a school dean nixed that idea. "Her advice to me was to 'Get a job,' since I was married with small children," Blackwell told *TeQnology*. He had married Marjilee Blackwell in 1961. The couple went on to have two sons and three daughters.

At about the same time, IBM Corporation visited the Wichita campus seeking minorities for its rapidly expanding firm. The dean arranged a meeting, and Blackwell was hired. "In those days, it wasn't necessary to have prior computer experience because nobody knew anything about computers," he told the *Brooks International* Web site. After 24 weeks of training in Chicago, Blackwell became a systems engineer, designing applications for hospitals and universities. In 1971, he shifted gears, moving to marketing and sales.

Abandoned Top IBM Spot to Go Solo

Except for a two-year stint as the assistant information technology director for the State of Kansas, Blackwell spent the next twenty years moving up IBM's ranks. By 1989, he was overseeing $250 million in sales to clients including Ameritech, Waste Management, and Inland Steel. In 1990 Blackwell became one of the highest ranking African Americans at IBM when he was appointed director of the company's Greater Chicago Consulting Services. He oversaw areas such as outsourcing, systems integration, application development, complex calling systems, value-added networks, and fee-based education. During a two-year tenure, he led a staff of 200 and saw the consultancy double in size each year.

At the height of his 26-year career, Blackwell decided to leave IBM and go solo. "I was running IBM's consulting services and I really liked it," he told *Brooks International*. "I thought having a consulting firm was something that didn't require a lot of capital and the barriers to entry were low." Another key factor in Blackwell's decision to launch his own firm was a shift he saw in IT's future. "Manufacturing had moved off shore and people were starting to outsource. And I knew there was going to be a market for information technology services," Blackwell told *Black Enterprise*.

Before leaving IBM, Blackwell solidified key relationships that would help him get started. After one of Blackwell's most important clients at IBM expressed dismay at his impending departure, Blackwell suggested the client ask IBM to sub-contract Blackwell's new firm in order to maintain their business relationship. "I worked like a dog to walk out the door with that one client, and as a result was able to start off renting an office and hiring people," Blackwell told *Inc. Magazine*.

Built Business as Father-Son Relationship Faltered

With son Robert Blackwell Jr. as a partner, Blackwell Consulting Services opened in 1992. Within 15 months, the firm had clocked more than $2 million in billings from IBM contracts alone. Despite this prodigious start, the company faced some major roadblocks. "The biggest obstacle was that we were a nobody," Blackwell told *Black Enterprise*. "We had no brand. No one knew who we were."

From day one, Blackwell Consulting was committed to "focusing on real technical problems people have," Blackwell explained to *Brooks International*. "We're not in some ivory tower somewhere contemplating what life should be about, but are actually down on the ground doing the project work." This turned out to be the firm's key to overcoming "nobody" status. Blackwell Consulting developed into the largest minority-owned IT consulting firm in the Midwest by focusing on package and custom application solutions, infrastructure and network solutions, and IT management services. By the end of 1993, the firm had landed two major clients, Waste Management and Abbot Laboratories, and revenues reached $2.7 million. Three years later that figure was $8 million.

As the company grew, so did a schism between father and son. Blackwell Sr. had a classic corporate mentality, steeped in discipline and hierarchy. Blackwell Jr. was an entrepreneur at heart, tuned in to the pulse of technological change. "You can see how there would have been a culture clash," the younger Blackwell told *Crain's Chicago Business*. The younger man did not take well to his father's direction, and the elder would not accept his son's freewheeling ways. After three years of fighting, Blackwell Jr. sold his share in the company and pulled out. No hard feelings lingered. "I just wanted my father to be my father," he told *Crain's*.

Catered to Employees and Diversity

Blackwell Consulting remained a family affair when Blackwell's daughter Pamela signed on in the mid-1990s. "The notion that your children can help grow your company is obviously pretty attractive," Blackwell told *Crain's*. However, he added, "First thing, you have to have a great company, so people want to come on board, even if they're not family."

To build a great company, Blackwell provided training programs, mentoring, and employee recognition awards. It has also instituted employee flex-time, allowing working parents to comfortably balance work and family. It was a reflection of Blackwell's personal philosophy. "My father sees this business as a family," Pamela Blackwell told the *Winning Work Places* Web site. "He always tells me, 'I have a wife and five kids at home and 300 kids at work.'"

Blackwell Consulting was also committed to diversity as a means of good business. "You have to focus on doing a better job than your competition, not your race," he told *Black Enterprise*. "You cannot overestimate the power of performance." In 2005 Blackwell told *Computerworld*, "We have 35 developers and architects whose first language is Spanish." He added, "We also have many Indians and Russians working for us. When you have these very diverse cultures coming together, you benefit from language expertise and differences in approaches."

Focused on Future of Continued Growth

In the late 1990s and early 2000s, Blackwell Consulting grew exponentially. By 1999, revenues were up to $18 million. The firm survived the dot.com crash to pull in $28 million in 2001. By 2003 that figure had swelled to $31.5 million, landing the firm on *Black Enterprise's* ranking of the top 100 black-owned Industrial/Service firms.

By 2004 family forces at Blackwell were once again shaping the company's future. Pamela Blackwell was promoted to president and chief operating officer (COO) after having served several years as chief financial officer and vice president of human resources. She promptly announced plans to increase revenues to $100 million by 2008.

Son Robert Blackwell Jr. also came back on board when his company Electronic Knowledge Interchange (EKI) merged with Blackwell Consulting Services to form BCS. EKI, specialized in software applications development, managed services, and web services, had sales of $15 million in 2004. "It's a very nice fit," Blackwell Sr. told *Computerworld*. With a family of leaders at its helm and a proven history of growth, BCS hoped to transcend the tag of largest African-American owned IT consulting firm to become one of America's largest IT consulting firms, period.

Sources

Periodicals

Black Enterprise, February 1, 2003.
Crain's Chicago Business, April 7, 2003; January 24, 2005.

On-line

"Brains for Hire," *Inc. Magazine,* www.inc.com/magazine/20040401/gettingstarted.html (April 7, 2005).
"Q&A: Minority IT Pros Face Glass Ceiling," *Computerworld,* www.computerworld.com/managementtopics/outsourcing/itservices/story/0,10801,99436,00.html (April 7, 2005).
"Robert Blackwell, Consumer Behavior," *Brooks International,* www.brooksinternational.com/Robert_Blackwell_372.htm#Second (April 7, 2005).
"Success Stories: Blackwell Consulting Services," *Winning Work Places,* www.winningworkplaces.org/library/success/success.php?sid=116 (April 7, 2005).
"Threads: Bob Blackwell," *TeQnology,* www.*TeQnology*.com/threads/pioneers/bblackwell/ (April 7, 2005).

—Candace LaBalle

Suzanne Boyd

1963—

Journalist

Magazine editor Suzanne Boyd launched *Suede,* a fashion magazine aimed at African-American women, in 2004. Unfortunately, *Suede* struggled financially through five issues before its parent company put it on indefinite hiatus. Future career prospects for Boyd—a Canadian of West Indian background—were unclear, but as *Globe & Mail* writer Simon Houpt noted, the longtime Toronto fashionista "presented a sizzling polyglot fabulousness that challenged the stiff British ice queen of the New York fashion magazine world, Anna Wintour," editor of American *Vogue.*

Boyd, Suzanne, photograph, Peter Kramer/Getty Images.

Born in Halifax, Nova Scotia, in 1963, Boyd was one of four children in her family. Her father, Donald, was a civil engineer originally from the Dominican Republic, who had met Donna, Boyd's mother and a native of Quebec, while a student at Dalhousie University. As a child, Boyd lived with her family in Barbados and also on Dominica, an island between Guadalupe and Martinique in the Caribbean. Her high-school years were spent in Jamaica, where she attended a Roman Catholic boarding school.

Boyd's first job in journalism was with *The Nation,* a Barbados newspaper, in 1982, for which she covered parliament and the tourism industry. Moving to Canada in 1984, she enrolled at York University in Toronto, where she majored in mass communications and English. She joined the staff of *Flare,* a leading Canadian fashion magazine for women, in 1990 as its associate beauty editor. Tragedy struck that same year, however, when her sister died in a plane crash. For a time, Boyd left *Flare* and freelanced for the *Toronto Star* and *Chatelaine,* another Canadian women's magazine, but returned to *Flare* in 1992 as its acting beauty editor. She rose to associate editor, and then editor-in-chief in 1996, which made her the first black woman to head a major Canadian publication.

Boyd retooled *Flare* and helped give it more uniquely Canadian focus. She championed homegrown designers, and emerged as a bona-fide Toronto celebrity herself. Statuesque at five-feet, ten-inches tall, with her hairstyle and perilously high heels sometimes adding another six inches, she regularly made it onto lists of Canada's best-dressed women. Her high profile attracted the attention of a New York publishing executive, Isolde Motley, at Time Inc., the print journalism arm of the Time-Warner empire. As Motley told Carr in

At a Glance . . .

Born January 17, 1963, in Halifax, Nova Scotia, Canada; daughter of daughter of Donald (a civil engineer) and Donna (deputy director of the YWCA) Boyd. *Education:* Attended York University, Toronto.

Career: *The Nation,* Barbados, reporter, 1982-84; *Flare* magazine, associate beauty editor, 1990; freelance writer for the *Toronto Star* and *Chatelaine,* 1990-92; *Flare,* acting beauty editor, 1992, became associate editor, and editor-in-chief, 1996-2004; Essence Communications Partners, editor-in-chief of *Suede* magazine, 2004.

Addresses: *Office*—Essence Communications Partners, 1500 Broadway, 6th Fl., New York, NY 10036.

the *New York Times* profile, she had first spotted Boyd on *Flare*'s Letter from the Editor page, with an accompanying photograph that showed her "wearing an evening dress that she had designed out of a Hudson Bay blanket," Motley recalled. "Years later, those dresses showed up on the runway."

Boyd and Motley kept in contact, and in early 2004 Boyd left *Flare* and relocated to New York City with a new job: Time Inc. had joined with *Essence* magazine's corporate parent to launch a new magazine division, and Boyd was hired to oversee the launch of a new title aimed at African-American women called *Suede.* Motley said when they discussed a new magazine for a younger African-American readership than the traditional *Essence* reader, Boyd already knew what it should look like. "This is a person who has a complete and passionate vision for what she wants to do," Motley enthused. "She already had the whole magazine in her head."

Suede, conceived in part as the younger, hipper sister to *Essence,* was determined to deliver style news to its reader in all its manifestations, from street fashion to haute couture. Boyd summed up her vision for it in *Advertising Age* interview with Jon Fine. Describing her target audience, she explained "They don't need to be told what to do—they do it anyway. Very expressive, like plumage—'birds of paradise,' I call these girls. Because it's all about color and energy."

Boyd brought some *Flare* staffers with her, including Canadian rocker Bryan Adams, whom she had regularly used as a photographer. She faced a tough market once the publication was on the newsstands, however.

A similar entry, *Honey,* had already folded thanks to financial troubles. Because of her high profile and successful track record, Boyd's Time Inc. and *Essence* bosses had considered her the crucial factor in *Suede*'s bid to lure the vital advertising dollars necessary to stay afloat. Though its account executives won some big contracts with cosmetics companies like Clinique and Lancôme, a cautious economic climate meant that *Suede*'s number of ad pages—the bellwether of a magazine's financial health—remained slim despite a well-received September 2004 launch issue.

Boyd put out another issue in 2004, and then geared up for a scheduled nine issues to hit newsstands in 2005. Carr, writing in the *New York Times* as the New Year loomed, critiqued the new title and termed it "frenetic in a way few fashion publications would dare to be. It can be exhausting to stare at. But sitting on a rack of me-too fashion magazines, it evokes significant exhilaration as well." In February of 2005, however, Essence Communication Partners announced that *Suede* would be going on hiatus. Reportedly, Boyd knew nothing prior to that day, and learned the news the same day as her 40-member staff. An April 2005 issue would be its last in its original, exuberant incarnation. Her boss, Ed Lewis, the chief executive officer of Essence Communications Partners, expressed his regrets about the decision. "The magazine is smart, exciting and provocative," Lewis said in the official announcement, according to the *Globe & Mail.* "However, although some of our most talented people have been working on *Suede,* it has become clear that more time and resources would be needed to further develop this brand."

Boyd was reportedly asked to stay on the job, but journalism-industry experts noted that it was rare for a magazine to come back from the dead, so to speak, and it seemed unlikely that *Suede* would have a future as defined by her original goals. Just two months earlier, she had reflected in the *New York Times* interview with Carr that the obstacles were many. "The expectation when it comes to black magazines is that they will be urban and that will be the end of it," she asserted. "There is supposed to be no taste level, no understanding of the runway aspects of fashion. We want to be fun and fashion correct."

Sources

Advertising Age, August 30, 2004, p. 17.
Contemporary Canadian Biographies, December 1997.
Globe & Mail (Toronto, Canada), February 25, 2005, p. A1.
Maclean's, April 7, 2003, p. 38.
Mediaweek, June 7, 2004, p. 32.
New York Times, December 7, 2004, p. E1.

—Carol Brennan

William Stanley Braithwaite

1878-1962

Critic, poet

Though in his lifetime William Stanley Braithwaite was termed the "Boston Dictator" for his formidable authority as an arbiter of taste in the world of American poetry, his influence later waned, and literary history seems to have forgotten him after his 1962 passing. An editor, anthologist, critic, and published poet himself, Braithwaite was a key figure in the revival of American poetry in the early decades of the twentieth century. From 1913 to 1929 he published the *Anthology of Magazine Verse,* an important annual collection that showcased the work of emerging poets on the American scene.

Braithwaite, because of the prominence he attained, was sometimes accused of ignoring issues of race to the point where detractors claimed that as a critic and poet he seemed ashamed of his own skin color. Later analysts have assessed his philosophy with a more balanced view, however, and his achievements were recognized by the National Association for the Advancement of Colored People (NAACP) when he was honored with its prestigious Spingarn Medal in 1918. "At a critical moment in our nation's literature, it was his voice which issued a clarion call for the support of American poetry," asserted Kenny J. Williams in the *Dictionary of Literary Biography* volume, *Afro-American Writers Before the Harlem Renaissance.* "At the same time, he was one of the first to explore the role of the Negro in literature and to champion the cause of the Afro-American writer in places where he could be heard."

Braithwaite was born in Boston on December 6, 1878. His parents, William Smith and Emma DeWolfe Braith-waite, were both of mixed-race heritage; his father's family was from the West Indies, while his maternal grandmother had been a North Carolina slave, and Braithwaite's mother likely the progeny of the property owner. In his own family, Braithwaite was the second of five children, all of which were home-schooled by their father, who was a stern disciplinarian with a British-colonial-bred sense of propriety. When his father died in 1886, Braithwaite and his siblings attended Boston public schools for a time, but by the time he was twelve Braithwaite had exchanged schoolwork for a job in order to help support the family.

Discovered English Romantic Poetry

Braithwaite was fortunate to land an apprenticeship at a Boston publishing house, Ginn and Company, where he learned typesetting. It was in this line of work that the 15-year-old fell under the spell of poetry—prompted, he later recalled, by John Keats's "Ode on a Grecian Urn." He began to read avidly, spending hours at the Boston Public Library, where he discovered that "the deeper I read, the more, and often discouragingly, I realized the difficulties confronting me," the *Dictionary of Literary Biography* essay quoted him as writing. He became particularly fond of the works of the English Romantic poets, among them Percy Bysshe Shelley and William Wordsworth, a penchant that would later filter into his own attempts at the form.

Around 1900, Braithwaite went to New York City and looked for a job in journalism there. Coming from Boston, a more egalitarian-minded city that had been

At a Glance . . .

Born William Stanley Beaumont Braithwaite on December 6, 1878, in Boston, MA; died following a brief illness on June 8, 1962; son of William Smith and Emma (DeWolfe) Braithwaite; married Emma Kelly, June 30, 1903; children: Fiona Lydia Rossetti, Katherine Keats, William Stanley Beaumont, Edith Carman, Paul Ledoux, Arnold DeWolfe, Francis Robinson. *Education:* Self-educated; apprenticed to a typesetter at Ginn and Company.

Career: *Colored American Magazine,* Boston, MA, editor, 1901-02; *Boston Evening Transcript,* Boston, literary editor and columnist, beginning in 1905; Atlanta University, Atlanta, GA, professor of creative literature, 1935-45. Publisher of *The Poetic Journal* in Boston, 1912-14; editor of *Poetry Review,* 1916-17; founder and editor of B. J. Brimmer Publishing Co., 1921-27; member of editorial board of *Phylon.* Contributor of book reviews, verse, essays, and articles to periodicals, including *Atlantic Monthly, Century, Crisis, Lippincott's, New York Times,* and the *New Republic,* among others. Braithwaite's papers are in the collection of the Syracuse University Library.

Memberships: Poetry Society of America, New England Poetry Society, Boston Authors' Club.

Awards: National Association for the Advancement of Colored People, Spingarn Medal, for outstanding achievement by a member of the colored race; honorary degrees from Atlanta University and Talladega College, 1918.

the center of the abolitionist movement in the nineteenth century, Braithwaite encountered a harsher reality. "I had a taste...of what the difficulties and injustices were for one of color who wanted to be accepted at his worth," he wrote later, according to a profile on his life and work in *Notable Black American Men.* Returning to Boston, he found a job with *Colored American Magazine,* and he wrote verse in his free time. Some of his earliest poems were published in *Voice of the Negro,* out of Atlanta, and *Crisis,* the magazine of the NAACP.

The first volume of Braithwaite's poetry, *Lyrics of Life and Love,* appeared in 1904. Like other novice writers, he was forced to seek out financial patronage to

help pay for the cost of printing his book. The verse in it, mostly Romantic in style with some homages to Keats, was not very well reviewed, however. "Braithwaite's poetry does not generally support in-depth analysis; rather it has a sort of surface fragility as it attempts to transmit something of the mystery of life and the awe of death," noted Williams in the *Dictionary of Literary Biography* essay. Moreover, the critics on both sides of the color bar wondered why there was so little mention of the black experience from his pen. A second collection, *The House of Falling Leaves,* appeared in 1908. Only in this volume does Braithwaite touch briefly on the issue of race in America, with one poem in commemoration of poet and abolitionist John Greenleaf Whittier. Yet here Braithwaite commends Whittier for abandoning poetry for the abolitionist cause, which seemed to reflect Braithwaite's belief that art and politics were, in the end, incompatible issues.

Edited Numerous Anthologies

Though Braithwaite would not publish another volume of his verse for 40 years, his influence on others was a profound one. His emergence as a poet came at a crucial moment: around 1905 there arose a sudden interest in poetry, a revival from an earlier generation which served to elevate it once more into a respected literary form in America. Poets of the previous century, among them Emily Dickinson and Walt Whitman, had enjoyed great prominence, but as a literary form American poetry had declined into mere magazine filler after that. In the first years of the twentieth century, however, a renaissance occurred, and a new generation of poets began to flourish. Several new literary forums sprang up that focused entirely on poetry, and there was a corresponding renewal of interest among the public as well.

In 1905, Braithwaite became the literary editor and columnist at the *Boston Evening Transcript*, an influential arts-focused paper in the city. His columns championed the work of new writers, and he interviewed such figures as Robert Frost for its pages. After abandoning his own attempts at writing verse, Braithwaite began to edit anthologies. Among these were *The Book of Elizabethan Verse*, which appeared in 1906, and *The Book of Restoration Verse* in 1910. These earned positive reviews from critics, and helped introduce American readers to the work of writers of previous eras who were nevertheless an influence on an emerging generation of contemporary poets.

Between 1912 and 1914, Braithwaite published several issues of *The Poetic Journal* out of Boston. It was one of several literary-focused financial ventures he attempted which failed to thrive, but he continued to be an increasingly important force in American poetry from behind the scenes. His rival, Chicago's Harriet Monroe, who had launched *Poetry: A Magazine of Verse* around the same time as his *Journal,* liked to call him the "Boston Dictator" and "Sir Oracle" because of his highly regarded authority and ability to launch a young poet's career. That influence was at its peak in his sole publishing venture to attain a modicum of financial success: the *Anthology of Magazine Verse,* which first appeared in 1913. To compile the annual, he combed through scores of journals, selecting poems from new and established writers. The measured assessments featured in his introductions to each volume introduced readers to new and emerging poets, and discussed the directions taken by more established poets in their current work. Contributors invited to participate included Frost, e. e. cummings, and Wallace Stevens, but he also included the work of African-American poets emerging in the Harlem Renaissance of the 1920s. This made his *Anthology* one of the first works of literary merit to feature the work of both black and white poets alongside one another.

Taught for a Decade

In the 1920s, Braithwaite launched a publishing house with poet Winifred Virginia Jackson. He served as its editor, and the company would issue the debut novel from future Pulitzer-Prize winner James Gould Cozzens, *Confusion,* in 1924. Yet the business venture did not earn much of a profit, and in 1927 Braithwaite was forced to file bankruptcy papers for it. The setback caused some financial hardship, for by then he was a husband and father of seven. In 1935, he took a post as a professor of creative literature at Atlanta University, a job that he would hold for a decade. The academic position was all the more remarkable given his lack of formal education credentials, but he became known as an excellent teacher and enthusiastic mentor to his students.

After retiring from academia in 1945, Braithwaite settled in the Harlem area of New York City. He lived in its Sugar Hill section, in an Edgecombe Avenue apartment building perched on a bluff overlooking the Bronx. That address survived to become an official New York City landmark, for it was home to a long roster of African-American luminaries, among them W.E.B. DuBois and Duke Ellington. From there Braithwaite continued to write about poetry, and his criticism appeared in many notable journalism forums, among them the *Atlantic Monthly, New Republic,* and *New York Times.* In 1958, he attempted to revive his *Anthology of Magazine Verse,* without success. Nevertheless, its earlier incarnation was a tremendous influence, asserted Williams in the *Dictionary of Literary Biography.* "The subsequent popularity," Williams noted, "of such anthologies and yearbooks as Edward J. O'Brien's annual collection of 'best' short stories and Burns Mantle's 'best' plays is due largely to Braithwaite having created an audience for that type of book."

The third and final book of Braithwaite's own verse was *Selected Poems,* which appeared in 1948. He died on June 8, 1962. His role in American literature spanned the era from Paul Laurence Dunbar, the first African American poet to achieve literary prominence, to Gwendolyn Brooks. Between that was a rich span of black-themed verse from writers such as Langston Hughes, Countee Cullen, and James Weldon Johnson, all of whom emerged out of the Harlem Renaissance of the 1920s. In his own verse and criticism, Braithwaite never addressed such topics as race or the social injustices faced by blacks in America—while in this pre-civil rights era others deemed it near-compulsory for African Americans of any prominence to raise awareness of such issues. He did, however, critique black writers with the same set of standards he applied to reviewing works by any poet. As Williams explained, Braithwaite's "insistence upon being part of the American scene was not predicated upon a view that race could or should be denied; rather, he felt race was simply a characteristic which did not have to be a motivating factor for one's life," the *Dictionary of Literary Biography* contributor asserted. "Ultimately, appreciating Braithwaite means accepting not only the diversity of Afro-American literature but also assuming that blackness and whiteness are not in themselves determining artistic or evaluative criteria."

Selected writings

Edited Anthologies

The Book of Elizabethan Verse, introduction by Thomas Wentworth Higginson, H. B. Turner, 1906, reprinted, FolcroftNorwood, 1980.
The Book of Georgian Verse, Brentano's, 1909, reprinted, Books for Libraries Press, two volumes, 1969.
The Book of Restoration Verse, Brentano's, 1910.
Anthology of Magazine Verse and Yearbook of American Poetry, seventeen volumes, G. Sully, 1913-29, reprinted, Books for Libraries Press, 1972.
(With Henry Thomas Schnittkind) *Representative American Poetry,* R. G. Badger, 1916.
The Poetic Year for 1916: A Critical Anthology, Small, Maynard, 1917.
The Golden Treasury of Magazine Verse, Small, Maynard, 1918.
The Book of Modern British Verse, Small, Maynard, 1919.
Victory! Celebrated by Thirty-Eight American Poets, introduction by Theodore Roosevelt, Small, Maynard, 1919.
Our Lady's Choir: A Contemporary Anthology of Verse by Catholic Sisters, foreword by Hugh Francis Blunt, introduction by Ralph Adams Cram, B. Humphries, 1931.

Poetry

Lyrics of Life and Love, H. B. Turner, 1904, reprinted, University Microfilms, 1971.

The House of Falling Leaves, J. W. Luce, 1908, reprinted, Mnemosyne Publishing, 1969.
Selected Poems, Coward-McCann, 1948.

Other

The Canadian (novel), Small, Maynard, 1901.
The Story of the Great War (juvenile; essays), F. A. Stokes, 1919.
Going Over Tindal: A Fragment Wrenched From the Life of Titus Jabson (novel), B. J. Brimmer, 1924.
John Myers O'Hara and the Grecian Influence, Smith and Sale, 1926.
The Bewitched Parsonage: The Story of the Brontes, Coward-McCann, 1950.
The William Stanley Braithwaite Reader, edited by Philip Butcher, University of Michigan Press, 1972.

Sources

Books

Dictionary of Literary Biography, Volume 50: *Afro-American Writers Before the Harlem Renaissance,* edited by Trudier Harris, Gale, 1986.
Notable Black American Men, Gale, 1998.

On-line

"William Stanley (Beaumont) Braithwaite," *Contemporary Authors Online,* Gale, http://galenet.gale group.com/servlet/BioRC (February 28, 2005).
"William Stanley (Beaumont) Braithwaite," *DISCovering Authors,* http://galenet.galegroup.com/servlet/BioRC (February 28, 2005).

—Carol Brennan

Sean Brown

1976—

Professional hockey player

Brown, Sean, photograph. Bruce Bennett Studios/Getty Images.

New Jersey Devils defenseman Sean Brown, one of just a handful of players of African descent in the National Hockey League (NHL), brings to the minds of many fans an earlier, more physical era of professional ice hockey. He is big (six-feet three-inches tall, 210 pounds), powerful, and a bit intimidating on the ice. Fights were on the decline in the NHL in the early 2000s, but Brown got into his share, and fans of the Boston Bruins, for whom Brown played from 2001 through 2003, dubbed him the Brown Bomber. He was part of several NHL playoff squads and was looking for his big break as hockey rinks were darkened by the players' strike and owners' lockout that led to the cancellation of the 2004-05 season.

Brown was born in Oshawa, Ontario, Canada, east of Toronto, on November 5, 1976. His life was consumed with hockey from a very early age, as he took to the ice as a defenseman in the local junior "pee wee" league. At one point his father gave him an autographed photo of Willie O'Ree, the Canadian-born black player who broke the NHL's color barrier in 1958. By the time Brown was in his late teens he had broken into organized hockey, playing 15 games for the Oshawa Legionnaires of the Ontario Junior Hockey League during the 1992-93 season.

Played in Ontario Hockey League

After beginning the 1993-94 campaign in another junior league in Manitoba, Brown moved on to the Belleville Bulls squad of the Ontario Hockey League, a prime breeding ground for NHL talent. He excelled over three years at Belleville, getting into the playoffs in 1994 and 1995 and consistently improving each year. Traded to the Sarnia Sting midway through the 1995-96 season, he returned to the playoffs once more and notched a strong 58 points (goals plus assists) for the split season even though he was never known primarily as an offensive threat. He was named to the OHL Second All-Star Team in 1996.

Brown also played for several seasons with the Knoxville Cherokees of the East Coast Hockey League in the United States, where hints of his combative on-ice personalilty began to surface. "We know they were just playing tough in their arena," he told *Knoxville News-Sentinel* reporter Nick Gates, referring to a series of illegal hits the Cherokees suffered in one game against

At a Glance . . .

Born on November 5, 1976, in Oshawa, Ontario, Canada.

Career: Belleville Bulls and Sarnia Sting, Ontario Hockey League, minor-league hockey player, 1993-96; Boston Bruins, National Hockey League, professional hockey player, 1995; Edmonton Oilers, National Hockey League, professional hockey player, 1996, 1998-2001; Boston Bruins, NHL, professional hockey player, 2002-03; New Jersey Devils, NHL, professional hockey player, 2003-04.

Addresses: *Office*—New Jersey Devils, 50 Route 120 North, P.O. Box 504, East Rutherford, NJ 07073.

the Jacksonville Lizard Kings. "(But) we file it away in the back of our minds. We know the next time we play them, we have a chance to get them back." Brown played both defense and offense in Knoxville, gaining some experience as a forward.

The NHL's Boston Bruins took note of Brown's strong statistics and chose him in the first round of the 1995 NHL draft; he was the 21st pick overall. Before getting the opportunity to play for the Bruins or enter their minor-league system, however, he was sent to the Edmonton Oilers in a complex trade. In the 1996-97 and 1997-98 season, Brown played mostly for the Oilers' Hamilton (Ontario) Bulldogs minor-league team in the American Hockey League (AHL), joining the parent squad for short periods.

Often Inhabited Penalty Box

In 1998, Brown began the first of four full seasons with the Oilers, earning, in the words of the *Bergen County (New Jersey) Record,* "a reputation as a stay-at-home, physical defender." He was a consistent player, blocking 29 shots over 51 games in his first seasons and improving to 46 blocked shots (with 12 points on offense) in his second. His most notable statistic as an Oiler player, however, related to his rough-and-tumble style of play: he spent over 100 minutes in the penalty box in each of his four seasons, with penalty stretches of 188 and 192 minutes in 1998-99 and 1999-2000 respectively.

Brown's playing time dropped somewhat over his last two seasons at Edmonton, even though he notched a career-best six goals in 2001-02. He was traded back to the Boston Bruins on March 19, 2002. He finished out the season with the Bruins, earning the admiration of fight-loving hockey fans by taking on a still-larger player, the six-foot six-inch Peter Worrell, in his second

night as a Bruin. During the off-season, the Bruins attempted to develop Brown's offensive skills as a forward. The move was beneficial for Brown's own career prospects. "I think it can definitely help me out," he told *Boston Herald* writer Steve Conroy. "You need someone who can go back and forth [between offense and defense]."

At Edmonton, Brown had been part of an unusual cluster of five black players, several of them Quebec-born athletes of Haitian descent. Blacks remained a rarity on NHL rinks, but the Edmonton squad had made strides toward diversity with the inclusion of black goalie Grant Fuhr on its Stanley Cup teams of the 1980s. Racial controversies flared several times in the NHL in the early 2000s, notably when AHL coach John Vanbiesbrouck used a racial slur against an opposing player in 2003. Brown, however, discounted the idea that racial tensions were on the rise in hockey generally, telling the *Providence Journal-Bulletin* that "There are all kinds of backgrounds playing the league, and they have respect for each other.... I don't think there's a problem."

Signed by Devils

Brown had limited success in his new dual role with the Bruins in the 2002-03 season as he struggled to master the team's complex offensive routines after a long layoff from the territory of the opposing goal. He got into 69 games, spending 117 minutes in the penalty box while playing mostly defense. At the end of the 2003 season, Brown became an unrestricted free agent. He was signed to a one-year contract, for $500,000, by the New Jersey Devils on July 24, 2003.

Early in the 2003-04 season, Brown was sent briefly to the Devils' Albany River Rats minor-league team. Accepting his new assignment with a characteristic positive attitude, he was quickly recalled to the parent team, at one point driving through a major blizzard to rejoin them. He got into 39 games with the playoff-bound Devils, shaving his penalty time to 44 minutes.

Off the ice, Brown kept busy as a mentor to younger black players, working with Willie O'Ree, who had become director of youth development for the NHL's Diversity Task Force, and instructing young skaters as a participant in New York's Hockey in Harlem program. During the 2004-05 strike, he was a member of a sports all-star team that raised funds for the Canadian Cancer Society's Relay for Life. Still well under 30 years old, he needed just one more defensive or offensive spark to his game in order to advance to the top levels of hockey stardom.

Sources

Periodicals

Boston Globe, September 28, 2002, p. F9; November 1, 2002, p. D1; January 26, 2003, p. C14.

Boston Herald, September 24, 2002, p. 75; October 6, 2002, p. B31; November 4, 2002, p. 88.

Edmonton Journal (Edmonton, Alberta, Canada), December 20, 2001, p. A1.

Jet, November 10, 2003, p. 46.

Knoxville (TN) *News Sentinel,* February 15, 1996, p. C1.

Providence Journal-Bulletin, March 12, 2003, p. D5.

Record (Bergen County, NJ), September 23, 2003, p. S2; October 22, 2003, p. S6.

Times Union (Albany, NY), December 12, 2003, p. C2.

USA Today, January 10, 2001, p. C1.

On-line

"Sean Brown," *National Hockey League Players Association,* www.nhlpa.com/WebStates/PlayerBiography.asp?ID=688 (March 2, 2005).

"Sean Brown," *New Jersey Devils,* www.newjersey devils.com (March 2, 2005).

"Sean Brown," *Sports Illustrated,* http://sports illustrated.cnn.com/hockey/nhl/players/1537 (March 2, 2005).

—James M. Manheim

Pierre Charles

1954-2004

Prime Minister of Dominica

Charles, Pierre, photograph. UN photo by Michelle Poire. Reproduced by permission.

On October 1, 2000, Roosevelt "Rosie" Douglas, prime minister of the Caribbean island-nation of Dominica, died of a heart attack after less than a year in office. Two days later Pierre Charles—popularly known as Pierro and deputy leader of the Dominica Labour Party (DLP)—was chosen as the new prime minister. A lifelong social and political activist, the longest-seated member of Parliament, and Minister of Communications and Works, Charles was the logical choice to lead the country through what was to become a major economic crisis.

Charles faced a difficult situation upon taking office. With a population of fewer than 100,000, Dominica—located between Guadeloupe and Martinique in the Lesser Antilles—was one of the poorest countries in the Caribbean. Hurricanes and globalization had devastated its traditional banana economy, and the terrorist attacks of September 11, 2001, and the ensuing worldwide economic downturn put Dominica's fledgling developments in ecotourism and offshore financial services on hold. Charles was forced to impose austerity measures that alienated his traditional poor and

working-class supporters, as well as business and political leaders.

Trained as a Teacher

Pierre Charles was born on June 30, 1954, in Grand Bay, on Dominica's south coast. The town of about 5,000 was a center of both Dominican culture and social and political activism. Pierre was one of seven sons and ten daughters born to Francis and Theodora (Francis) Charles. Pierre was educated at Grand Bay Boys' School and the Dominica Grammar School before completing high school at St. Mary's Academy in 1972. As a student he was a sergeant in the Cadet Corps, representing Dominica at the 1972 Regional Cadet Camp in Jamaica. That year he became a teacher at the Grand Bay Primary School.

Charles married Justina Musgrave, a nurse, and fathered three children. His son Camilo was named for the Cuban revolutionary hero Camilo Cienfuego. Charles was a member of the National Basketball League of Dominica, a Boy Scout leader, and belonged to a choral group called "La Jeune Etoile," which revived Dominican folk music. Later he managed the "Midnight Groovers" band.

In 1975 Charles and his friends formed the activist group L'Echelle (The Ladder). Inspired by the left-wing Caribbean political ideology of the times, their goal was to raise social consciousness among the young people of Grand Bay and involve them in the fight for Dominican independence from Great Britain. L'Echelle formed a loose-knit network with activists from neighboring islands, including Grenada, St. Vincent, and St. Lucia. The group's motto was "work and study." Charles worked with the Dominica Literacy Project and the Library Project at Tetre Lalay Grandbay.

In July of 1978 Charles defied the Dominican government by leading a group to the 11th World Festival of Youth and Students in Havana, Cuba. He was a founding member of the Dominica Cuba Friendship Society, which led to a Cuban government scholarship program that enabled hundreds of Dominicans to attend university in Cuba.

Joined the Independence Movement

Charles became involved with Rosie Douglas's Popular Movement for Independence for Dominica and in 1977 he led Dominica's National Youth Council into the movement. The Commonwealth of Dominica

gained independence from Great Britain in 1978. The following year Charles gave up teaching.

During the May 1979 political uprising against the government of Prime Minister Patrick John, Charles represented the National Youth Council on the Committee for National Salvation, which negotiated a settlement. In June Charles was appointed a senator in the Dominica Interim Government. In the July 1980 general election he ran unsuccessfully for the Grand Bay parliamentary seat on the ticket of the left-wing Dominica Liberation Movement Alliance.

Charles was a leader of the reconstruction efforts after Hurricane David devastated Grand Bay in August of 1979. He served on the Grand Bay Village Council for more than a decade, eventually becoming chairman. In 1979 Charles helped establish an agricultural trade organization called Farm to Market. As operations manager and later field manager, he worked to develop markets for Dominica's small-farm produce.

Elected to Parliament

In 1985 Charles—now a member of the major opposition party, the social democratic DLP—was elected to parliament from Grand Bay. He was reelected in each general election through 2000, when the DLP, in a coalition with the Dominica Freedom Party, took power for the first time in 20 years. As deputy leader of the DLP, Charles organized party branches throughout the island and joined Prime Minister Douglas's cabinet. Eight months later he became the DLP leader and prime minister of Dominica.

In addition to his role as prime minister, Charles was in charge of finance, economic planning, and Caribbean and foreign affairs. He promised to attract foreign investment, create jobs, and diversify the island's economy.

Always an outspoken critic of American foreign policy in the Caribbean and elsewhere, Charles protested the United States' hostile treatment of Cuba and its invasion of Afghanistan. One of his first acts as prime minister was to establish diplomatic relations with Libya. However, Charles also began to seek closer relations with the United States, Canada, Europe, and especially Japan.

Imposed Austerity Measures

Charles was a strong supporter of the integration of Caribbean economies as a means of dealing with globalization. However, from his first months in office, he faced a worsening economic crisis. Unemployment was at 23%. Between 2000 and 2002—after the World Trade Organization forced European Union members to phase out preferential treatment for their former colonies—Dominica's banana export revenue dropped by 32%. The island's stagnant tourist industry slumped after September 11th, 2001. The global economic downturn meant that Dominicans working abroad no longer had money to send home. The nation lacked educational opportunities, health care, and adequate infrastructure. Dominica's debt equaled about 75% of its gross domestic product.

To meet this economic crisis Charles was forced to undertake drastic economic measures that were at odds with his political inclinations. In 2002, yielding to pressure from the International Monetary Fund (IMF), the World Bank, and the Eastern Caribbean Central Bank, Charles imposed a 4% stabilization levy on all salaries and a 5% tax on telephone and television services and all petroleum products except kerosene. Public spending was cut 15% and Charles downsized his government. Strikes, protests, and the largest mass demonstrations in two decades erupted in response to these measures. The government was under siege by trade unions, industry organizations, and the main opposition party.

In 2002 the Caribbean Community (CARICOM) launched a $250-million stabilization fund to help the region's struggling economies, particularly Dominica. That fall, frightened by the Dominican crisis, the Organization of Eastern Caribbean States moved to initiate the creation of an economic union. By the end of 2003, following the imposition of new austerity measures, the IMF granted Dominica special financing for poverty-relief programs.

Died in Office

Charles underwent heart surgery twice in 2003. In November he took a three-week medical leave. Some members of his own party, as well as the opposition, called for him to step down. On January 6, 2004, while being driven home from an evening cabinet meeting, the 49-year-old prime minister died of a heart attack.

At Charles's state funeral at the Grand Bay Roman Catholic Church, Cristin Gregoire, Dominica's ambassador to the United Nations, was quoted on the *CNN* Web site: "He was like a fighter in the ring. He took the punches that were thrown at him, and was still able to smile and radiate the love and kindness for which he was well known."

In a tribute to Charles on the Dominica Academy of Arts and Sciences Web site, Gabriel J. Christian wrote: "Whatever we may have thought of him, Pierre Charles was an independence hero, a man who stood for social justice. One who died at his post, giving his last full measure for Dominica. In respecting his legacy, we will be respecting ourselves and so encourage the principle that patriotic and selfless service to one's country is a blessed virtue."

One year after Charles's death, the Dominican government renamed the Grand Bay Secondary School and a road in Grand Bay after the late prime minister. The Pierre Charles Foundation was established to provide student scholarships. At the 2005 ceremony, Dominica's Prime Minister Roosevelt Skerrit was quoted by the *Asia Africa Intelligence Wire*: "To have moved from a negative 5 per cent growth to seeking to achieve in 2004-05 a growth of about 3 per cent is the fruits of the efforts of Pierre Charles. He will be remembered in the history of Dominica for really taking the bold and necessary decisions in the best interest of Dominicans."

Selected writings

Address, United Nations General Assembly, 56th Session, 51st Plenary Meeting, New York, November 13, 2001.

Sources

Periodicals

Asia Africa Intelligence Wire, January 8, 2005.
Global Information Network (New York), July 15, 2002, p. 1; October 17, 2002, p. 1.

On-line

"Dominica Prime Minister Honored in State Funeral," *CNN.com*, www.cnn.com/2004/WORLD/americas/01/17/dominica.charles.ap/ (April 25, 2005).
"Pierre Charles," *Biography Resource Center*, www.galenet.com/servlet/BioRC (May 19, 2005).
"Tributes & Condolences to late Hon. Pierre Charles," *Dominica Academy of Arts and Sciences*, www.da-academy.org/bios.html (April 25, 2005).

—Margaret Alic

Don Cheadle

1964—

Actor, director, writer, musician

Don Cheadle has carved as unique niche for himself in Hollywood. He is, as *Esquire* dubbed him, "the thinking man's character actor." Cheadle selects his roles with care, relishing the opportunity to try new things. Cheadle has won extensive critical acclaim for his vast array of characters, including his turns as a district attorney on television's *Picket Fences,* as Denzel Washington's horrifying sidekick Mouse in *Devil in a Blue Dress,* as a porn star in *Boogie Nights,* and as a dancing and singing Sammy Davis, Jr., in *Rat Pack.* But his lead role in *Hotel Rwanda* catapulted him to stardom. His portrayal of Paul Rusesabagina, the Rwandan hotel manager who protected over 1,000 Tutsis from harm when his country erupted in civil war in 1994, earned him an Oscar nomination and "the luxury of picking and choosing what movies he'll perform in," according to *Ebony.*

Found Work Early On

Cheadle was born on November 29, 1964, in Kansas City, Missouri, the second of three children of a psychologist father and a schoolteacher mother. His father's pursuit of educational and job opportunities took the family to Lincoln, Nebraska, and Denver, Colorado. The role of Templeton the Rat in a fifth grade production of *Charlotte's Web* got him interested in acting. "I remember carrying my script around and studying it like I do now—I don't know why, but I was serious about acting even then," Cheadle told Kristine McKenna of the *Los Angeles Times.* After performing in numerous high school plays and musicals, Cheadle moved on to the California Institute for the Arts in Valencia, California, near Los Angeles. "I loved Cal Arts. I knew I would be acting all the time there. You might not get the part you want, but you know you're going to be in twenty-four plays no matter what," Cheadle told *Interview.*

Typical struggling actor jobs such as waiting on tables or parking cars are not part of Cheadle's story. "I've been blessed beyond belief. I've only been an actor to support myself. To complain would be sinful," Cheadle told Justine Elias of *Interview.* Landing his first paying acting jobs while still in drama school, Cheadle has been working steadily in films, television, and theater since 1985. Upon graduation in 1986, Cheadle was given five hundred dollars by his parents to help him start off his professional career. Fortunately, after a about a month, just as the money was running out, Cheadle landed a role in the film *Hamburger Hill,* a drama about a group of soldiers battling to secure a strategic hill during the Vietnam War. Shot on location in the Philippines, the film was directed by John Irvin and featured a roster of new young performers including Dylan McDermott, Courtney B. Vance, and Steven Weber, along with Cheadle.

Returning from the Philippines, Cheadle quickly found work at the Guthrie Theater in Minneapolis in a production of Jean Genet's *The Screens* staged by renowned experimental director JoAnne Akalaitis. From there Cheadle moved on to the film *Colors,* a gritty tale of Los Angeles gang warfare between the Bloods and the Crips. Directed by Dennis Hopper, the film starred Robert Duvall and Sean Penn as police

At a Glance . . .

Born on November 29, 1964, in Kansas City, MO; the son of a psychologist and a teacher; partner: Bridgid Coulter; children: two daughters. *Education*: California Institute of the Arts, Valencia, CA, BFA, 1986.

Career: Actor, playwright, director, 1980s–; musician (saxophone player); Elemental Prose, founder.

Memberships: none.

Awards: National Society of Film Critics and the Los Angeles Film Critics Association, Best Supporting Actor Award, 1995, for *Devil in a Blue Dress*; Los Angeles Film Critics Association, Best Supporting Actor Award, 1995, for *Devil in a Blue Dress*; Golden Globe Award, 1998, for *The Rat Pack*.

Addresses: *Publicist*—Steven Huvane, Huvane, Baum, Halls Public Relations, 8383 Wilshire Boulevard, Suite 444, Beverly Hills, CA 90211.

officers investigating a "drive-by" shooting of a gang member. Cheadle played Rocket, the leader of the Crips who dies in a shoot out at the film's end. A happier film project was 1993's *The Meteor Man*, a socially conscious fantasy about a man who finds himself with superhuman power after being struck by a meteor and uses the new power to clean up his troubled neighborhood. Robert Townsend wrote, directed, and starred in the film. Again, Cheadle played a gang member, only this time for satirical humor.

Cheadle's breakthrough film was *Devil in a Blue Dress*, a moody "film noir" based on a Walter Mosley mystery novel. Released in 1995, the film starred Denzel Washington as Easy Rawlins, an unemployed aircraft worker turned private detective investigating a murder in Los Angeles' vibrant black community in the 1940s. Cheadle played Mouse, Rawlins' violent and vicious friend who became his partner in the investigation. "Don Cheadle does a frighteningly funny turn as a completely amoral little man who finds it easier to kill someone than to talk to him," wrote David Denby in *New York*. And film critic Sibylla Nash wrote in the *Los Angeles Sentinel* that "Cheadle almost steals the show from Washington with his matter-of-fact humor." But Cheadle told Stephen Farber of the *New York Times*: "At first I was surprised that audiences laughed at Mouse. I wasn't attempting to get laughs. But in any farce, the energy a character spends pursuing a single

goal is funny. And it's scary, too. I think one reason people laugh is that they're feeling 'I'm glad I'm not in that room with Mouse.'"

Devil in a Blue Dress was directed by Carl Franklin, in whose American Film Institute student film, *Punk*, Cheadle had appeared several years before. Initially Franklin did not want Cheadle for the role of Mouse, thinking him too young to play a contemporary of fortyish Washington. Cheadle was refused an audition. Fortunately, an accidental encounter between Cheadle and Franklin at a doctor's office lead to Cheadle being asked to read for the part. A second reading with Washington, during which the two actors clicked, secured the part for Cheadle. "I had six weeks to prepare so I did lots of research that included spending a week in Houston, which is where Mouse is from. I met a few people from the '40s who were of the world Mouse lived in, and having talked with some of them I can tell you that gangsters of that era were different from gangsters today. There was more honor among thieves then, and they had a strong sense of community and all kept each other in check. Crack, of course, has put an end to all that," Cheadle told the *Los Angeles Times*.

Won Critical Acclaim as Mouse

Though well received by critics, *Devil in a Blue Dress* failed at the box office. "That was very disappointing because it was a wonderful film, with wonderful performances," critic Orlando Peters explained to the *Jacksonville Free Press*. "I would have bet a bundle that film would have done well. It had a proven star, and it was based on a popular book. It wasn't even a matter of it failing to cross over, because black people alone could have made that film a success, and the final numbers say black audiences were not interested in the film." For his work as Mouse, Cheadle was named best supporting actor by the Los Angeles Film Critics Association and by the National Society of Film Critics. Cheadle's name, however, was not on the list of Academy Award nominees. "Now that I know how [Oscar nominees] get picked, and how the selection process works, I could give a (expletive) if I ever get one. I mean it would be nice because your money goes up, and it shows appreciation on a wide level, but what does my performance have to do with the political lobbying and machinations that go on inside the Academy that I am not privy to? Nothing. If I never get an Oscar, it doesn't mean anything about my work," Cheadle told Mark Ebner of *Premiere*. Although many critics felt Cheadle's not earning an Academy Award nomination for *Devil in a Blue Dress* was an outrage, Cheadle tried to take a more practical view of the situation. "My folks sent me a slew of magazine and newspaper articles that asked why I wasn't nominated, so in the end I got more buzz for being overlooked," Cheadle told Elias.

Though Cheadle spent his early years landing distinct supporting character roles, he played the lead in

Rebound: The Legend of Earl "The Goat" Manigault. Made for the Home Box Office (HBO) cable channel in 1996, *Rebound* told the near-autobiographical story of a Harlem basketball wizard of the 1960s whose chance for a career in professional basketball was ruined by his descent into drug addiction and crime. Manigault's eventual recovery from addiction and his work with New York City youth were also depicted. "Cheadle's performance in portraying the once promising basketball star who traded his skills for the foolish pleasures of snorting and injecting his way to a temporary high is superb," wrote Jaime C. Harris in the *Amsterdam News. Rebound* was directed by actor Eriq LaSalle, of television's *ER,* and featured James Earl Jones, Forrest Whitaker, and Clarence Williams III.

Another story based on past events in which Cheadle appeared was *Rosewood,* a look at the burning down by angry, bigoted whites of Rosewood, an African American community in central Florida. Believing a white woman's false accusation that she had been attacked by a Rosewood man, and jealous of Rosewood's prosperity, white residents of the neighboring mill town of Sumner torched the nearly all-black town in 1923. Cheadle played Sylvester Carrier, a piano teacher who risked his life by deciding to stand his ground and not run away from the racist mob. The film was directed by John Singleton. "I had seen Don Cheadle's portrayal of Mouse in *Devil in a Blue Dress* and was impressed with his performance. I called him up afterward and told him we had to work together. I didn't know what it would be at the time, but when we were casting *Rosewood,* I realized he would be a great Sylvester," Singleton told the *Indianapolis Recorder.* Released in 1997, *Rosewood* garnered some excellent reviews. Joan H. Allen of the *Amsterdam News* called the film "powerful and compelling." Despite critical praise, *Rosewood* barely registered at the box office. "It was a hard sell," Cheadle explained to Elias. "Very few movies take on the risk of trying to teach you something, or illuminate something so that people who just want escapism will digest it too…The Rosewood tragedy wasn't that long ago: It took place in our grandparents' day, and the xenophobic attitude it shows is prevalent today. And when the mirror is held up to that attitude, well, I think people feel pretty resentful when they've just paid $7.50," he continued.

Cheadle admitted that money was the primary impetus for his appearance in the disaster film *Volcano,* in which an unprepared Los Angeles is threatened with an overwhelming flow of lava. His role in the 1997 film as assistant chief of the city's emergency management squad was not written specifically for a black actor. Cheadle said non-race specific roles are relatively rare and not necessarily desirable. "Color blindness is ridiculous…You don't need to ignore your race…There are issues you can't not confront. I'm glad people try to write roles that anyone can do, but I also don't ever want to end up in movies where the fact that I'm a black man is a nonissue. In America, it's always an issue," Cheadle told *Interview.*

In *Boogie Nights,* an unsparingly frank examination of the pornographic film industry of the 1970s, Cheadle played Buck Swope, an X-rated movie star. "My backstory on him would be that he's from a broken home, and he's fallen into this family of misfits that have welcomed him," Cheadle said of his character in the film to Ebner. At first, Cheadle was reluctant to accept the part, worried that the film might be tawdry. He requested that he not have to take off his clothes for the camera. "I didn't want to be naked and exploited. I wanted the film to take a deep look at these people and it does," Cheadle recalled in *Interview.*

Appeared on TV

On series television, Cheadle's most notable work was his two years as a straight-arrow district attorney on the quirky small town life drama *Picket Fences.* He also had a regular role on the situation comedy *The Golden Palace,* an unsuccessful sequel to *The Golden Girls,* and recurring roles on *Fame* and *The Fresh Prince of Bel Air.* More television is not something Cheadle sees in his future, hoever. "I plan to focus on films and theater because with television you're forced to deal with major script changes every day. There's no time to refine things, and they so often cut things that are key to where you're trying to take your character. I find it very frustrating," Cheadle said in the *Los Angeles Times.*

Cheadle's concentration on landing roles that he could dig his teeth into paid off. For his portrayal of Sammy Davis, Jr., in the made-for-television movie the *Rat Pack,* Cheadle won a Golden Globe award. Cheadle also won critical praise for his lead role in *Hotel Rwanda,* the real-life story of the 1994 civil war in Rwanda. *Hollywood Reporter* called it "an African version of 1993's *Schindler's List.*" Cheadle plays hotel manager Paul Rusesabagina, a Hutu, who from April to July 1994 protected 1,200 Tutsis from the rampaging Hutu militias in the Rwandan capital of Kigali. *Variety* lauded his performance as "exquisitely crafted," *Interview* found it "breathtaking," and *Newsweek* called it Cheadle's "richest role since *Devil in a Blue Dress.*" Cheadle earned an Oscar nomination for it. Cheadle's five-year experience working on *Hotel Rwanda* touched him deeply. He became a political activist, raising awareness of the atrocities of the Rwandan civil war and trying to drum up support to stop the ongoing civil war in Sudan.

Cheadle followed *Hotel Rwanda* with *Crash. Crash* uses a variety of incidents—including a traffic accident and a burglary—happening in Los Angeles over a 36-hour period to show how different people act toward each other based on first impressions, skin color, and accents. Cheadle, who also produced the film, played an L.A. police detective. The cast included actors Sandra Bullock, Matt Dillon, and Michael Pena. *People* film critic Leah Rozen praised the film, writing: "Movies don't come better acted, as lucidly written or, most importantly, more capable of grabbing a viewer emotionally and intellectually than this exceptional ensemble drama about racial and ethnic relations in urban America today."

Although a seasoned professional, Cheadle's work seemed to have only just begun in the early 2000s. He was widely sought after as an actor; he wrote and directed plays; and he continued to produce films. Cheadle also made his feature film directorial debut with an adaptation of Elmore Leonard's novel, *Tishomingo Blues*. In the film, which remained in production in 2005, Cheadle plays Robert Taylor, a gangster from Detroit. But as his children grew, Cheadle again eyed television as a good outlet for his talents because it required less traveling than film work. He had taken his daughters to South Africa with him for the filming of *Hotel Rwanda,* and did not feel that he could ask them to pick up and move whenever he found an interesting film. "I don't want to have them going from place to place just because this is what I want to do," Cheadle told *Ebony*. Nevertheless, Cheadle did not expect to lower his standards for interesting and compelling roles.

Cheadle, who lives in Venice, California, with actress Bridgid Coulter and their two young daughters, is pleased with how his life and career have evolved. He told *Premiere*: "When I sit back and think about it, relaxed on my front porch, feeling a breeze and listening to the wind chimes, I go, 'Damn, this came out right. This is really nice.'"

Selected works

Films

Hamburger Hill, 1987.
Colors, 1988.
Roadside Prophets, 1992.
Meteor Man, 1993.
Things to Do in Denver When You're Dead, 1995.
Devil in a Blue Dress, 1995.
Rosewood, 1997.
Volcano, 1997.
Boogie Nights, 1997.
Bulworth, 1998.
Out of Sight, 1998.
Family Man, 2000.
Traffic, 2000.
Ocean's Eleven, 2001.
Swordfish, 2001.
Hotel Rwanda, 2004.
Ocean's Twelve, 2004.
Crash, 2004.

Plays

The Screens and *Leon, Lena and Lenz*, Guthrie Theatre, Minneapolis, MN.
The Grapes of Wrath and *Liquid Skin*, Mixed Blood Theatre, Minneapolis, MN.
Cymbeline, Public Theater, New York City, 1989.
'Tis a Pity She's a Whore, Goodman Theatre, Chicago, IL.
The Blood Knot, Complex Theatre, Hollywood, CA.
Groomed, New Works Festival, the Mark Taper Forum, Los Angeles, CA, 1997.
Topdog/Underdog, 2001.

Television

Fame, c. 1985.
The Fresh Prince of Bel Air, c. 1990.
The Golden Palace, 1992-1993.
Picket Fences, 1993-1995.
Rebound: The Legend of Earl "The Goat" Manigault (television movie), 1996.
The Rat Pack (television movie), 1998.
A Lesson Before Dying (television movie), 1999.

Sources

Periodicals

Amsterdam News (New York), November 23, 1996, p. 56.
Bay State Banner (Boston), March 20, 1997.
Ebony, June 2005, p. 178.
Entertainment Weekly, October 10, 1997, p. 66.
Esquire, January 2005, p. 24.
Hollywood Reporter, December 2004, p. 30.
Indianapolis Recorder, February 22, 1997, p. B2.
Interview, August 1997, p. 80-85; December 2004, p. 66.
Jacksonville Free Press, March 5, 1997, p. 13; June 4, 1997, p. 11.
Los Angeles Sentinel, October 4, 1995, p. A3.
Los Angeles Times, September 30, 1995, p. F1.
Newsweek, December 27, 2004, p. 80.
New York, October 2, 1995, p. 82.
New York Beacon, May 14, 1997, p. 26.
New York Times, October 22, 1995, sect. 2, p. 18.
Philadelphia Tribune, January 31, 1997, magazine section, p. 4.
Pittsburgh Courier, February 12, 1997, p. B3.
Sun Reporter, February 20, 1997, p. 9; April 24, 1997, p. 9.
Variety, September 20, 2004, p. 60.

On-line

"Movies: Interviews: Don Cheadle," *BBC*, www.bbc.co.uk/films/2005/02/24/don_cheadle_hotel_rwanda_interview.shtml (June 7, 2005).

"*Swordfish* Interview: Don Cheadle," *Film Force,* http://filmforce.ign.com/articles/300/300420p1. html (June 7, 2005).

Other

Information also provided by Huvane, Baum, Halls Public Relations.

—Mary Kalfatovic and Sara Pendergast

Kenneth B. Clark

1914-2005

Psychologist, educator, writer

Kenneth Bancroft Clark will remain among the most prominent black social scientists of the twentieth century. For many years a professor of psychology at City College of New York (now City College of the City University of New York), Clark achieved national recognition when his work was cited by the U.S. Supreme Court in its 1954 ruling that racially segregated schools were inherently unequal and therefore unconstitutional. That decision was a catalyst for the civil rights movement of the 1960s, and Clark went on to author a series of highly influential books about ghetto life, education, and the war on poverty. After retiring from teaching in 1975, Clark established a consulting firm to assist corporations and other large employers with their racial policies and minority hiring programs. Until his death in 2005, Clark worked diligently to pressure American society to acknowledge the social ills of segregation.

Mother Sought Opportunity in United States

Clark was born in 1914 in the Panama Canal Zone, the son of Miriam Clark and Arthur Bancroft Clark, a native of the West Indies who worked as a superintendent of cargo for the United Fruit Company. Despite the family's relatively comfortable situation in Panama, Miriam Clark, a Jamaican woman of stubborn courage, insisted that the Clark children should be raised in the United States, where they would get better education and employment opportunities than in Panama. Kenneth and his sister, Beulah, accordingly moved with

their mother to the Harlem district of New York City when Kenneth was four-and-a-half; their father, however, refused to relocate to a country where his color would prevent him from holding a job similar to his position with United Fruit. Undeterred, Miriam Clark found work in Harlem as a seamstress and proceeded to raise the children on her own.

In later life, Clark became famous as an uncompromising advocate of integrated schooling, and it is not surprising that his own education took place in the culturally diverse setting of 1920s Harlem. At that time Harlem was home to immigrants of various nationalities, especially those of Irish and Jewish origin, and was also the center of a rapidly growing black population.

Attending classes in New York City schools, young Clark was held to the same high standards as his fellow students, most of whom were white. As he told New Yorker magazine many years later, "When I went to the board in Mr. Ruprecht's algebra class,... I had to do those equations, and if I wasn't able to do them he wanted to find out why. He didn't expect any less of me because I was black." That is a capsule description of the educational philosophy Clark would maintain for the rest of his life: schools must be open to students of every race, and teachers must expect the same performance from each child. In such an environment, some students will naturally perform better than others, but not according to racial categories.

When he finished the ninth grade, Kenneth Clark was faced with a critical juncture in his education. School counselors advised most black youths to attend

At a Glance . . .

Born Kenneth Bancroft Clark on July 24, 1914, in Panama Canal Zone; died on May 1, 2005, in Hastings-on-Hudson, NY; son of Arthur Bancroft (a cargo superintendent for United Fruit) and Miriam (a seamstress; maiden name, Hanson) Clark; married Mamie Phipps (a psychologist), April 14, 1938 (died, 1983); children: Kate Miriam, Hilton Bancroft. *Education*: Howard University, BA, 1935, MS, 1936; Columbia University, PhD, 1940. *Religion*: Episcopalian.

Career: Howard University, Washington, D.C., psychology instructor, 1936; Hampton Institute, Hampton, VA, psychology instructor, 1940; worked for U.S. Office of War Information, 1941-42; City College of New York (now City College of the City University of New York), instructor, 1942-49, assistant professor, 1949-1960, professor, 1960-70, distinguished professor of psychology, 1970-75, became professor emeritus, 1975. Harlem Youth Opportunities Unlimited (HARYOU), chairman of board of directors, 1962-64; Metropolitan Applied Research Center, Inc. (MARC Corp.), president, 1967-75; Clark, Phipps, Clark & Harris, Inc. (consulting firm), president and chairman of the board, 1975-(?).

Memberships: New York State Board of Regents, 1966(?)-1986.

Awards: Rosenwald fellow, 1940-41; Spingarn Medal, National Association for the Advancement of Colored People, 1961; Board for the Advancement of Psychology in the Public Interest, Committee on Psychology in the Public Interest Award, 1978; Franklin Delano Roosevelt Four Freedoms Award, Franklin and Eleanor Roosevelt Institute, 1985; National Alliance of Black School Educators, Living Legend Award, 1995. Honorary degrees from Columbia University, Johns Hopkins University, Princeton University, and others.

Excelled Academically

Instead, Kenneth was sent to George Washington High School, where he excelled in all subjects and grew especially fond of economics. He had thoughts of becoming an economist until he was denied an award for excellence in economics by a teacher who apparently could not bring himself to so honor a black student. Clark remembers this as his first direct experience of discrimination, and it may well have prepared the ground for his subsequent decision to study psychology, particularly the psychology of racism.

Upon entering Howard University in 1931, Clark originally intended to become a medical doctor. In his second year at the all-black institution he took a class in psychology taught by Francis Sumner that changed forever the course of his studies. "What this professor showed me," Clark told the *New Yorker*, "was the promise of getting some systematic understanding of the complexities of human behavior and human interaction,…the seemingly intractable nature of racism, for example." Clark determined that he would follow the example of Sumner in the field of psychology, and after receiving a master's degree in 1936, he joined the faculty of Howard for a year of teaching.

At that point Clark came to another critical fork in his career. He could have remained at Howard, teaching with either his master's degree or a doctorate, but at the urging of his mentor Sumner and a number of other outstanding faculty members, Clark went on to Columbia University with the express purpose of obtaining his doctorate and teaching at an integrated college. He became the first black doctoral candidate in psychology at Columbia and completed his degree in 1940.

Clark was married in 1938 to Mamie Phipps, a fellow psychology student at Howard who would coauthor many of the articles that later made the couple famous. After graduating from Columbia, Clark taught briefly at Hampton Institute in Virginia, a very traditional black college whose most famous alumnus was Booker T. Washington. Hampton was far too conservative a school for Clark, who left after one term rather than teach a form of psychology based on the subjugation of blacks. Following a two-year stint with the U.S. Government's Office of War Information, Clark joined the faculty of City College of New York in 1942, becoming an assistant professor seven years later and, by 1960, a full professor—the first black academic to be so honored in the history of New York's city colleges.

Investigated the Psychology of Segregation

As a black psychologist, Clark had always been deeply concerned with the nature of racism, and in the 1940s he and his wife, Mamie, began publishing the results of their research concerning the effects of segregated

vocational high school, where they could learn skills appropriate to the limited employment opportunities available to blacks. When Clark's mother heard of this plan she went directly to the counselor's office and told him that under no circumstances would her son go to trade school; she had not come all the way from Panama to raise a factory worker.

schooling on kindergarten students in Washington, D.C. Between 1939 and 1950 the Clarks wrote five articles on the subject and became nationally known for their work in the field.

In 1950 Kenneth Clark wrote an article for the Mid-century White House Conference on Children and Youth, summarizing his own work and other psychological literature on segregation. This report came to the attention of the National Association for the Advancement of Colored People (NAACP) during its post-World War II campaign to overturn legalized segregation. In its landmark 1954 decision declaring such segregation unconstitutional, the U.S. Supreme Court cited the Clark report as representative of "modern authority" on the subject.

Clark was intimately involved in the long legal struggle which culminated in *Brown v. Board of Education*, as the court's 1954 desegregation decision was titled. He testified as an expert witness at three of the four cases leading up to the Supreme Court's review of *Brown*, and his report on the psychology of segregation was read carefully by the justices. Psychological findings were critical to the NAACP's case, in which they asked the court to overturn its earlier decision (*Plessy v. Ferguson*, 1896) that "separate but equal" schooling for the two races did not violate individual rights under the Constitution.

In *Plessy v. Ferguson*, the court had held that as long as separate schools were of equal quality, they did not inherently "deny...the equal protection of the laws" guaranteed by the Fourteenth Amendment. The NAACP challenged the Plessy decision by asserting that, in reality, separate meant unequal for blacks–especially black schoolchildren. In his testimony before one of the lower courts, Clark defined the harmful effects of segregated schooling as "a confusion in the child's own self esteem–basic feelings of inferiority, conflict, confusion in his self-image, resentment, hostility toward himself." Such effects would be felt, Clark and the NAACP argued, regardless of the relative merits of the schools involved; or, as the court eventually stated, "Separate educational facilities are inherently unequal."

Brown v. Board of Education was not only a milestone in the modern civil rights movement, it also made Kenneth Clark into something of an academic superstar. Clark went on to become the most influential black social scientist of his generation. He received honorary degrees from more than a dozen of the nation's finest colleges and universities, but his larger goal of integrated, adequate schooling for blacks had not become a reality even four decades after the announcement of the monumental court decision.

Studied School System in Harlem

America's schools did not suddenly integrate themselves the day after *Brown v. Board of Education*; in most urban areas the growth of black ghettoes only reinforced the segregation of black and white schoolchildren. Clark understood that in order to improve the education of students of color, the African American community as a whole needed to lobby for a massive infusion of capital and commitment from the federal government and from private citizens. After sparring unsuccessfully with the New York City Board of Education during the late 1950s over issues of segregation, Clark was given a unique opportunity to effect a wholesale reformation of the school system in Harlem. As part of the "Great Society" plans inaugurated by the administrations of President John F. Kennedy and his successor, Lyndon B. Johnson, federal funds were provided in 1962 to create Harlem Youth Opportunities Unlimited (HARYOU), the task of which was to study and suggest remedies for the causes of juvenile delinquency in the Harlem area.

Clark was appointed chairman of HARYOU, which over the next two years produced a 620-page report recommending, among other things, the "thorough reorganization of the schools" in Harlem. This would include increased integration, a massive program to improve reading skills among students, stricter review of teacher performance, and, most importantly, a high level of participation by the residents of Harlem in implementing these changes. HARYOU was the first example of what would later be known as a community-action program.

HARYOU was sabotaged by political power bargaining in New York, and few if any of its recommendations were followed. As Clark commented in the *New Yorker*, "As it turned out, all we did at HARYOU was to produce a document." Clark's community-based approach inspired many subsequent programs in the "War on Poverty," but with few exceptions they too fell victim to the complexities of urban politics. Although his experience with HARYOU must be counted as a failure in terms of political reality, it did spur Clark to write the book for which he is best known, *Dark Ghetto: Dilemmas of Social Power*. In this work, Clark goes beyond his HARYOU research to write what he describes in the introduction as "no report at all, but rather the anguished cry of its author"–an overview of black ghetto life that has become required reading in sociology classes around the country.

In 1967 Clark formed and presided over a nonprofit corporation known as MARC Corp. (the Metropolitan Applied Research Center), composed of a group of social scientists and other professionals who hoped to identify and solve problems of the urban poor. MARC's most significant work was undertaken in 1970, when the school board of Washington, D.C., asked Clark and his associates to design a new educational program for the city's 150,000 schoolchildren, 90% of whom were black and the majority of whom were poor.

In an era of radical social and political experimentation, the Washington, D.C. school system offered Clark the chance to test his theories of education on a large scale and under ideal conditions. Clark outlined a program similar to the HARYOU program for New York, calling for a massive and immediate upgrading of reading skills, teacher evaluation based on student performance, and community involvement in the schooling process.

Once again, however, real life proved far more complex than theory: the Washington, D.C. teachers refused to make their pay and position dependent on the outcome of student tests, and a new superintendent of schools (elected in 1971) refused to cooperate with the plan and even challenged Clark's central thesis that children of the ghetto could and should be expected to perform at "normal" levels. Ghetto life, argued this administrator, was anything but normal, and it would be unfair to hold teachers and schools responsible for the performance of students handicapped by living in the ghetto.

Such a claim flew in the face of everything Kenneth Clark had learned and fought for since he was a grade school student. It also contradicted the findings of *Brown v. Board of Education*: if ghetto children could not be held to the same standards as other children, then the schools they were attending were obviously *not* "equal." Clark's defeat at the hands of political reality did not dampen his belief in integrated schooling, however; nor did he cave in to the demands of the politically fashionable black separatist movement in the late 1960s and early 1970s. He opposed the creation of any organization based on racial exclusivity, including such projects as a black dormitory at the University of Chicago and Antioch College's Afro American Institute. As a result, Clark was attacked as a "moderate" at a time of black radicalism, in some instances receiving personal threats for his adamant rejection of racial separatism.

Continued Working for Educational Equality

After his retirement from City College in 1975, Clark and his wife and children founded a consulting firm called Clark, Phipps, Clark & Harris, Inc., helping large corporations design and implement minority hiring programs. The firm flourished, attracting prestigious clients such as AT&T, Chemical Bank, and Consolidated Edison, and Clark remained active in the burgeoning field of minority concerns in the 1990s workplace.

Back in 1982, Clark admitted in the *New Yorker* that the educational outlook was poor for children of color. "Things are worse. In the schools…more black kids are being put on the dung heap every year." His wife, Mamie, was even more frank, stating: "More people are without hope now…. I really don't know what the answer is." Viewing this discouraging prospect eight

years later, Clark admitted that even he was beginning to doubt the possibility of racial harmony through integration. "I look back and I shudder," he told the *Washington Post*, "and say, 'Oh God, you really were as naive as some people said you were.'"

With the commitment of U.S. president Bill Clinton's administration to equalize opportunities for all Americans, Clark continued to voice his outrage over the country's lack of educational progress–in academic, social, and psychological terms–but offered a mandate for change in the nineties. In a 1993 essay for *Newsweek* titled "Unfinished Business: The Toll of Psychic Violence," Clark commented: "We have not yet made education a process whereby students are taught to respect the inalienable dignity of other human beings…. [But] social sensitivity can be internalized as a genuine component of being educated. This is nonviolence in its truest sense. By encouraging and rewarding empathetic behavior in all of our children—both minority and majority youth—we will be protecting them from ignorance and cruelty. We will be helping them to understand the commonality of being human. We will be *educating* them."

Clark did not live to see his life's work fulfilled, however. The 2002 Harvard's Civil Rights Project "A Multiracial Society with Segregated Schools: Are We Losing the Dream?" described a resegregation of the nation's public schools, finding that while "the South remains the nation's most integrated region for both blacks and whites, it is the region that is most rapidly going backwards as the courts terminate many major and successful desegregation orders," according to the *Antioch Review*. Clark died in his home on May 1, 2005, at the age of 90. But his legacy lives on. New York journalist Woody Klein collected Clark's more than fifty years of work in *Racial Identity in Context: The Legacy of Kenneth B. Clark*. The collection provides behind-the-scenes stories of Clark's studies of black public school children that became the proof behind the *Brown v. Board of Education* case. Other scholarly works provide insight into Clark's contributions to American society and the field of psychology. He will be remembered as an unwavering voice against racism.

Selected writings

Prejudice and Your Child, Beacon Press, 1955, reprinted, University Press of New England, 1988.

(With Lawrence Plotkin) *The Negro Student at Integrated Colleges*, National Scholarship Service and Fund for Negro Students, 1963.

The Negro Protest: James Baldwin, Malcolm X, Martin Luther King Talk with Kenneth B. Clark, Beacon Press, 1963, published as *King, Malcolm, Baldwin: Three Interviews*, University Press of New England, 1985.

Dark Ghetto: Dilemmas of Social Power, Harper, 1965, reprinted, University Press of New England, 1989.

Social and Economic Implications of Integration in the Public Schools, U.S. Department of Labor, 1965.

(Editor with Talcott Parsons) *The Negro American*, Houghton, 1966.

(With Jeannette Hopkins) *A Relevant War Against Poverty: A Study of Community Action Programs and Observable Change*, Harper, 1969.

(With Harold Howe) *Racism and American Education: A Dialogue and Agenda for Action*, Harper, 1970.

(Editor with Meyer Weinberg) *W. E. B. Du Bois: A Reader*, Harper, 1970.

Pathos of Power, Harper, 1974.

Author, with wife, Mamie Phipps, of a series of articles on the effects of school segregation. Also author of numerous articles published in journals of psychology and sociology.

Sources

Books

Clark, Kenneth B., *Dark Ghetto: Dilemmas of Social Power*, Harper, 1965.

Clark, Kenneth B., *Pathos of Power*, Harper, 1974.

Keppel, Ben. *The Work of Democracy: Ralph Bunche, Kenneth B. Clark, Lorraine Hansberry, and the Cultural Politics of Race,* Harvard University Press, 1995.

Bowser, Benjamin P., and Louis Kushnick with Paul Grant, eds., *Against the Odds: Scholars Who Challenged Racism in the Twentieth Century,* University of Massachusetts, 2002.

Klein, Woody, ed., *Toward Humanity and Justice: The Writings of Kenneth B. Clark. Scholar of the 1954 Brown v. Board of Education Decision,* Praeger, 2004.

Philogene, Gina. *Racial Identity in Context: The Legacy of Kenneth B. Clark,* APA, 2004.

Periodicals

American Psychologist, January 2002.
Antioch Review, Spring 2004.
Commentary, November 1971.
New Yorker, August 23, 1982.
New York Times, May 2, 2005.
Newsweek, January 11, 1993.
Washington Post, March 4, 1990.

—Jonathan Martin and Sara Pendergast

Helen Claytor

1907-2005

YWCA President

A staunch advocate of racial equality and a life long supporter of the Young Women's Christian Association (YWCA), Helen Claytor spent her career working tirelessly and courageously to ensure minority rights. The first black president of the National YWCA, she dedicated her talents to the organization and to the cause of betterment for all. Also active in the Urban League and the National Association for the Advancement of Colored People, her pioneering role paved the way for hundreds of women.

The third of four daughters, Helen was born in Minneapolis in 1907, where her father, a Pullman porter from Ohio, and her mother had decided to raise their family. The young couple had met during one of his train runs, when Helen's mother, a woman from Virginia, was on her way to Pierre, South Dakota, where she was going to teach cooking. In an interview with Mary Mead Fuger reprinted in *Grand River Valley History*, Helen elaborated, "My father, as he was running on the road, was also reading law in a lawyer's office. It was back in the days when you could pass the bar if you knew enough law, and he was the first black man to pass the bar in South Dakota."

Hoping early on that their children would attend college, Helen's enterprising parents wanted to live near a university, hoping to save on room and board when the time came for their daughters to enroll. They built a home near the University of Minnesota campus, though local whites unsuccessfully tried to buy them out. As Claytor related to the *Grand Rapids Free Press*, though the offers became extravagant, her father finally told the eager buyers, "you're wasting your time. There is no amount of money you can offer because my principles are not for sale." Those principles and her parents' push towards education gave Helen what she believed was something better than a silver spoon.

Claytor's involvement with the YWCA (or "Y" in popular vernacular) began in the seventh grade, when she joined the YWCA Girl Reserves. She would remain active with the group throughout high school and college. As hoped for, Claytor attended the University of Minnesota, graduating cum laude in 1928 as valedictorian of her class and as a member of Phi Beta Kappa. She had hoped to enter the teaching profession but was faced with the fact that teaching jobs for blacks were nonexistent—even for someone with her credentials. Most blacks in her position looked for employment in the South, but Claytor instead turned her thoughts to the YWCA, already a big influence on her life.

Claytor was directed to the Trenton, New Jersey, branch of the Y, which at the time was racially segregated. Having a main community YWCA for whites and a branch located a few blocks away for blacks was not uncommon. As Claytor explained to Fuger in *Grand River Valley History*, "Back then they had a lot of black branches of the YWCA. There [was] only one YWCA in a community, and anything else [was] a branch." Two years later, having fulfilled the promise she had made to her mother that she would work for a time before marrying, Helen married Earl Wilkins. The brother of former National Association for the Advancement of Colored People (NAACP) executive

At a Glance . . .

Born April 12, 1907, in Minneapolis, Minnesota; died on May 10, 2005, in Grand Rapids, MI; daughter of a Pullman porter and a cooking instructor; married Earl Wilkins, c. 1920s (died 1941); married Robert Claytor, 1943 (died 1989); children: Roger (first marriage), Judith (second marriage), Sharon (second marriage). *Education*: University of Minnesota, education degree, 1928.

Career: YWCA-Trenton YWCA, NJ, Girl Reserves secretary, c. 1920s; YWCA-Kansas City, MO, c. 1930s; National YWCA, secretary for interracial education, c. 1940s; YWCA-Grand Rapids, MI, volunteer, c. 1945-48, president, 1949; YWCA World Council, 1946-52, 1967-73; National YWCA Board of Directors, member, 1946-73; National YWCA of U.S.A., president, 1967-73.

Memberships: Phi Beta Kappa, 1928; National YWCA Board of Directors, honorary member, 1973-2005; Urban League; National Association for the Advancement of Colored People; Grand Rapids Human Relations Commission, charter member, 1955; League of Women Voters; Kent County Medical Auxiliary; Women's City Club, Grand Rapids, MI; National Women's Advisory Committee for Civil Rights; National Office of Equal Opportunity; Widowed Persons Service.

Awards: Honorary Doctor of Humanities, Eastern Michigan University, 1968; Outstanding Achievement Award, University of Minnesota, 1968; Honorary Doctor of Public Service, Western Michigan University, 1972; Helen J. Claytor Merit of Distinction, YWCA-Grand Rapids, 1983; Michigan Women's Hall of Fame, 1984; named a "Woman of Courage," Michigan Women's Foundation, 1994.

director Roy Wilkins, Earl had been a college classmate of Claytor's and was working as a journalist in Kansas City, Missouri. Claytor spent the next ten years with her husband in Missouri. After Wilkins died of tuberculosis in the late 1930s, Helen resumed her activities with the YWCA, choosing to remain in Kansas City with the couple's son.

The work she did there brought her to the attention of the National YWCA board in New York City, which offered her the position of secretary of interracial education. Upon accepting, Claytor joined a team whose responsibilities included traveling to other Ys, lending technical assistance and studying interracial practices that would eventually lead to desegregation within the organization.

Traveling to Michigan on behalf of the National YWCA, she met her second husband, Dr. Robert Claytor, the first black physician in Grand Rapids and a member of board of the local Community Chest (the United Way precursor). The two met during a meeting of local leaders. According to former Grand Rapids YWCA board president Marilyn Martin in the *YWCA Focus*, Claytor had been asked to address the Michigan "State Public Affairs Committee of the YWCA, regarding the organization's role in the [Second World] war effort." Amongst local leaders gathered to hear her speak that evening was Dr. Claytor, who later took her to dinner and escorted her back to the train station. What Helen would later describe as "love at first sight" in the *YWCA Focus*, resulted in marriage one year later, in 1943.

The Claytors early years in Grand Rapids were marred by racial incidents, including housing discrimination. Realtors would show the new couple small, houses unsuitable for their "extended" family. Such occurrences brought back to Helen memories of what her father had encountered in Minnesota. The discrimination was obvious and very frustrating for the Claytors, especially when they believed they had a house one day only to be told the next that it had been sold to other buyers. As word quickly spread that the prospective buyers were blacks, neighbors and realtors banded together to protest the Claytor's eventual purchase of a home on the northeast side of town. Little did the protesters know that the house would become a permanent residence for the family.

Discrimination came from other quarters of the city as well. Martin recounted that the Kent County Medical Auxiliary and the American Association of University Women did not invite Helen to join, although she met all the criteria for membership—except, apparently, skin color. When she joined the League of Women Voters, the group was politely asked to find a new home, and thus relocated from the Women's City Club to the more "race-friendly" Grand Rapids Public Museum. Not until many years later was Claytor admitted to both the Medical Auxiliary and the Women's City Club. Meanwhile, Claytor had resigned her position with the National YWCA and had begun volunteering at the Grand Rapids branch. Martin noted in the *YWCA Focus* that Claytor was initially unaware that relations between the Grand Rapids YWCA and the black community were poor. Practices such as barring black children from the swimming pool and segregated classes were the rule of the day.

The struggle for equal treatment continued, when, in 1949, Claytor was nominated to the YWCA's highest position—president of the board. The initial impact on the community was negative; the idea of a black in such a position was theretofore unheard of, creating, in Claytor's own words, "a lot of fuss." Pressure to withdraw from the race mounted, culminating in the resignation of three members of the board of directors. Claytor found it difficult to have the same group of women perfectly willing to serve with her on the board, but unwilling to have her preside over them as their board president. "They were perfectly willing to be on the board with me, but they thought it would be disastrous to have a black person as president," she assessed in the *Grand River Valley History*.

Fortunately support came from two key figures: treasurer Gertrude Skipper, who firmly stated her intentions to remain in place, and Tirzah McCandless, the candidate nominated to replace Claytor. At first McCandless did not know of the circumstances surrounding her own nomination, but according to Martin in the *YWCA Focus*, "When Tirzah learned the truth, she withdrew her name and renominated Helen, who was then elected the first Negro YWCA president in the United States. It was a sweet victory." Claytor clarified in the *Grand River Valley History*, "It was the first time anyplace in the country that a black woman had been elected president of a community [as opposed to a branch] YWCA."

After proving her talents as president of the Grand Rapids YWCA, Claytor assumed the presidency of the National YWCA Board of Directors in 1967. Once again she was the first black woman in history to hold the post. That year she was also selected for a second stint with the YWCA World Council, having previously served from 1946 to 1952. One of the biggest highlights of Claytor's career occurred in 1970, during the first YWCA national convention over which she presided. There she witnessed the results of the study of interracial practices with which she had assisted for many years come into fruition. The justice and equality imperative, specifically "the elimination of racism wherever it exists and by any means necessary" was adopted and became a tenet of all YWCAs.

At that point, having filled a variety of roles during her long involvement with the YWCA, many in leadership capacities, including vice president at large and chair of the central region, Claytor contemplated retiring from the national board in 1970, only to find herself nominated and elected to a second three-year term as national board president. Claytor finally resigned from the National YWCA's board of directors in 1974, but retirement did not slow Claytor down, prompting her mother to comment, as Claytor fondly related to Fuger, that Helen was into "everything except the fire department." Claytor went on to serve on the National Women's Advisory Committee for Civil Rights and the National Office of Equal Opportunity and continued to be active in such groups as the NAACP and the Urban League.

A longtime volunteer at the St. Phillip's Episcopal Church, Claytor also maintained her involvement in local human rights issues. She clearly remembered the resistance faced by Grand Rapids mayor Paul Goebel as he was appointing a committee to study whether the establishment of a Human Relations Commission was warranted. Quite a few people felt the need for such a committee was nonexistent, but Claytor and a group nicknamed "the girls" persisted. In the *Grand River Valley History*, Claytor revealed to Fuger that "the thing I am proudest of, for the service that I've done in Grand Rapids, is that I was one of the people who helped to found what we called then the Human Relations Commission, but which is now the Equal Opportunity Office (EOO)." The EOO brought to light existing discrimination in such areas as housing and employment and exposed other gaps in living conditions in the community. The City of Grand Rapids honored Claytor's civic contributions by creating the Helen Jackson Claytor Civil Rights Award.

Throughout the years, Claytor received much recognition for her involvement and contribution in public service. In 1968, she was awarded an honorary Doctor of Humanities by Eastern Michigan University and in the same year received an Outstanding Achievement Award from the University of Minnesota. In 1983 the Grand Rapids YWCA held a special tribute for her, establishing the Helen J. Claytor Merit of Distinction—a biannual award given to volunteers who have made valuable service contributions to the YWCA organization—and making her the first recipient. Nationally recognized civil rights activist Dorothy Height was the keynote speaker at the well-attended event. And in 1994, Claytor, along with civil rights heroine Rosa Parks, was named a "Woman of Courage" by the Michigan Women's Foundation. The ceremony's co-chair was quoted by the *Grand Rapids Free Press* as saying, "the women we are honoring have served as an inspiration to generations of women, not only in Michigan, but throughout the nation and the world. Through their perseverance and dedication, they have made a real difference in promoting equality for individuals regardless of gender or race."

Upon her retirement from the national YWCA Board of Directors, Helen set forth the philosophy that guided her throughout her life and so enriched the lives of others. In her farewell address she declared: "I have done what I could all my life for the cause of human dignity, multiplying my efforts by those of all the members of this organization, who, motivated by the barrier-breaking love of God, have kept on a road they cannot and would not get off. This has helped me keep my equilibrium—kept me from falling into despair or depression, knowing that, if my faith has validity, the quality of life for which the YWCA struggles must ultimately succeed. It also seems to me that despite the multiplicity of ills still besetting the world, more and more people are aware of them and are willing to commit their lives to healing them, and I know that I must stay in the number." Indeed she did, remaining active in her church and community until her death. Coretta Scott King described Claytor's career as an "eloquent testament to the great things an individual can accomplish," according to the African American Registry. Claytor died at the age of 98 on May 10, 2005, in her home in Grand Rapids, Michigan.

Sources

Periodicals

Grand Rapids Free Press, April, 1994, p. B3.
Grand Rapids Press, May 11, 2005, p. A1.
Grand River Valley History, 1995, pp. 14-18.
Star Tribune (Minneapolis, MN), May 12, 2005, p. B8.
Washington Post, May 14, 2005, p. B14.

YWCA Focus (Grand Rapids), Winter, 1993, p. 1; Spring, 1996, pp. 1-2.

On-line

"Helen Claytor, a YWCA Original...," *African American Registry,* www.aaregistry.com/african_american_history/2739/Helen_Claytor_a_YWCA_original (June 6, 2005).

Other

Additional information for this profile was obtained through YWCA- Grand Rapids press releases dated 1983 and January 28, 1985; the Helen J. Claytor Merit of Distinction Award Dinner program, April 22, 1983; and the Michigan Women's Foundation Award program, 1994.

—Doris H. Mabunda and Sara Pendergast

Johnnie Cochran

1937-2005

Lawyer

Johnnie L. Cochran, Jr. led the winning team of lawyers in what has been known as the "trial of the century," and in the process became arguably the most famous lawyer in the world. Cochran's successful defense of former football great O. J. Simpson against charges of murder in the televised trial was followed by millions of Americans. Although his trial tactics still spark debate, his legal acumen and ability to sway a jury characterized his distinguished legal career. While the *People v. O. J. Simpson* is perhaps Cochran's most well known courtroom victory, it was proceeded and followed by a string of significant court cases, some involving superstars such as Michael Jackson and others involving ordinary people thrust into extraordinary circumstances. *Ebony* magazine once described Cochran as "a litigator who'd taken the cases people said he *might* win when hell freezes over, then laughed all the way to the bank when the multimillion-dollar verdicts came rolling in."

Handsome and well spoken, Cochran was established in the West-Coast power elite well before his defense of O. J. Simpson. After the trial, he was one of America's foremost attorney celebrities. Though he was detested in some circles as an opportunist, he was just as widely admired as an African-American success story. Cochran told *Essence* that he was never bothered by his detractors. "I have learned not to be thin-skinned, especially when I think I'm doing the right thing," he said. "It's not about money, it's about using the law as a device for change."

Longed for the Good Life

Johnnie Cochran, Jr. was born in 1937 in Shreveport, Louisiana, and is the great-grandson of a slave. He grew up in a prosperous and stable family, with a father and mother who stressed education, independence, and a color-blind attitude. While Cochran was still young the family moved to Los Angeles, and he attended public schools there, earning excellent grades. Although his father had a good job with the Golden State Mutual Life Insurance Company, Cochran always managed to find friends who had more money and more luxuries than he did. "If you were a person who integrated well, as I was, you got to go to people's houses and envision another life," he recalled in *The American Lawyer*. "I knew kids who had things I could only dream of, I remember going to someone's house and seeing a swimming pool. I was like, 'That's great!' Another guy had an archery range in his loft. An archery range! I could not believe it. I had never thought about archery! But it made me get off my butt and say, 'Hey, I can do this!'"

Cochran earned a bachelor's degree from the University of California, Los Angeles, in 1959, supporting himself by selling insurance policies for his father's company. He was accepted by the Loyola Marymount University School of Law and began his studies there in the autumn of 1959. "I was the kind of student that didn't want to look like a jerk, always raising my hand," Cochran recalled in *The American Lawyer*. "But I would sit there and pray that I would be called on. That was my competitive spirit lying in wait."

At a Glance . . .

Born Johnnie L. Cochran, Jr. on October 2, 1937, in Shreveport, LA; died on March 29, 2005, in Los Angeles, CA; son of Johnnie L. (an insurance company executive) and Hattie Cochran; married Barbara Berry Cochran, 1959 (divorced 1977); married Sylvia Dale, 1985; children: (first marriage) Tiffany, Melodie; (with former girlfriend) Jonathan. *Education*: University of California, Los Angeles, BA, 1959; Loyola Marymount University School of Law, JD, 1962. *Politics*: Democrat.

Career: Attorney, 1963-2005. City of Los Angeles, deputy city attorney, 1963-65; private attorney, 1965-78; Los Angeles County, assistant district attorney, 1978-82; private attorney and head of law firm, 1982-2005; Cochran Firm, founder, 2001. University of California, Los Angeles School of Law and Loyola University School of Law, former adjunct professor of law. Democratic National Convention, Rules Committee, chairman, 1984. Served on special congressional committee for ethics and official conduct.

Selected Memberships: Criminal Courts Bar Assn., board of directors; Langston Bar Assn, board of directors; Los Angeles Urban League, board of directors; Los Angeles African American Chamber of Commerce, board of directors; Black Business Assn of Los Angeles, president, 1989; Lawyers Mutual Insurance Co., board of directors, 1991; American Bar Foundation, fellow, 1991; Rebuild LA Project, board of directors, 1992; Daniel Freeman Hosp, board of directors, 1993; TransAfrica Forum, board member, 2002.

Selected Awards: John M Langston Bar Assn, Honorable Loren Miller Award as Trial Lawyer of the Year, 1983; California Assn of Black Lawyers, Loren Miller Award as Trial Lawyer of the Year, 1983; Legal Defense Fund of the NAACP, Equal Justice in Law Award, 1984; Los Angeles Trial Lawyers Assn, Trial Lawyer of the Year, 1990; Trumpet Award, Turner Broadcasting System, 1995.

Having finished his law studies and passing the California bar by 1963, Cochran took a job with the city of Los Angeles, serving as a deputy city attorney in the criminal division. There he worked as a prosecutor. In 1965 he entered private practice with the late Gerald Lenoir, a well-known local criminal lawyer. After a short period with Lenoir, he formed his own firm, Cochran, Atkins & Evans. "That was the closest to a storefront I ever had," Cochran remembered in *The American Lawyer*. Johnnie Cochran's career was launched from this office with a highly publicized and inflammatory case.

Took First Race-Related Case

In May of 1966, a young black man named Leonard Deadwyler was shot dead by police as he tried to rush his pregnant wife to the hospital. Cochran represented Deadwyler's family, who accused the police of needless brutality in their son's murder. The Los Angeles Police Department insisted that the officers had acted in self-defense. "To me, this was clearly a bad shooting," Cochran maintained in *The American Lawyer*. "But the [district attorney] did not file charges, and when our firm filed a civil suit we lost. Those were extremely difficult cases to win in those days. But what Deadwyler confirmed for me was that this issue of police abuse really galvanized the minority community. It taught me that these cases could really get attention."

Another memorable case further steered Cochran toward working on behalf of his race. In the early 1970s he went to court in defense of Geronimo Pratt, a Vietnam War veteran who was convicted of a murder on a tennis court in Santa Monica, California. Many speculated that he was put away because of his leadership role in the Black Panther Party. Cochran lost that case too, but he insisted that Pratt was railroaded by the F.B.I. and local police. "White America just can't come to grips with this," Cochran explained in *Essence*. "To them the police are as they should be: saving children, acting like heroes in the community. They aren't setting up people, they're not lying, they aren't using their racist beliefs as an excuse to go after certain people." Cochran continued to work on the case long after Pratt was imprisoned, and finally in 1997 he was able to get an Orange County judge to overturn Pratt's sentence and free him. He sued the state of California for wrongful imprisonment and won Pratt $4.5 million.

Such headline-grabbing cases quickly made Cochran's name known among the black community in Los Angeles. By the late 1970s, he was handling a number of police brutality and other criminal cases. In an abrupt about-face in 1978, however, he joined the Los Angeles County district attorney's office. Cochran has said that he took the job because he wanted to broaden his political contacts and refashion his image. "In those days, if you were a criminal defense lawyer, even though you might be very good, you were not considered one of the good guys, one of the very top rung," he explained in *The American Lawyer*.

Cochran's position at the district attorney's office did not spare him a brush with racist police. One afternoon as he drove his two young daughters across town in his Rolls Royce, he was pulled over. The police yelled at him to get out of the car with his hands up, and when he did he could see that they had drawn their guns. "Well, talk about an illegal search and seizure!" Cochran exclaimed in *The American Lawyer*, recalling the event. "These guys just go through ripping through my bag. Suddenly this cop goes gray. He sees my number three badge from the D.A.'s office! He's like, 'Ahh! Ahh!' They all go apologetic. I never got stopped again, but I'm careful not to make any weird moves. I might get shot!"

Cochran never publicized the incident, but he was deeply disturbed about its effect on his two daughters. "I didn't want to tell them it was because of racism," he added. "I didn't want to tell them it happened because their daddy was a black guy in a Rolls, so they thought he was a pimp. So I tried to smooth things over.... As an African American, you hope and pray that things will be better for your children. And you don't want them to feel hatred."

Became the "Best in the West"

Returning to private practice in 1983, Cochran established himself as "the best in the West," to quote *Ebony* magazine. One of his first major victories occurred in the case of Ron Settles, a college football player who police said had hanged himself in a jail cell after having been picked up for speeding. On behalf of Settles' family, Cochran demanded that the athlete's body be exhumed and examined. A coroner determined that Settles had been strangled by a police choke hold. A pre-trial settlement brought the grieving family $760,000.

The Settles case was the first in a series of damage awards that Cochran won for clients—some observers estimate he has won between $40 and $43 million from various California municipalities and police districts in judgments for his clients. *Essence* reporter Diane Weathers wrote: "Cochran is not just another rich celebrity lawyer. His specialty is suing City Hall on behalf of many fameless people who don't sing, dance or score touchdowns and who have been framed, beaten up, shot at, humiliated and sometimes killed at the hands of the notorious LAPD."

Success bred success for Cochran. The Settles case was followed by another emotional case in which an off-duty police officer molested a teenager and threatened her with bodily harm if she told anyone. In that case Cochran spurned an out-of-court settlement of six figures and took the issue to the courtroom, where a jury awarded his client $9.4 million. A post-verdict settlement paid the young woman $4.6 million.

Took Celebrity Cases

As Cochran's fame grew, his client list began to include more celebrities, which included pop singer Michael Jackson. On Jackson's behalf, Cochran arranged an out-of-court settlement with a boy who had accused the singer of molestation. Cochran had the case retired in such a way that the charges against Jackson were withdrawn, and Jackson could publicly proclaim his complete innocence. Cochran also engineered an acquittal for *Diff'rent Strokes* star Todd Bridges, who stood accused of attempted murder.

No celebrity trial was more closely followed than O. J. Simpson's trial, however. In the summer of 1994, Simpson was arrested and charged with the murders of his ex-wife, Nicole Brown Simpson, and her friend Ron Goldman. Simpson declared that he was innocent, and he engaged Cochran as part of an expensive "dream team" of lawyers dedicated to his defense. Before long, Cochran had replaced Robert Shapiro as leader of the "dream team" as the matter was brought to trial. Calling the O. J. Simpson trial a "classic rush-to-judgment case," Cochran vowed to win an acquittal for the football star-turned-television celebrity. Responding to questions about the nickname for his legal team, Cochran told *Time*: "We certainly don't refer to *ourselves* as the Dream Team. We're just a collection of lawyers...trying to do the best we can."

One week into the Simpson trial in February of 1995, *Time* reported that Cochran had "unveiled an unexpectedly strong defense." With his engaging manner and sincerity, Cochran sought to poke holes in the case against Simpson as presented by district attorneys Marcia Clark and Christopher Darden. Piece by piece he challenged the evidence, paying special attention to the racist attitudes of one of the investigating officers, Mark Fuhrman.

Cochran was effective—and controversial—in his closing arguments on Simpson's behalf. He claimed his client had been framed by a racist police officer, and that if such injustice were allowed to persist, it could lead to genocide as practiced by Nazi dictator Adolf Hitler. Speaking to the jury, Cochran concluded: "If you don't speak out, if you don't stand up, if you don't do what's right, this kind of conduct will continue on forever." After deliberating only four hours, the mostly black jury found Simpson not guilty on all counts.

Observers called Cochran's remarks the "race card," and some castigated the attorney for proceeding in this manner. Cochran offered no apologies for his strategy, claiming that his scenario represented the truth as he saw it. "I think race plays a part of everything in America, let alone this trial," he maintained in a *Newsweek* interview. "That's one of the problems in America. People don't want to face up to the fact that we do have some racial divisions."

Life After O.J.

After handling the post-trial publicity, Cochran returned to other cases, including pending civil litigation against Simpson. The trial had a huge impact on Cochran's life. Once a celebrity lawyer only in Los Angeles, he became a celebrity lawyer across America. Cochran had his share of negative publicity as well. His first wife, Barbara Berry Cochran, wrote a memoir during the Simpson trial in which she accused Cochran of abuse and infidelity. "I did a lot of stupid things," Cochran admitted in *Essence* when asked about his private life. "I paid a price with my eldest daughter and with my [first] marriage. I would like young lawyers not to make the mistakes I made." In response to many of the questions and practices he had followed both professionally and personally, Cochran published *Journey to Justice*, an autobiographical work that focused on his early influences, his career path up to and including the Simpson case, and where he hoped to take his passion for civil rights activism through law in the future. He also began appearing regularly on the Courtroom Television Network first as a co-contributor on the show *Court TV: Inside America's Courts* and then on his own show a few years later.

Many people speculated that Cochran might retire after settling the Pratt case, as he had off-handedly commented on many occasions, but Cochran forged ahead in his fight against police and governmental abuse against African Americans. In early 1998 he took on the case of four men who were shot by New Jersey police during what Cochran called a "racial profiling" traffic stop. When asked why he was taking on the case, Cochran commented during a New York City news conference that, "this case is a catalyst more then anything else," hoping to stir the American public into taking interest in what their protection agencies were actually doing while on the streets.

Even though Cochran was at the top of his game professionally, he still faced trials and tribulations in his personal life. In November of 1998, Cochran's brother RaLonzo Phlectron Cochran was found murdered in Los Angeles from gunshot wounds. In a statement released by the Cochran family, RaLonzo was described as "yet another victim of the senseless violence that so often permeates our society." Added to this was a long arduous case that Cochran brought against the *New York Post* for libel, claiming that remarks made about him in a column hurt his reputation and caused him emotional distress. The case was eventually settled out of court, but no retraction was ever published.

None of this seemed to slow Cochran as he continued to take on high profile cases. In 2001 Cochran represented Sean "P. Diddy" Combs against charges of gun possession and purportedly bribing a witness to change his testimony. Cochran, true to his track record, was able to convince a jury that Combs had not broken any laws. Cochran also brought a case to the courts in

2001 where he represented numerous clients who had begun smoking before the age of 18 and wished to reclaim the money they spent on smoking from the tobacco companies, alleging that the tobacco companies unfairly advertised to their age bracket and coaxed them into buying cigarettes.

In late 2001 Cochran opened the Cochran Firm in Memphis, Tennessee, to practice civil law. Along with four other attorneys, Cochran hoped to use his name to help clients who would not otherwise get what he considered "proper" representation. As Julian Bolton, the managing partner of the Cochran Firm's Memphis office put it to the Knight Ridder/Tribune News Service, "We have seen a large segment of the population that feels somewhat powerless in the courtroom and in official circles.... They want and need a hero like Mr. Cochran." The Cochran firm eventually established offices in thirteen states. Cochran also found time to join new organizations, becoming a board member of TransAfrica Forum, a group looking to foster constructive United States policies towards Africa and the Caribbean.

Engaged Larger Social Issues

Cochran felt that the battle for fairness for all Americans was long from over. Along with his move to open the Cochran Firm, Cochran also turned his attention from police abuse to the broader scope of racial inequality in all facets of society. One of his first major cases in this vein was when he joined a team lead by Cyrus Mehri in a suit against the Coca-Cola company in 2000, accusing them of unfairness to African Americans in the form of unequal wages, prejudiced evaluations, and lack of promotions. Coca-Cola settled out of court, but refused to admit to any wrongdoing. Cochran and Mehri did not stop there, however, instead turning their sights on industry giant Johnson & Johnson, which they claimed was guilty of similar practices. The case had not yet settled, but when asked to comment on why he targeted such large companies, Cochran joked to the *Corporate Counsel*, "The bigger the giant, the bigger the fall."

Cochran also hoped to gain the support of the American public in his crusade against racism and unfair practices in sports. In early 2002 he brought an anti-trust suit against stock car racing giant NASCAR, owned by the France family, claiming that they were discriminating against smaller companies such as Speedway Motorsports Inc. by owning both the organization that runs all of the major stock car races in the United States as well as International Speedway Corporation which owns 13 of the major tracks where NASCAR is raced yearly. Almost a year later, he took the fight to one of the oldest sports in the United States, challenging the National Football League (NFL) to hire more minority coaches or face a lawsuit dealing with unfair hiring practices based on race. As Cochran told the Knight Ridder/Tribune News Service, "There are many problems, but one of the biggest is that there doesn't seem to be a hiring criteria where blacks are concerned." Well before a suit was filed, the NFL began making changes to its internal processes.

Quite wealthy and married for a second time, Cochran lived in a luxurious home overlooking the Los Angeles basin. Approaching the age of 70, Cochran told *Newsweek* that he wanted to initiate a "healing" between the races in America. If that is to happen, he believed, white America will have to become more sympathetic to the hardships facing African Americans. "It doesn't make sense for us to go back into our individual camps after this is over," he noted. "African Americans... respond to what I have to say. I spoke what they feel is happening, and I spoke it as an African American lawyer.... I don't want to exacerbate racial problems. But you have to be true to who you are.... This is not for the timid." Cochran's dream was not yet realized when he passed away as the result of an inoperable brain tumor at his home on March 29, 2005. He was widely eulogized as one of the finest African American lawyers of the twentieth century, a man who used his vast talents to pursue justice for his people.

Sources

Books

Clarke, Caroline V. *Take a Lesson: Today's Black Achievers on How They Made It and What They Learned along the Way,* John Wiley, 2001.

Cochran Berry, Barbara, *Life After Johnnie Cochran: Why I Left the Sweetest-Talking, Most Successful Black Lawyer in L.A.,* BasicBooks, 1995.

Newsmakers, Issue 1, Gale Group, 1996.

Periodicals

Africa News Service, October 10, 2001.

American Lawyer, May 1994, p. 56.

Black Enterprise, June 2005, p. 11.

Black Issues in Higher Education, April 21, 2005, p. 20.

Corporate Counsel, April 2002, p. 13-14.

Ebony, April 1994, pp. 112-16; November 1996, pp. 92-96; June 2005, p. 184.

Entertainment Weekly, February 9, 2001, p. 13.

Essence, November 1995, p. 86.

Jet, May 17, 1999, p. 37; April 25, 2005, p. 5. May 30, 2005, p. 4.

Knight Ridder/Tribune News Service, May 24, 2001; October 4, 2001; April 7, 2002; November 26, 2002; February 27, 2003.

MediaWeek, January 13, 1997, p. 41.

Newsweek, January 16, 1995, p. 60; October 9, 1995, pp. 31, 34; October 16, 1995, pp. 37-39, 42.

People, April 10, 1995, pp. 55-56.

The Source, January 1996, p. 34.

Time, January 30, 1995, pp. 43-44; February 6, 1995, pp. 58-63; January 1, 1996, pp. 102-03.

U.S. News and World Report, January 23, 1995, pp. 32-35.

On-line

Cochran Firm, www.cochranfirm.com (June 8, 2005).

—Ashyia Henderson, Mark Kram, Ralph G. Zerbonia, and Tom Pendergast

Agbani Darego

1982—

Model

Darego, Agbani, photograph. Yoav Lemmer/AFP/Getty Images.

Nigeria's Agbani Darego was crowned Miss World in 2001, making her the first black woman from an African country ever to win the pageant. Darego spent much of her Miss World year making public appearances around the globe and serving as an unofficial ambassador for her country, and even her continent. "People think that Africa is a backward, poverty-stricken place, that everyone who lives there is suffering," she told Lesley Garner of the *Evening Standard,* a London newspaper. "There are parts that are like that, but in Nigeria a lot of people are well-to-do."

Born in 1982, Darego hails from a town called Abonnema in the Rivers State area of southern Nigeria. Her full name is Ibiagbanidokibubo Asenite Darego, and she was the sixth of eight children in her family. Her father was a customs official, while her mother, Inaewo, had a rice-trading business which necessitated frequent travel; on her trips Inaewo bought clothing and sold it in a clothing boutique where Darego spent many hours as a little girl, paging through foreign fashion magazines. But Darego was sent off to a boarding school when she was ten years old. Two years later, her mother died of breast cancer, and Darego later realized she had been

sent away to shield her from her mother's condition. "I wasn't too happy at first, but it prepared me for my life now," she reflected about being away from home in an interview with Julia Llewellyn Smith of the *Mail on Sunday.* "I learned to be on my own. It makes you independent."

During her teens, Darego dreamed of becoming a model, a career plan dismissed by her father. At six feet, she was unusually tall for a Nigerian—all in her family are of above-average height—and she was slimmer than the prevailing standard of beauty. "The way most women look in Nigeria is not the Western ideal," she explained to Garner in the *Evening Standard* interview. "In my country, short, curvy women are thought beautiful, not me." Such extra pounds are considered a sign of health and prosperity, and some brides-to-be in Nigeria even cloister themselves in what is known as a "fattening room" two weeks before the wedding in order to gain weight.

Darego had a back-up plan, to study computer science, and had won a place at a university. She deferred it, however, and began making the rounds of modeling agencies in Lagos, Nigeria's main city, and began

At a Glance . . .

Born Ibiagbanidokibubo Asenite Darego in 1982, in Abonnema, Rivers State, Nigeria; daughter of Chief Asenite Darego Kaladokubo Jack V (a retired customs official) and Inaewo Darego (a rice-trading business owner and boutique proprietor). *Religion:* Christian.

Career: Model; signed with L'Oreal Cosmetics, 2002.

Awards: "The Face of Africa" modeling contest, runner-up, c. 1998; "Most Beautiful Girl in Nigeria" beauty pageant winner, 2001; crowned Miss World, 2001; made honorary member of Nigeria's Council of Chiefs, 2001.

Addresses: *Office*—c/o L'Oreal SA, Centre Eugene Schueller, 41, rue Clichy, F-92117, France.

entering pageants. In "The Face of Africa" modeling contest, she placed as a runner-up. In January of 2001 she won the "Most Beautiful Girl in Nigeria" contest, which made her eligible for the Miss World pageant later that year. The global-beauty event was held in Sun City, South Africa, and that year was hosted by American television personality Jerry Springer. Initially, Darego was a long shot to win, but that year's contest had a new feature: television viewers could phone in a vote for their favorite contestant. On that November evening, Darego became Miss World 2001, and failed to erupt in tears—the first time in recent memory that the winner had maintained her composure.

Darego was the first Nigerian to win the Miss World crown, but more importantly was the first black woman from an African country to win it. Black women had won the title before, but they hailed from Caribbean lands. Three other women from African nations had taken the crown over the years, but two were white women from South Africa, and the other an Arabic contestant from Egypt in the 1950s. There were massive celebrations in Nigerian cities the same night that Darego was crowned, and when she returned to Nigeria for her first official visit she met with government ministers and took part in a four-day celebration. She was even made an honorary member of the Council of Chiefs in Lagos, an extraordinary honor for a woman as young as she was and one that made her the country's youngest chief.

Darego chose to become a patron of a breast-cancer awareness program and dedicated her crown to her mother. She also devoted time during her Miss World year to an anti-malaria campaign. "I had malaria as a child, but I was privileged to have hospital treatments," she explained in the *Mail on Sunday* interview with Smith. "So many others die because they can't get drugs." She spent much of the year traveling, but used London as her base, in a home she shared with her younger sister. All told, she walked the Great Wall of China, attended the Cannes Film Festival and England's Royal Ascot—where she wore a stunning fuchsia ensemble and requisite elaborate hat—and was photographed for American *Vogue*. She also invested some of her cash prize in a parcel of land back in Nigeria.

Darego's year as Miss World was a successful one, but blighted in its last weeks by a political and religious controversy that had little to do with her: she was set to relinquish her crown at the next Miss World pageant in Nigeria, which was slated to be held in her country as an honor to her, but at the time, another young woman from Nigeria, Amina Lawal, had been sentenced to death by stoning on charges of adultery. Women's-rights groups from around the world called attention to the spectacle of holding a beauty pageant in a country where a woman was about to be executed for such a transgression. Perhaps seeking to defuse some of the tension, a Nigerian newspaper journalist wrote that were the prophet Mohammed, founder of Islam, alive today he might have selected a wife from among the contestants. Parts of Nigeria are predominantly Muslim, and the comments incited even more of a controversy. Widespread riots left 200 dead, and Darego and the new Miss World contestants were confined to their hotel for their personal safety. In the end, the pageant locale was hurriedly switched to London, and Darego crowned Miss Turkey as the new Miss World.

Darego landed a three-year contract with L'Oreal, the cosmetics giant, during her Miss World year. A born-again Christian, she does not drink or smoke, and had rarely even worn makeup prior to her Miss World year. She had ambitious plans for the rest of her career. "I'm not going to be a model for the rest of my life," she told the *Evening Standard*'s Garner. "I want to be a successful businesswoman. I want to be good at everything."

Sources

Asia Africa Intelligence Wire, March 27, 2003.
Evening Standard (London, England), May 7, 2003, p. 23.
Mail on Sunday (London, England), June 16, 2002, p. 29.
Sun (London, England), June 11, 2002, p. 28.

—Carol Brennan

O. R. Dathorne

1934—

Novelist, poet, critic, professor

Dathorne, O.R., Photograph. Courtesy of O.R. Dathorne. Reproduced by permission.

Author and educator O.R. Dathorne earned an international reputation for his work exploring and illuminating the experience of colonized cultures. Born and raised in the complex and diverse society of colonial Guyana, Dathorne was quite young when he began to learn about the social conflicts of race, class, and status that result when one nation takes possession of another. As a child growing up in a black family trying to achieve middle class status in a society ruled by white Europeans, Dathorne was all too aware of the divisions in the world around him. Perhaps because he did not fit comfortably into any one group, he became a questioner and a challenger, a social critic with little patience for the hypocrisy and unfairness he saw around him. Though his challenges have often brought him into conflict with those in authority, Dathorne remains a creative thinker and a respected expert on the effects of colonization and the literature of colonized peoples.

Situated in northern South America, between Suriname and Venezuela on the Atlantic Ocean, Guyana means "Land of Many Waters." First encountered by Europeans in 1498, the small, fertile country was almost immediately colonized by the Dutch, who brought African slaves to work on their sugar and tobacco plantations. The British, who took over the colony at the beginning of the nineteenth century, continued to use black slave labor to operate plantations until the 1830s, when the slavery was officially ended. After the abolition of slavery, British plantation owners brought in other workers to serve as cheap plantation labor, first from Portugal, then from India.

Grew Up in a British Colony

This resulted in a highly diverse society, made up of large black and Indian populations, with minorities of Portuguese, Chinese, and Native Americans, dominated by a British minority. Into this complex culture, Oscar Ronald Dathorne was born in the fall of 1934. The family lived in Guyana's capital city, Georgetown. Oscar Robertson Dathorne was an electrical engineer, and his wife Rosalie Belona Dathorne worked at home caring for young Ronald and his six brothers and sisters. Though many Guyanese blacks did not have

At a Glance . . .

Born Oscar Ronald Dathorne on November 19, 1934, in Georgetown, Guyana; married Hilde Ostermaier, 1959; children: Cecily, Alexander. *Education:* University of Sheffield, England, BA, English, 1958; University of London, Certificate of Education, 1959; University of Sheffield, MA, English, 1960; PhD, English, 1966; University of London, Diploma in Education, English as a foreign language, 1967; University of Miami, MBA, business administration, and MPA, public affairs, 1983.

Career: Ahmadu Bello University, Zaria, Nigeria, assistant professor, 1959-63; University of Ibadan, Nigeria, associate professor, 1963-6; United Nations Educational, Scientific and Cultural Organization Milton Magai Training College, 1967-70; University of Sierra Leone at Njala, English Department, chair and professor of English literature and Black literature, 1967-70; Yale University, visiting professor, 1970; Howard University, Department of African Studies, professor, 1970-1; University of Wisconsin, Department of Afro-American Studies, professor, 1970-1; Ohio State University, Department of English, professor, Department of Black Studies, professor and co-director, 1971-7; University of Miami, Caribbean, African and African-American Studies Program, director and professor of English, 1977-87; University of Kentucky, English department, professor, 1987–; *Journal of Caribbean Studies,* editor, 1979–.

Membership: Association of Caribbean Studies, director.

Awards: Ohio State University, Distinguished Teacher of the Year, 1976; University of Miami, Distinguished Teacher of the Year, 1980; National Association of Journalists, "Best Column Award," 1987; Alliance of Cuban Community Workers Award, 1987; Student Motivational and Recruitment Team (SMART) award for support and encouragement, 1988.

Addresses: *Office*—1325 Patterson Office Tower £0027, University of Kentucky, Lexington, KY 40506.

such skilled professions, Dathorne's family had worked hard to become educated and improve their status.

Even his mother's father had studied in England and had become an engineer.

Having achieved some degree of financial and social success, the Dathornes were protective of their children and did not want them to associate with poorer black children who lived nearby. As a child, Ronald often felt suffocated and confined when his parents discouraged him from making friends with children of a lower class. He was already beginning to learn how difficult it could be to navigate the divisions of a colonial society.

Eager to introduce him to friends of a better class, Dathorne's parents got him a government scholarship to the prestigious Queen's College, a boys' school which had been opened in Georgetown during the mid-1800s. Because its founders were British, Queen's College was organized in much the same way as exclusive British academies. The school accepted students of all races, but the principal and most of the teachers were white. In school Dathorne was taught that there were six races of people inhabiting Guyana: the English, the Indians, the blacks, the Amerindians, the Chinese, and the Portuguese. It interested him to learn that the English did not even consider their fellow Europeans the Portuguese to be members of their race.

Though he did well in his studies, young Ronald Dathorne was not happy at Queen's College. He was acutely aware of racial prejudice and resented the easy assurance of the white students who unthinkingly accepted the privileges of their race, interrupting other students and taking the best places without even seeming to notice. In addition to this, he was not athletically inclined and could not use sports to achieve success, the way many other black students did. However, he was inspired and encouraged by his history teacher Sir James Cameron Tudor, one of the few black teachers at Queen's College.

Attended College in England

In 1953, after his graduation from high school, Dathorne went to England to continue his education, as his grandfather had before him. He worked for two years as a clerk in the office of the London County Council while he studied the advanced Latin he needed to be accepted into a British university. In 1955, he entered the University of Sheffield in central England. He received his bachelor's degree in English in 1958 and studied education at the University of London for a year before returning to Sheffield to pursue his master's and doctoral degrees.

In 1963, armed with a Ph.D. in English, he began to look for a teaching job in England. However, he soon found that few English universities were willing to offer a black colonial the kind of teaching work that Dathorne was qualified to do. He sought job opportunities abroad and was hired to teach at the University of Ibadan in the west central African nation of Nigeria. Over the next six years, he would teach at several African colleges and universities, both in Nigeria and in the tiny coastal country of Sierra Leone.

Like Dathorne's home South America, the continent of Africa has also been conquered and colonized by a variety of European nations. Coming from England to live in Africa, Dathorne began to understand a bit of the experience of the English in Guyana. Far from feeling that he had come "home," Dathorne's education, accent, and even his name announced him as a foreigner, even among the African friends he made. His professor's salary enabled him to live like a wealthy man in Nigeria. As a member of the educated class, he was attended by servants, and even called "master" by working people. Very uncomfortable in this upper class role, he invited the man who served his meals to sit and eat with him. When this gesture only made the servant uncomfortable as well, Dathorne realized that he had learned one more twist in the complicated maze of race and class divisions that are part of a colonized society.

Developed Interest in African Literature

While teaching in Nigeria, Dathorne began to meet artists, publishers, and writers. Inspired by his new friends, he started using books by African writers in his literature classes. In the past, "African literature" had mainly consisted of books written by Europeans about Africans. In these works, Africans had been presented as the "Other," that is, strange and foreign beings who were only seen through the eyes of the European colonizers. Dathorne had learned from his own experience that it was damaging to native peoples to be seen only through the eyes of those who had conquered them. Along with some other literature professors of African ancestry, such as Molly Mahood, Dathorne began to redefine African literature to be works written by Africans.

In 1969 Yale University invited Dathorne as a guest lecturer. During the late 1960s, the civil rights movement had begun to evolve into a Black Power movement that celebrated African culture and heritage. Colleges and universities all over the United States were becoming interested in African and African-American studies. Yale offered Dathorne a permanent job, but only as an associate professor. At his last job at the University of Sierra Leone at Njala, he had not only had a full professorship, but had headed the English department. Always reluctant to take a job that was below his capabilities, Dathorne instead went to work at Howard University in Washington, D.C., where he became professor of African studies.

While moving to Nigeria had placed him in the master class, moving to the expensive United States left

Dathorne broke. Following in the tradition of hard-working colonials everywhere, he took a second job to help pay the bills. Along with his job at Howard, he became professor of African-American studies at the University of Wisconsin. Unfortunately, working at two different institutions is severely frowned upon in the academic world. When university officials complained about Dathorne's two jobs, he resigned both and went to work at Ohio State University.

Pioneered Black Studies in the United States

He spent the next 15 years working at Ohio and the University of Miami, establishing and directing African, Caribbean, and African-American studies programs. Though he had a great love for African and Caribbean literature and culture, he often found working within universities to be frustrating and competitive. Too often he felt that the schools did not have a serious commitment to black studies, and that they only wanted to quiet the demands of African-American students by offering a few courses. Though he was not always successful, Dathorne worked to create strong programs that offered students a chance to major in African-American studies. Often his struggles brought him into conflict with those who employed him, and he changed jobs several times because of these conflicts.

In 1987 he left the University of Miami, having worked unsuccessfully for many years to establish a black studies major. He took a job as a professor in the English department at the University of Kentucky. Along with teaching, he continues to direct the Association of Caribbean Studies, which he founded in 1979. He has also been the editor of the *Journal of Caribbean Studies* since 1979.

During the mid-1960s, Dathorne had begun to write poetry and novels to describe his experiences and the feelings they aroused in him. *Dumplings in the Soup* was inspired by his years as a student in England, and *The Scholar-Man* describes the academic world in Africa. He also wrote critical works about the literature he was teaching. During the mid-1970s, as he worked to establish African studies in U.S. academics, he published *The Black Mind: A History of African Literature, African Literature in the Twentieth Century,* and, in 1981, *Dark Ancestor: The Literature of the Black Man in the Caribbean.*

In the 1990s and early 2000s, Dathorne returned to the issue that has perhaps influenced him more than any other—the multi-layered experience of colonized people. In books such as *In Europe's Image: The Need for American Multiculturalism, Imagining the World: Mythical Belief Versus Reality in Global Encounters, Asian Voyages: Two Thousand Years of Constructing the Other,* and *Worlds Apart: Race in the Modern Period,* Dathorne explores the ways that

European colonists have affected the nations they colonized, even many years after the colony has achieved independence. He also points out the deep effect that Africans have had on culture and society in the Americas and the Caribbean.

In many of his works, Dathorne has continued to examine the way that viewing the colonized person as the "Other," or outsider, has allowed colonizers to mistreat native people. In many ways, Dathorne points out, the entire concept of race itself, of "blackness" or "whiteness," stems from the colonizers' need to separate themselves from the "Other." Dathorne's own complex life as a black man from a colonized country, who has lived in various parts of the world, serves as an illustration that both black and white have many different shades.

Selected writings

Criticism

The Black Mind: A History of African Literature, University of Minnesota Press, 1974.

African Literature in the Twentieth Century, University of Minnesota Press, 1976.

Dark Ancestor: The Literature of the Black Man in the Caribbean, Louisiana State University Press, 1981.

In Europe's Image: The Need for American Multiculturalism, Greenwood Publishing Group, 1994.

Imagining the World: Mythical Belief Versus Reality in Global Encounters, Greenwood Publishing Group, 1994.

Asian Voyages: Two Thousand Years of Constructing the Other, Greenwood Publishing Group, 1996.

Worlds Apart: Race in the Modern Period, Greenwood Publishing Group, 2001.

Novels

Dumplings in the Soup, Cassell, 1963.
The Scholar-Man, Cassell, 1964.
Dele's Child, Lynne Rienner Publishers, Incorporated, 1986.

Poetry

Songs for a New World, Association of Caribbean Studies Press, 1988.

Sources

On-line

"History of the Republic of Guyana," *Guyana News and Information,* www.guyana.org/history.html (February 14, 2005).

"Oscar Ronald Dathorne," *Senior Paper: Anglophone Authors Project,* www.yudev.com/mfo/britlit/dathorne_oscar_ronald.htm (February 14, 2005).

"We Are More than the Other. We Are the Same," *Mots Pluriels,* www.arts.uwa.edu.au/MotsPluriels/MP1400ord.html (February 14, 2005).

Other

Information for this profile was obtained through an interview with O.R. Dathorne on February 19, 2005.

—Tina Gianoulis

George Dixon

1870-1909

Boxer

Known as "Little Chocolate" or "The Chocolate Drop," Canadian-born boxer George Dixon became the first black boxer to hold a world championship when he defeated British fighter Nunc Wallace in 1890 to take the bantamweight crown. He later won the world featherweight championship as well, becoming the first boxer of any ethnicity to hold two championships of different weight classes. Dixon was noted for his defensive skills and precise style, and for many years after his retirement in 1906 he was hailed as a pioneer of "scientific" boxing. Considered one of the best small boxers of all time, Dixon faced racial hostility when he defeated prominent white fighters of the day.

Dixon was born in Africville, an African-Canadian community near Halifax, Nova Scotia, Canada, on July 29, 1870. He spent time in Boston, Massachusetts, with his family as a child, becoming inspired to try his hand at boxing after being sent to a match one day while he was working in a photographer's shop. Dixon stood five feet, three and a half inches and weighed only 87 pounds when he first stepped into the ring professionally in Halifax on November 1, 1886, but he knocked out opponent Young Johnson in the third round.

May Have Fought 800 Bouts

That bout was the beginning of a boxing career that would be considered insanely strenuous by today's standards. Various figures have been given for his official record; the *Boxing Registry* credits him with 50 wins, 26 losses, and 44 draws. Those 120 fights,

however, were just the beginning. Boxing was Dixon's life, and the main source of financing for what became deepening addictions to gambling and alcohol. Dixon spent his life on the road in the United States, England, and Canada, giving boxing exhibitions and taking on anyone who was willing to fight him for money. Matches at that time ran until one fighter was knocked out or exhausted, often running 50 rounds or more, and boxing gloves were used only intermittently. The Cyber Boxing Zone Web site lists over 230 Dixon bouts, and estimates of how many matches he participated in have ranged as high as 800.

In 1888, after several victories in Boston over top fighters, Dixon claimed the world bantamweight championship. The sport's governing bodies at the time had an even less well-defined hierarchy than they do today, however, and others laid claim to the championship as well; one was Charles "Cal" McCarthy, against whom Dixon fought a grueling 70-round draw on February 7, 1890. Dixon sailed for England with his lifelong manager Tom O'Rourke on May 3 of that year, and after he knocked out the previously invincible Wallace in 18 rounds on June 27 he was widely recognized as the bantamweight champion.

Dixon defended his bantamweight title with a 40-round victory over Johnny Murphy in Providence, Rhode Island on October 23. By this time he weighed about 115 pounds, and he gave up his bantamweight title and moved up to the featherweight class. In a Troy, New York fight against Cal McCarthy on March 31, 1891, Dixon earned the title of featherweight champion of the world and an unprecedented title at a second

At a Glance . . .

Born on July 29, 1870, in Africville, near Halifax, Nova Scotia, Canada; died on January 6, 1909, in New York. *Education:* Worked as photographer's apprentice, Boston, MA.

Career: Featherweight and bantamweight boxer, 1886-1906; world bantamweight champion, 1888 (recognized, 1890); world featherweight champion, 1891-1900 (with periodic, brief losses of his title); fought famed 25-round draw against Australian boxer Young Griffo, 1895; lost championship to Terry McGovern, 1900; credited with at least 230 and perhaps as many as 800 matches.

weight class with a 40-round knockout. He quickly defended his title against Abe Willis on July 28 in San Francisco, and he held the featherweight belt for most of the following nine years.

Fought Twice in One Day

He lost occasionally, but several came back to win in a rematch against the same fighter. On October 4, 1897, Dixon relinquished his title to Solly Smith in a 20-round loss in San Francisco, but he came back to win a series of bouts in 1898 and 1899 that were billed as championships. Between 1890 and 1900 he lost only a handful of fights even as he took on numerous boxers in exhibition matches. On May 2, 1893 he fought against James "Sun" Ashe and Billy Nally within the course of a single day. On March 7, 1895 in New York, Dixon took on and beat Sam Bolen, who outweighed him by 20 pounds.

Dixon had many admirers in the white boxing community, and old-timers of later eras would fondly remember his career. In 1893 he wrote an autobiography, *A Lesson in Boxing.* But some of the same racial controversies that swirled around the career of heavyweight boxer Jack Johnson also plagued the high-living, sharp-dressing Dixon, who married the sister of his manager O'Rourke. After he knocked out Jack Skelly at the Olympia Club in New Orleans, Louisiana, on September 6, 1892, the club banned mixed-race bouts. His fight against "Torpedo" Billy Murphy on December 15, 1893, ended in a riot.

Still, some of Dixon's fights were considered classics. An example was Dixon's 25-round draw against Australia's Young Griffo on January 19, 1895. Those who attended the fight on Coney Island in New York, noted the *Washington Post* in 1915, "had the opportunity of witnessing an encounter between two boys who have certainly never been excelled, and probably never equaled, in the matter of ring science."

Paid Cost of High Living

On January 9, 1900, Dixon came out on the losing end of an eight-round knockout at the hands of "Terrible Terry" McGovern in New York. Although Dixon claimed that McGovern had not made weight for the fight, he lost again to McGovern later that year. Dixon fought Abe Attell for the featherweight title in 1901, but his long period of dominance was over. "Loose living," noted the *Washington Post,* "had made inroads on his constitution." The aging fighter toured England from late 1902 through 1905, hoping to stave off financial problems that had left him with little more in the way of assets than a home he owned in Boston; he was reported to have burned through winnings of more than $100,000. After a December 10, 1906, loss to a boxer named Monk the Newsboy, Dixon retired from the ring.

Hospitalized because of complications from alcoholism, Dixon died in New York on January 6, 1909. He was remembered after his death by boxing tacticians, who admired his artistic style; never a brawler, Dixon was a quick, agile fighter who could duck punches with ease and who anticipated the counterpunching styles of a later era of the sport. Dixon was inducted into the Boxing Hall of Fame in 1956 and the International Boxing Hall of Fame in 1990, and several boxing historians ranked him among the top bantamweights of all time.

Sources

Books

Hickok, Ralph, *A Who's Who of Sports Champions: Their Stories and Records,* Houghton Mifflin, 1995.
Roberts, James B., and Alexander G. Skutt, *The Boxing Register,* McBooks, 2002.

Periodicals

Los Angeles Times, October 4, 1913, section 3, p. 3.
Washington Post, November 23, 1913, p. S2; December 20, 1914, p. S3; November January 31, 1915, Sports section, p. 4.

On-line

"George Dixon ('Little Chocolate')," *Cyber Boxing Zone,* www.cyberboxingzone.com/boxing/dixon-g. htm (April 24, 2005).
"Ring Champions: Dixon, Buirns, McLarnin & Langford," *Canada's Digital Collections,* http://collections.ic.gc.ca/heirloom_series/volumb4/tributes. htm (April 24, 2005).

—James M. Manheim

Howard Dodson, Jr.

1939—

Historian, educator, curator

Howard Dodson, Jr., has committed his professional life to the retrieval, preservation, interpretation, and dissemination of the history and culture of African and African American peoples. Since 1984, he has served as chief of the New York Public Library's Schomburg Center for Research in Black Culture, the world's leading and most prestigious repository for materials and artifacts on black cultural life.

A scholar, consultant, lecturer, and educator, Dodson has guided the Schomburg Center through major fundraising and expansion projects, including successful capital campaigns and multi-million-dollar construction and renovation projects. In the spring of 1991, the Center celebrated its 65th anniversary with the opening of the newly expanded complex, which included an auditorium, an exhibition hall, the Moving Image and Recorded Sound Division, and much-needed additional space for acquisitions. By 2005 the Center had well-established educational and cultural programs, including seminars, exhibitions, forums, film screenings, performing arts programs, readings, and special events, to complement and interpret its collections. The programming was carefully developed to highlight the resources of the library as a research center, however. Dodson told *American Visions* that "There has been the recurring question of the role educational and cultural programs and exhibits play in the life of an institution like this. We see our interpretive programming as a means of focusing attention on the collection and on the issues and themes in the African and African-American diasporan experience."

The Schomburg Center's yearly exhibitions featuring art objects, photographs, documents, published works and artifacts drawn from its own holdings, as well as resources from other institutions, have been critically praised. Each exhibition explores issues and themes in the history and culture of people of African descent throughout the world. The 2005 exhibition *Malcolm X: A Search for the Truth* offered audiences opportunities to view the Center's extensive collection of Malcolm X's published and unpublished writings.

Center Preserves and Shares Knowledge

In the mid-1980s Dodson instituted the Schomburg's scholars-in-residence program, which provides six- and twelve-month fellowships and use of the Schomburg collections for scholars, researchers, and writers. In an interview with *Contemporary Black Biography (CBB)*, Dodson explained that he sees the Center as the "platform for one mission: to foster an understanding of the history and culture of people of African descent." The research of the scholars over the years has tapped the Center's resources in a variety of different ways. In 2001 scholar Samuel Kelton Roberts worked on his project: *Infectious Fear: Tuberculosis, Public Health, and the Logic of Race and Illness in the Urban South, 1880-1930* and the following year Winston Kennedy pursued his work on *Out of the Shadows: The African American Image in Print* while George A. Priestley studied for his work on *George Westerman and West Indian-Panamanians*

At a Glance . . .

Born on June 1, 1939, in Chester, PA; son of Howard and Lou Birda (Jones) Dodson; married Jualynne White (marriage ended); children: Alyce Christine, David Primus Luta. *Education*: West Chester State College, BS, 1961; Villanova University, MA, 1964; University of California, Berkeley, ABD, 1974.

Career: National Credit Union Education Federation of Ecuador, education programs director, 1964-66; U.S. Peace Corps, volunteer in Ecuador, 1964-66, office staffer, 1966-69, recruiting director, 1967-68; Institute of the Black World, Atlanta, executive director, 1974-79, director of Black Studies curriculum development, 1980-83; The Schomburg Center for Research in Black Culture, chief, 1984–, director, scholars-in-residence program, 1986–. Emory University, lecturer in Afro-American history, 1976-79; National Endowment for the Humanities, consultant to director, 1979-82; also consultant to African American Museums Association, Library of Congress, U.S. Department of Education, Congressional Black Caucus, and National Council of Churches; Chairman, Black Theology Project.

Memberships: Association for the Study of Afro-American Life and History (ASALH), National Council for Black Studies, Organization of American Historians, Southern Historical Association, 100 Black Men.

Awards: ASALH Service Award, 1976; Chairman's Award, Black and Puerto Rican Caucus; Governor's Award for African Americans of Distinction, 1982; honorary degree from Widener College, 1987.

Addresses: *Office*—The Schomburg Center for Research in Black Culture, 515 Malcolm X Boulevard, New York, NY 10037-1801.

most outstanding historians of the decade, Arthur A. Schomburg, was a Puerto Rican of African descent. His library, as Dodson described it, contained over five thousand books, three thousand manuscripts, two thousand etchings and portraits, and several thousand pamphlets. The Schomburg library provided the resources for many of the artists and intellectuals during the Harlem Renaissance of the 1920s. In 1926 the New York Public Library acquired Schomburg's collection for its newly opened special branch on 135th Street, the Division of Negro Literature, History, and Prints. This acquisition formed the basis for today's Schomburg Center for Research in Black Culture.

According to Dodson, Schomburg was driven by a belief in the necessity of preserving and reconstructing the historical past of "the American Negro...as a stimulating and inspiring tradition for the coming generations." In Alain Locke's 1925 book *The New Negro*, Schomburg had drawn three conclusions: "First, that the Negro has been throughout the centuries of controversy an active collaborator, and often a pioneer, in the struggle for his own freedom and advancement. Second, that by virtue of their being regarded as something 'exceptional,' even by friends and well-wishers, Negroes of attainment and genius have been unfairly disassociated from the group, and group credit lost accordingly. Third, that the remote racial origins of the Negro, far from being what the race and the world have been given to understand, offer a record of credible group achievement when scientifically viewed, and more important still, that they are of vital general interest because of their bearing upon the beginnings and early development of culture." These conclusions, almost seventy years later, continue to motivate Howard Dodson's mission.

Inspired to Study Cultural Histories

Howard Dodson, Jr., was born in Chester, Pennsylvania, on June 1, 1939, the oldest of four children and the only son of Lou Birda Jones and Howard Dodson. With the support of his family, teachers, and church, Dodson was enabled and encouraged "to navigate dangerous waters," he told *CBB*. His parents' advice to "be all that you can be" encouraged him to achieve an outstanding academic record throughout his junior high and high school years. He was academically ranked first or second in his class each year and was one of only nine of the 89 students who entered Chester High School's academic program to graduate and attend college.

Living at home and earning tuition and book scholarships, Dodson received a B.S. in social studies and secondary education from West Chester State College in 1961 and was admitted to the graduate program in history and political science at Villanova University, where he earned a master's degree in 1964. Dodson was fascinated by African and African American history, but Villanova's history department offered only

in the 20th Century: Negotiating Identity, Culture and Nationality.

Dodson continues a long tradition of preserving and disseminating black literature and cultural artifacts—a tradition that began in Harlem in the 1920s. With the migration of millions of people of color from various regions of the United States, the Caribbean, and Africa and the resulting intensity of artistic and intellectual activities, Harlem became known as the "black capital" of the United States during the early 1920s. One of the one course in black studies—African politics; black American history classes did not exist. "I had to shoe horn my way into black studies through the back door," Dodson told *CBB*.

During this time, Dodson's major interest was the comparative histories of black peoples throughout the Western Hemisphere. His curiosity about the Western Hemisphere was inspired by his understanding that during the first 300 years of European colonization (1492-1776), only one million of the six-and-one- half million peoples who survived the Atlantic Ocean crossing were actually Europeans; the rest were Africans who were taken to the United States, the Caribbean, and South America. Dodson's desire to learn about the differences among the cultural histories of African peoples in these three major geographical areas led to his decision to go to South America instead of Africa with the U.S. Peace Corps in the early 1960s.

Moved by King Assassination

The real turning point in his search for knowledge about black culture and history, however, occurred with the 1968 assassination of Dr. Martin Luther King, Jr. Dodson recalled in the *CBB* interview that at this time, he faced a major choice: to become a permanent expatriate or to return to his country of birth—the United States—with its increasing racial hostility and violence. Because of his work in the Peace Corps, Dodson had been offered several permanent positions overseas. But he didn't like what he saw happening to expatriates—particularly their loss of racial identity. Also, Dodson said, he feared that if he accepted a long-term position overseas, he might never return to the United States, a decision he felt he didn't have a right to make because so many others had invested in him. "My domestic debts were still unpaid," Dodson reported to *CBB*. Dr. King's death thus propelled him to take another course of action.

In his despair and disillusionment over hearing of King's assassination, Dodson decided to go into "retirement," as he called it. He traveled to San Juan, Puerto Rico, to spend a year reading, studying, and contemplating the convergence of various social and historical factors that had resulted in the civil rights and Black Power movements of the 1960s, taking with him ten boxes of books that he had acquired over the years. Dodson explained to *CBB* that by 1968, the tremendous amount of interest in the Black Power movement had resulted in the publication of many dissertations, articles, and other works on black history and literature, but that the majority of the books he took with him were secondhand copies of classics in black studies. During his "retirement" he read continuously and supplemented his own collection of books with research at the nearby library in Mayaquez.

Dr. King's assassination had "de-centered the very foundations" of Dodson's own code of living. In the interview with *CBB*, Dodson commented that the violent nature of King's death actually caused him to consider an equally violent response to it. But Dodson's ethical and moral principles, which he now identified as being closely tied to King's, enabled him to understand that this was not a personally acceptable response for him; the core of King's message was the belief that a substantial percentage of the white population was capable of being "redeemed." With King's death, however, Dodson realized that he now had no clear path to travel, and his solution to this sense of "de-centering" was "to return to history for new bases for assessing this particular moment in time." Dodson told *CBB* that he needed to connect with the "best of moral and ethical traditions," which he was to find in his extensive studies of black history and literature.

Joined Leading Black History Scholars

Puerto Rico was a neutral ground for Dodson. He had been there during his tenure with the Peace Corps, so it represented a "comforting" place, yet he knew he would not be tempted to remain there permanently away from his own country. At the end of his year of study, he had come to realize that "neither the social sciences nor other fields of study could adequately explain what was going on" in the United States during the 1960s.

This awareness motivated him to enter the doctoral program in Black History and Race Relations at the University of California at Berkeley in 1969—the only such program of its kind in the United States at that time. There he studied under such distinguished scholars as Winthrop Jordan, who established the program, Lawrence Levine, Leon Litwack, Kenneth Stampp, and Nathan Huggins. Dodson and other graduate students were also offered internships during this time at the Institute of the Black World, the research arm of the Martin Luther King, Jr., Center for Nonviolent Social Change in Atlanta.

Dodson told *CBB* that he had been attracted to the work of the Institute during the first months of 1968, during which he awoke every morning at 5:30 a.m. to watch another installment of Black Heritage, a 102-episode series produced by Vincent Harding. Dodson told *CBB* that these 30-minute segments, televised on CBS, constituted his "real education." His subsequent internship at the Institute allowed him to continue his education under the guidance of Harding, Stephen Henderson, Lerone Bennett, Jr., St. Clair Drake, and other leading scholars of black history and culture. Dodson went on to become director of the Institute from 1974 to 1979.

Continued the Schomberg Legacy

Dodson's research for his Ph. D. dissertation at Berkeley was a culmination of his earlier interests in comparative histories of African people in the Western Hemisphere, his own personal reading and involvement in the Black Power movement, and his education at the hands of leading black scholars in California and Atlanta. Although Dodson's doctoral research has yet to be formally compiled, his conclusions make a viable contribution to contemporary revisionist discourses of black American history.

Choosing "The Political Economy in South Carolina: 1780-1830" as his topic, Dodson draws a picture of African Americans who were generative agents in the development of the southern plantation political economy—people who were contributors to, not passive victims of, a complex economic system. By approaching his topic from the perspective of the planter class's economic dependence on the black population, Dodson reverses commonly held myth-making assumptions, which focus primarily on the perceived dependence of the black population on the planter class. Dodson said that he chose South Carolina as the focus of his study because it was the only "mainland colony to have a majority black population"; he further added that from the founding of South Carolina in 1640, the black population was primarily transported from Barbados, which gave South Carolinian blacks a uniquely homogeneous cultural heritage.

From his decision to study the black experience forward, Dodson has continuously worked to improve the research and scholarly opportunities for investigating African and African American culture. Dodson wrote of his vision for the future of the Schomburg Center in an essay for the *Dictionary of Literary Biography*. There he expresses his continuing commitment to furthering the understanding of the cultural and historical contributions of black peoples throughout the world: "The Schomburg Center is looking toward the twenty-first century as it expands its services, facilities, and technology to meet the contemporary needs of writers, scholars, artists, and others who are studying and making contributions to black culture. In the tradition established by [Arthur] Schomburg the center continues to be a repository for materials documenting black life and a participant in the evolution of black culture." Under his leadership the center has grown to include more than five million items, including many digitally accessible sources, and Dodson has contributed to several important studies of the black experience.

Selected writings

Editor in chief, *Black World View*, 1977.
(With Madelon Bedell) *Thinking and Rethinking U.S. History*, Council on Interracial Books for Children, Inc., 1988.
(With Deborah Willis) *Black Photographers Bear Witness:100 Years of Social Protest*, Williams College Museum of Art, 1989.
The Black New Yorkers, Schomburg Center, 1999.
Jubilee: The Emergence of African-American Culture, New York Public Library and National Geographic Society, 2003.
Editor (with Sylviane Diouf) *In Motion: The African-American Migration Experience,* National Geographic Books, 2005.

Television

Project director, *The Other American Revolution* (television series), 1982-84.
Producer/executive producer, "Paul Robeson: A 90th Birthday Tribute," Schubert Theater, 1988.
Producer/executive producer, "Ella Fitzgerald: A 75th Birthday Tribute," Carnegie Hall, 1992.

Sources

Books

Dictionary of Literary Biography, Volume 76: Afro-American Writers, 1940-1955, Gale, 1988, pp. 242-55.
Schomburg, Arthur A., "The Negro Digs Up His Past," in *The New Negro*, revised edition, edited by Alain Locke, Atheneum, 1969, pp. 231-37.

Periodicals

American Vision, April-May 1993, p. 18.
Ebony, February 2005, p. 12.

On-line

The Schomburg Center for Research in Black Culture, www.schomburgcenter.org (June 8, 2005).

Other

CBB spoke with Howard Dodson at the Schomburg Center on November 8, 1993.

—Mary Katherine Wainwright and Sara Pendergast

Karl Dorrell

1963—

Football coach

One of just a few African-American head football coaches serving at Division I college programs in the mid-2000s, Karl Dorrell faced doubters on a variety of fronts when he took the helm for the University of California at Los Angeles (UCLA) Bruins in the fall of 2003. Dorrell was not yet 40 years old at the time, and the plum UCLA post was his first head coaching job. In his first two years, however, Dorrell made significant strides toward rebuilding UCLA's floundering football program. Just as importantly, he set his team on a path toward discipline, focus, and good behavior.

Dorrell's leadership skills were evident even when he was a child growing up in San Diego, California. A native of Alameda in the northern part of the state, Dorrell moved south with his family as his father John's career in the United States Navy required. Dorrell's skills in logistical thinking may have come from his father, who was chief petty officer on an aircraft carrier. By the time he was eight or nine, Dorrell was not only quarterbacking his neighborhood street football team but also putting together written playbooks. His motivational talents surfaced as he talked friends into completing the hilly sections of his newspaper delivery route for him, telling them that they would strengthen their leg muscles by climbing San Diego's hills.

Criticized Father's Study Habits

John Dorrell instilled a sense of discipline in his son—so much so that sometimes it was the son who did the disciplining. "I remember when I was retiring from the Navy and taking some math classes at Gross-

mont College," the elder Dorrell told Ed Graney of the *San Diego Union-Tribune*. "Karl sat down one night to help me with my homework and became very impatient with me. He knew I hadn't studied." At San Diego's Helix High School, Karl Dorrell was a standout in several sports. He led the football squad to a sectional title as a junior in 1980 and was named honorable mention All-America in 1981. Prior to graduating in 1982 he was courted by several colleges, including San Diego State University, but chose to attend UCLA.

Beginning his athletic career at UCLA in both football and basketball, Dorrell soon began to focus on football and to improve dramatically, playing at the position of wide receiver. As a sophomore in 1983 he caught 26 passes for 390 yards and six touchdowns, adding five catches and two touchdowns in UCLA's 45-9 Rose Bowl victory over Illinois. He had already played on the team's 1982 Rose Bowl-winning squad, and after a year lost to injuries he paced the Bruins to a Rose Bowl win once again in 1985. When he graduated in 1987, he ranked second in UCLA team history in pass receptions with 108, and fourth in total receiving yards gained with 1,517.

A computer enthusiast, Dorrell looked forward to a career with the IBM corporation after graduation. But UCLA coach Terry Donahue encouraged his detail-oriented star to think about a coaching career himself after a short stint with pro football's Dallas Cowboys ended with an injury. "He said, 'Karl, as a young minority coach, you'll climb the ladder so fast, you won't know what hit you,'" Dorrell recalled to Graney.

At a Glance . . .

Born December 18, 1963, in Alameda, CA; married to Kim Dorrell; children: Chandler and Lauren. *Education:* University of California at Los Angeles (UCLA), BA, 1987.

Career: Dallas Cowboys, professional football player, 1987; UCLA, graduate assistant, 1988; University of Central Florida, receivers coach, 1989; University of Northern Arizona, offensive coordinator and receivers coach, 1990-91; University of Colorado, wide receivers coach, 1992-93; Arizona State University, receivers coach, 1994; University of Colorado, offensive coordinator and wide receivers coach, 1995-98; University of Washington, offensive coordinator, 1999; Denver Broncos, National Football League (NFL), wide receivers coach, 2000-02; UCLA, head coach, 2002–.

Selected awards: NFL Minority Coaches Fellowship Program, participant, 1993 and 1999.

Address: *Office*—UCLA Athletics, J.D. Morgan Center, P.O. Box 24044, Los Angeles, CA 90024.

Dorrell became a graduate assistant under Donahue and quickly moved on to a receivers coach slot at the University of Central Florida in 1989. There, he helped shape the skills of future National Football League (NFL) stalwart Shawn Jefferson.

Guided Careers of Future Pro Players

Donahue's prophecy came true as Dorrell quickly ascended to new coaching positions, generally gaining more responsibility or moving to a larger school. He became offensive coordinator at the University of Northern Arizona in 1990 and 1991, wide receivers coach at the University of Colorado in 1992 and 1993, wide receivers coach at Arizona State University in 1994, offensive coordinator at Colorado from 1995 through 1998, and offensive coordinator at the University of Washington in 1999. His rising career resulted not from his minority status, however, but from the stellar performances of his players on the field; over the course of his collegiate career prior to coming to UCLA, Dorrell coached six receivers who went on to play in the NFL. Three became first-round draft picks. Helping steer the Colorado Buffaloes to five postsea-

son bowl appearances in the 1990s, he raised the total number of bowl games he participated in as a player or coach to 12.

After stints with the Denver Broncos training camp coaching staff under the auspices of the NFL's Minority Coaching Fellowship Program in 1993 and 1999, Dorrell joined the Broncos full time in 2000 as wide receivers coach. The players for whom he was responsible—receivers Ed McCaffrey and Rod Smith—turned in franchise-record performances during his first year. Thrust into the pro spotlight, Dorrell also dealt with personal tragedy: his sister Debra died of colon cancer at age 46, and he donated stem cells in the course of his brother Kent's battle against leukemia. The last words Dorrell's sister spoke to him, he told Graney, were "Your dream will come true. You're going to be a head coach."

That dream was realized on December 18, 2002, Dorrell's 39th birthday, when he was hired as UCLA's head coach to replace Bob Toledo. The appointment of Dorrell, who had never held a head coaching job, to one of the top jobs in the college football world was a surprise to many, but UCLA athletic director Dan Guerrero pointed out Dorrell's UCLA roots to Jeremy Rutherford of the *St. Louis Post-Dispatch*. Guerrero wanted a coach who "knows something about rivalries…and the importance of those kinds of things in a city like Los Angeles." Bruin fans, for example, were deeply disturbed by UCLA's four consecutive losses to the University of Southern California (USC) under Toledo.

Steered Players Away from Trouble

With off-the-field player behavior said to be part of the reason for Toledo's firing, Dorrell set clear boundaries from the start. His first words at his first UCLA team meeting, according to Matt Hayes of *The Sporting News*, were "Don't jeopardize your integrity." The approach paid off, even as crimes by players for other teams were making headlines around the country. "We've had one transgression among over 100 players since the time Karl came in here last spring," Guerrero told *USA Today* in the fall of 2003. "The word is out in terms of what the expectation is for the student-athletes and what we want as a program overall."

On the field, Dorrell's results weren't so immediate. After an opening-game loss to Colorado and a 1-2 start, however, UCLA won four straight games. They were in contention for a bowl slot in the stretch run but finished with a 6-7 record after a string of five late-season losses including one to arch-rival USC. Dorrell, dissatisfied with his own performance, declined a one-year contract extension, telling Lonnie White of the *Los Angeles Times* that "In my mind, we did not accomplish enough of our goals."

Several players on the Bruins' offense made strong showings, however, and Dorrell's second season brought promising signs of improvement. After a discouraging loss to Oklahoma State in the season opener, UCLA once again put together a streak of four straight victories. They finished 6-5 overall and, despite being picked to finish eighth in the Pacific 10 Conference, finished fifth with a 4-4 league record. Most encouraging was a close 29-24 loss to a powerhouse USC squad. UCLA went to the Las Vegas Bowl on December 23, losing a 24-21 heartbreaker to Wyoming. After having turned down a contract extension the previous year, Dorrell now agreed to a two-year addition running through the year 2010. "It takes a great deal of patience and perseverance before you start seeing the fruits of your labor," Dorrell told White. "We're starting to get ourselves out of the clouds and we're starting to see the reason why we do things a certain way."

Sources

Periodicals

Los Angeles Times, November 12, 2004, p. D1; December 18, 2004, p. D1; December 20, 2004, p. D1.

San Diego Union-Tribune, December 19, 2002, p. D1; August 29, 2003, p. D1; September 5, 2004, p. C11.

St. Louis Post-Dispatch, September 12, 2003, p. D10.

Sporting News, November 10, 2003, p. 68.

USA Today, September 4, 2003, p. C3.

On-line

"Karl Dorrell," *UCLA Bruins,* http://uclabruins.collegesports.com/sports/m-footbl/mtt/dorrell_karl00.html (June 9, 2005).

—James M. Manheim

Aaron P. Dworkin

1970—

Violinist, organization leader

Dworkin, Aaron, photograph. AP/Wide World Photos.

From the first time he heard a violin, Aaron P. Dworkin has been in love with classical music. He attended a prestigious music academy and earned a master's degree in music. He swooned over orchestral performances and gave several of his own. Yet, there was something wrong. He told the *New York Times* that of all the musical situations he had been in, from rehearsals to performances, "I was either the only minority or one of less than a handful." Dworkin decided to change this statistic by launching the Sphinx Organization. In under a decade the group has helped open up classical music to thousands of minorities and has made diversity a reality in orchestras around the nation. Sphinx's success is due in large part to Dworkin's spirit. A top administrator from Dworkin's alma mater, the University of Michigan, recalled to the *Michigan Difference*, "One of Aaron's professors told me, 'I've taught more advanced musicians than Aaron Dworkin, but I never taught someone who changed the world.'"

Embraced Music as an Early Escape

Aaron Paul Dworkin was born on September 11, 1970, in Monticello, New York, and promptly given up for adoption. Two weeks later, Barry and Susan Dworkin, white, neuroscience professors from Manhattan, adopted him. Dworkin reunited with his birth parents, Vaughn and Audeen Moore, an inter-racial couple from upstate New York, in 2001. "It was the kind of experience music was created for," Dworkin told *People Weekly*. "I couldn't express it in words." It was Dworkin's adoptive mother, an amateur violinist, who introduced him to classical music. He told the *New York Times* that the first time he heard her play Bach, he was hooked. "I just loved it and I picked it up right away."

When Dworkin was ten, his family moved to Hershey, Pennsylvania. "There was only one black family," he told *People Weekly*. "I got Racial Issues 101, with a heavy dose of ostracism. I used music to escape." Dworkin pursued classical violin with a passion and for the final two years of high school attended the prestigious Interlochen Arts Academy in Michigan. "[It] literally saved my life, because in Hershey I'd been on a downward spiral," he told the *Metro Times*. "I was a young kid with a huge Afro; I was black, yet I had an older brother who's white; and in the school system, I played the violin. It was too strange for most people."

At a Glance . . .

Born in 1970, in Monticello, NY; married Carrie Dworkin, 1997 (divorced 2003); children: Noah. *Education*: University of Michigan, BM, violin, 1997; University of Michigan, MM, music, 1998.

Career: Sphinx Organization, Detroit, MI, founder, executive director, 1996–.

Memberships: University Musical Society, Ann Arbor, MI, board member; Walnut Hill School, Natick, MA, board of visitors; ArtServe Michigan, board of directors; MetLife Awards for Excellence in Community Engagement, panelist; Alternative Strings Awards, advisory board.

Awards: University of Michigan, African-American Alumni Council, 5 Under 10 Award, 2002; New Detroit, Close the Gap Award, 2003; *Detroit News*, Michiganian of the Year, 2003; Black Entertainment Television (BET), History Makers in the Making, 2003.

Addresses: *Office*—Sphinx Organization, 400 Renaissance Center, Suite 2120, Detroit, MI 48243.

After graduating from Interlochen, Dworkin returned home and enrolled in Pennsylvania State University to study business. He also served as concertmaster for the Penn State Philharmonic. After financial strains forced him to withdraw he decided to move to Michigan where he married Carrie, a student he had met at Interlochen. In Michigan Dworkin worked a variety of jobs in sales and marketing. He landed in non-profit administration and eventually founded Jumpstart, a homeless organization. It was not easy. "We spent years with pretty rough times," Dworkin told *People Weekly*. "Poverty, getting evicted. But I also got experience with nonprofits."

Love of Classical Led to Launch of Sphinx

Drawn back to music, Dworkin enrolled in the University of Michigan and earned a bachelor's degree in violin in 1997 and a master's degree in music the following year. He got the idea for Sphinx while attending orchestral concerts at Ann Arbor's Hill Auditorium. "I'd see no minorities on the stage," he told the *Detroit News*. "I wondered why there should be no place for minorities in classical music, something that was very important to me—something I loved." Around

the same time Dworkin also came across the work of African-American composer William Grant Still. "I was upset with myself," he told the *New Crisis*. "I thought, how could I not have known about this music? And had I known, what motivation might it have given me, and how much more focused might I have been?"

Dworkin told the *New York Times*, "So, out of that came this idea of how to increase the representation of minorities in the audience and onstage, and I thought a competition would be a good vehicle." Dworkin drew up his plan and named it the Sphinx Organization after the mythical Egyptian figure which for many represents the African continent. For Dworkin the Sphinx also represented a mystery which he equated with music. "Like the Sphinx, it is up to the beholder, the listener, to interpret and appreciate from the music what is ultimately a reflection of internal emotions and spiritual experiences," noted the Sphinx Web site.

With characteristic enthusiasm, Dworkin sent an appeal to James Wolfensohn, then-president of the World Bank. Wolfensohn replied with a personal note and a check for $10,000. Dworkin raised another $70,000 to get the competition off the ground. A spokesman for Texaco, an early corporate sponsor, told the *Detroit Free Press*, "The quality of Aaron's leadership was very impressive. He had such a clear plan, knew what the need was and knew how to have an impact."

Built Community for Minority Classical Musicians

The first Sphinx competition was held in 1996. Open to African-American and Latino classical string players from junior high school through college, the competition brought 18 semi-finalists in two categories—junior and senior—to Michigan each year. Three from each group were chosen laureates, ranked from one to three. They received financial stipends as well as guest appearances with prominent orchestras. In addition all semi-finalists received scholarships, musical training, and if needed, the one-year loan of a high-quality instrument. Professional development was offered from renowned musicians such as cellist Yo-Yo Ma. "Most kids who grow up in urban environments don't have the resources to pay for those kinds of teachers," Dworkin told *Strings Magazine*.

"The competition was like camp—it was so much fun. I pretty much forgot it was a competition the second I got there, because everyone was so nurturing and supportive," 2003 junior winner, Elena Urioste told the *Michigan Difference*. That the competition is more like a convention is by design. "I'm actually not a fan of competitions," Dworkin told *Strings Magazine*. "Often times, you demotivate more people than you motivate." Sphinx motivates, building a community where there was none before. "I can't express how it is to learn that you're not alone, that there are other African Americans your age doing the same thing," 2002 senior division winner Patrice Jackson told the *New York Times*.

Sphinx has done more than build solidarity among young minorities in classical music. It has also provided a bridge to the world of the professional orchestra. For each competition, Dworkin brings together a group of professional minority musicians from around the nation to form the Sphinx Symphony. The musicians offer mentoring and accompany the laureates during the finals. "It's our mission to build a sense of peer group and to give the players a sense through the Sphinx Symphony that there was a generation of pioneers before them. That this is a world they belong to," Dworkin told the *Detroit Free Press*.

Drove Orchestras to Build Diversity

The driving vision that motivated Dworkin to found Sphinx was a world in which classical music reflected cultural diversity. "A big goal of ours is to increase the numbers across the board, in audiences and in orchestras and in music schools and faculty, and hopefully, potentially as a soloist," he told the *New York Times*. When Dworkin started the organization there were just a handful of minority musicians in the nation's professional orchestras. As of 2005 the figure was still dismal—less than 3 percent of all orchestral members nationwide, or just one or two minorities per 80-member orchestra. Not only has this problem been vexing for minority musicians, it has also been of concern to orchestras who want their membership to better reflect the social makeup of society.

"Orchestras have traditionally insisted that the minority talent simply wasn't out there," Dworkin told the *Detroit News*. "And now at least they're saying, 'Yes, the talent's there but we're not seeing those musicians at our auditions.' Getting these kids spotlighted in front of the orchestras is going to change all that." The connections the kids make with Sphinx Symphony members help, as does the guest performances with professional orchestras. "I'd never have imagined I'd play with the Boston Pops or the National Symphony in DC," 2002 junior winner Gareth Johnson told *People Weekly*. "The experience of performing with an orchestra is both invaluable and very hard to get," Dworkin told *Strings Magazine*. "It makes them infinitely better musicians and acclimates them to life in an orchestra." Dworkin predicted that Sphinx alumni would start auditioning for spots on professional orchestras by 2006.

Dworkin has highlighted another essential element in the diversification of classical music—the need for young people to embrace the music in the first place. Cultural factors have long pushed minority youth towards pop, rap, or hip-hop music. Classical has been considered the bastion of wealthy, white patrons. To counter that, Sphinx created Musical Encounters, an inner-city music program which sends Sphinx laureates into underprivileged schools to perform and meet the students. "We ask our kids to go back to their communities and be ambassadors for the music—to play in church concerts, play in local community concerts, play for friends, etc.," Dworkin told the *Metro Times*. "Because the same thing that sparked them to start is what's going to happen when they play."

Instruments Poised for More Success

In January of 2005 Sphinx held its eighth competition. By that time Dworkin and crew had established artistic partnerships with 25 professional symphonies, 16 music academies, and scores of professional classical musicians. Five major universities, including the Julliard School, had created scholarship programs in conjunction with Sphinx. In addition, the competition had given way to the development of musical outreach programs, recital series, and mentoring programs, potentially reaching tens of thousands of minority youth nationwide. "What the Sphinx Competition is doing couldn't possibly be more important," Guillermo Figueroa, music director of the Puerto Rico and New Mexico Symphony Orchestras, told *The Detroit News*.

Yet Dworkin recognized that there was still a long way to go. Though Sphinx's budget had grown from an initial $80,000 to $1.5 million by 2004, thanks in large part to corporate sponsorships, the whole program could be jeopardized if even one major sponsor pulled out. To counter that, Dworkin announced plans to seek a $20 million endowment to assure the program's future. Kenneth C. Fischer, president of the University Musical Society in Ann Arbor, did not doubt Dworkin could do it. "He's irresistible," he told the *Detroit News*. "He simply doesn't take no for an answer. He's an inspiration to anybody in any kind of arts organization. You see what vision and persistence and hard work can accomplish."

Dworkin has been the feature of a documentary called *Breaking the Sound Barrier* and has garnered numerous awards including a 2003 nod from Black Entertainment Television (BET) as a History Maker in the Making. He was looking forward to seeing that history made. Dworkin, who has recorded two CDs and published a book of poetry, told *People Weekly*, "My hope is that one day nobody makes a big deal about hiring a minority classical musician. I hope there's no need for a Sphinx Organization and I can go off to write poetry and play my violin."

Selected works

Albums

Ebony Rhythm, Ethnovibe Records.
Bar-talk, Ethnovibe Records.

Books

They Said I Wasn't Really Black, Ethnovibe Publishing, 1999.

Sources

Periodicals

Detroit Free Press, February 6, 2002; January 25, 2005.
Detroit News, February 15, 2003; February 17, 2004; January 22, 2005.
People Weekly, November 22, 2004.
New York Times, March 3, 2002.
New Crisis, September/October 2002.

On-line

"Behind the Sphinx," *Metro Times,* www.metrotimes. com/editorial/story.asp?id=4628 (February 22, 2005).
"Changing the Face of Classical Music," *Michigan Difference,* www.giving.umich.edu/leadersbest/fall2004/classical.htm (February 22, 2005).
"Mystery of the Sphinx," *Metro Times,* www.metro times.com/editorial/story.asp?id=4626 (February 22, 2005).
"The Sphinx Stands Alone," *Strings Magazine,* http://stringsmagazine.com/issues/strings107/coverstory .html (February 22, 2005).

Other

Additional information for this profile was obtained from www.sphinxmusic.org.

—Candace LaBalle

Gnassingbé Eyadéma

1937-2005

President of Togo

General Gnassingbé Eyadéma was one of the world's longest-serving national leaders, having run the West African nation of Togo from 1967 to his death in 2005. Eyadéma's hold on presidential power in Togo was consolidated by both force and by political machination in a career that included military coups, suspicious murders, assassination attempts on opposition leaders, and dramatic appeals to "national unity" at the expense of free expression.

While other self-imposed rulers in Africa bowed to demands for multiparty democracy—most often relinquishing power in the process—Eyadéma retained his hold on the Togolese government in spite of national unrest and international censure. Even a 1993 general election, which Eyadéma won by a large margin, seemed nothing more than a deceptive show designed to guarantee the general's continued power. *Africa Report* contributor Colleen Lowe Morna characterized the government of Togo as "essentially an authoritarian state, with the president dominating all branches and functions of government, and ruling by decree"; but legislative elections held in February of 1994 indicate that the opposition may soon gain a voice in Togo's government.

Africa Report correspondent Peter Da Costa noted that Eyadéma "has shown remarkable survival skills, clawing back his powers stripped by a national conference in 1990.... With his 1993 election victory, Eyadéma's bully-boy tactics, which cost hundreds of lives, appear to have paid off." Eyadéma's style of autocratic rule, which he held to tightly through contested elections in 1998 and 2003, led observers to call Togo

"one of the [African] continent's most closed and repressive nations," to quote *New York Times* contributor Kenneth B. Noble.

Only 30 miles wide and 360 miles long, Togo is a tiny country that borders the Atlantic Ocean in West Africa. Formerly a French colony with strong ethnic ties to neighboring Ghana, the nation became independent in 1960. Most Togolese citizens are subsistence farmers, but the country does export coffee, cocoa, and phosphates. Many imports and funds for development come from France, Germany, and other Western nations, including the United States. Seagoing commerce is centered in Lome, the capital city, which is quite close to the Ghana-Togo border.

The two principal ethnic groups in Togo are the Ewe and the Kabiye. As is the case elsewhere in Africa, tensions between the two peoples present a continuing political concern, especially since neighboring Ghana contains a sizeable population of Ewes. Gnassingbé Eyadéma was of Kabiye descent. As leader of the Togolese military starting in 1963, he oversaw the promotion of Kabiye soldiers to all ranks in the army. Eyadéma's own ascent in the Togolese army ranks was swift. He received his military training with the French Army and served with French troops in such places as Indochina and Algeria before accepting a commission in Togo in 1961. At the age of 26 he was named a commander in the Togolese Army after he led a successful revolt against then-president Sylvanus Olympio.

After engineering the coup that resulted in Olympio's death in 1963, Eyadéma invited Nicolas Grunitzky,

At a Glance . . .

Born Étienne Gnassingbe Eyadéma on December 26, 1937, in Pya, Lama-Kara, Togo; died on February 5, 2005; son of Gnassingbé and N'Danida Eyadéma; married; several children.

Career: French Army officer, 1953-61, serving in Indochina, Dahoney, Niger, and Algeria; Togolese Army, commander, 1963; Togolese Army chief of staff, 1965; president of Togo, chief of armed forces, and minister of defense, 1967-2005.

Awards: Named Chevalier du Legion d'Honneur (France).

Togo's first prime minister, back to head the country. (Grunitzky had lost power to Olympio in 1958.) Grunitzky attempted to institute a constitutional multiparty government in Togo, but his efforts came to naught, and the increasingly popular Eyadéma began to court support among the military and the civilian populace. In January of 1967, Eyadéma, by then army chief of staff, assumed the political leadership of Togo in a nonviolent coup. He reorganized the government, named himself president, and scheduled a referendum on a new constitution. That referendum was later canceled, and by 1969 Eyadéma had enough popular support that he was able to form and head a new political party, the Togolese People's Rally (RPT). The RPT was Togo's only legal political party until the 1990s, and its simple platform rested on theories of "national unity" and "cultural authenticity." Under his authority many members of the Kabiye tribe came to dominate leadership in Togo's military and political institutions.

Eyadéma's dictatorship could not entirely quell opposition, however. As early as 1970 he was forced to suppress a plot to overthrow him, and by the mid-1970s several exiled dissenters—including the sons of ex-president Olympio—were viewed as real threats to the regime. On the other hand, foreign aid from France, Germany, and the United States introduced new industries into Togo, and a growing world market for phosphates brought improvement to the country's economy. As the relative prosperity continued into the 1980s, Togo became known as "Africa's little Switzerland." The capital of Lome, stocked with luxurious imports from Europe and America, was also a regional banking center and a bustling deepwater port.

Colleen Lowe Morna noted that the trappings of prosperity failed to cover severe problems in Togo. "The casual visitor might be forgiven for concluding that Togo is at the top of the African achievement league," she wrote. "Ironically, in 1982, Togo, along with a handful of other Third World countries, was officially designated by the UN General Assembly as one of the 'least developed countries among developing nations.' With an average GNP per capita of $300 per annum, Togo's 3 million people rank among the poorest in the world." A downturn in the phosphate market late in the 1980s accelerated an economic decline and, not surprisingly, produced new hostility toward the Eyadéma regime.

A series of bomb attacks in Lome during the summer of 1985 led to the arrest of more than a dozen people who were subsequently accused of terrorism and distributing subversive literature. The Togolese Movement for Democracy (MTD), made up of a group of exiled dissenters, claimed that members of Eyadéma's government had perpetrated the bombings and then used them as an excuse to launch a "wave of repression." When one of the detainees charged with the bombings died mysteriously in prison—and allegations surfaced that others may have been tortured—the human rights organization Amnesty International tried to send investigators to Togo. They were unable to enter the country, but a delegation of French observers did report evidence of torture among political prisoners. Eyadéma responded to these charges by issuing a presidential pardon to several of the detainees.

A more serious coup attempt against the Eyadéma regime occurred in September of 1986. A paramilitary unit occupied the Lome military barracks, the RPT headquarters, and the national radio station, killing about a dozen people during the attack. Eyadéma appealed to his French allies for assistance, and France sent 250 paratroopers to restore order. In December of 1986, 13 people were sentenced to death, and 14 to life imprisonment for the attack. One of three people to receive the death sentence in absentia was Gilchrist Olympio, an exiled son of the former Togolese president.

These and other demonstrations against Eyadéma's regime were the first harbingers of resistance to the dictator and his one-party rule. In an effort to silence the opposition, Eyadéma called for an election in the winter of 1986. Kenneth Noble described the voting procedure in the *New York Times*: "Gnassingbe Eyadéma held a referendum on his reign as President of [Togo]. As soldiers stood guard, voters were obliged to hold up a card of one color for 'yes' or another for 'no.' Given these circumstances, there were visible few signs of discontent, and Mr. Eyadéma, the sole candidate, polled 99 percent of the vote." Eyadéma was shrewd enough to realize, however, that he could not ignore the calls for multiparty democracy. By 1989 he was assuring the United States government—and his own people—that the process of democratization of Togo would begin shortly.

Opposition parties multiplied both within Togo and outside its borders, especially in Ghana, while unrest swelled in Lome especially. After another round of politically-motivated arrests in 1990—and more allegations of torture of political prisoners—widespread strikes erupted in the capital city. Eyadéma's forces clashed with protesters who attacked public property; eventually almost 200 people were arrested. As in previous cases of organized unrest, Eyadéma blamed "international machinations" and foreign influence for the troubles, pointing a finger most notably at Ghana. Likewise, he once again resisted efforts to investigate human rights violations, issuing widespread presidential pardons to those arrested in the demonstrations.

Protests continued in Togo, gaining momentum as other African nations ousted long-standing dictators in favor of democratic governments. By the spring of 1991 Eyadéma was compelled to agree to widespread reforms. The most dramatic demonstration of his loss of power came in the summer of 1991, when an umbrella group representing ten political parties, the Collective of Democratic Opposition (COD), organized a general strike, tore down the statue of Eyadéma in Lome, and convened a national conference to address Togo's political problems.

That conference, attended by numerous opposition parties, government representatives, students, union leaders, and clergymen, became a forum from which Togo's citizenry denounced the Eyadéma administration and sought to overthrow it. Four days after convening on July 8, the conference declared its sovereignty. "The tide was already turning against the military regime," wrote Mark Huband in *Africa Report*. "The country's post-independence history was thrown into the spotlight, and very quickly the pillars of government began to crumble." Huband added that the conference highlighted both human rights abuses and cases of financial mismanagement that could be tied directly to the Eyadéma regime. "Accusations by the human rights activist Me Kwami Occansey that Eyadéma was no better than [German political leader and Nazi party founder Adolf] Hitler received rapturous applause in the conference hall," the reporter stated.

The 1991 national conference in Togo effectively removed Eyadéma from power and installed an archrival, Joseph Kokou Koffigoh, as leader of a new provisional government. The victory was short-lived, however. Armed forces loyal to Eyadéma mounted a siege of Lome's government establishments in the winter of 1991, taking Koffigoh prisoner. By mid-1992 Koffigoh had named a number of Eyadéma deputies to his inner circle, and by year's end he was little more than a figurehead. According to Da Costa, Koffigoh, "a human rights lawyer elected to lead the transitional government through to the elections and threatened, even kidnapped, by Eyadéma loyalists, [became] a shadow of his former self."

The political crisis continued through 1992 and into 1993, with strikers demanding immediate elections and neutral armed forces. Hundreds of thousands of Togolese citizens fled to Ghana and Benin, and the international community was stunned by an assassination attempt on opposition leader Gilchrist Olympio. In March of 1993 Eyadéma's residence in Lome came under armed attack by dissenters within the military ranks. Eyadéma survived the coup attempt and proceeded to negotiate a timetable for presidential elections with the leaders of Togo's principal political parties.

The presidential election, held late in the summer of 1993, was beset by numerous controversies. Observers from the international community—including former U.S. President Jimmy Carter—refused to endorse the results, citing "hasty planning, the lack of a credible opposition, and question marks over voter lists and cards," to quote Da Costa. Indeed, Eyadéma's principal opponent—Gilchrist Olympio—was not allowed to run because he would not agree to be examined by Togolese doctors to confirm his health. Olympio, who had documentation of a thorough examination by French doctors, complained that he could not safely enter Togo to undergo the examination. In Olympio's stead, Eyadéma faced the leaders of three opposition parties. When the results of the August 25th election were polled, Eyadéma had received 96.42 percent of the popular vote.

Da Costa wrote: "Eyadéma, with close to three decades of self-imposed autocratic rule under his belt, will find it difficult to claim that his victory in Togo's…presidential elections gives him an undisputed right to remain at the helm of the West African country…. The context behind Eyadéma's huge margin—the lack of credible opponents, as well as a paltry turnout officially put at 39.5 percent—confirmed the landmark in Togo's march toward democracy as little more than a sham, an exercise in self-delusion by a man reluctant to surrender to the mass of forces ranged against him." Da Costa felt that Togo would face further violence and unrest as long as Eyadéma wielded power, but other observers offered a different view. For instance, in an election-day appeal to his fellow citizens, Koffigoh characterized Eyadéma as a man who "could guarantee security, peace, and stability for Togo."

At least one citizen interviewed by Da Costa echoed Koffigoh's optimism. "I voted for Eyadéma because he's not just our patron, he's our god," a Lome taxi driver told *Africa Report*. "The city used to be safe, you could taxi…24 hours a day and even sleep in the streets. But now Lome is in a mess. It's democracy that's done this. Only Eyadéma can solve our problems."

Over the next decade, Eyadéma remained in power. Although he won multiparty elections in both 1998 and 2003, Eyadéma was widely considered to have held power by intimidation and other unfair means. Over his many years as leader of Togo, Eyadéma had placed himself so squarely in the center of Togo's affairs that when he died of a heart attack on February

5, 2005, he left his country with "no reliable mechanisms for resolving disputes without him," according to the *Economist*. Eyadéma's legacy was seen when his loyal army quickly named his 39-year-old son, Faure Gnassingbé, as Togo's president, a move that went against Togo's constitution. A successful business man, Faure Gnassingbé had limited political experience, having served as his father's minister for public works, mines, and telecommunications. Gnassingbé's appointment as president caused such outrage in Togo and western Africa that he stepped down in order for a proper election to be held in April. He later won the presidential election and was sworn into office on May 4, 2005. Violent protests of the election and flow of refugees from Togo to neighboring countries caused ongoing instability as Gnassingbé took office. It remains to be seen if he rules with the iron fist of his father.

Sources

Books

Africa South of the Sahara: 1994, 23rd edition, Europa, 1994.

Periodicals

Africa Report, September-October 1990, pp. 36-38; November-December 1991, pp. 18-20; November-December 1993, pp. 61-65; March-April 1994, p. 7.

Economist, April 27, 1991, p. 48; December 7, 1991, p. 50; February 13, 1993, p. 48; August 21, 1993, p. 34; February 12, 2005, p. 48.

New African, March 2005, p. 20; April 2005, p. 4, 27.

New York Times, July 25, 1991, p. A-6; August 29, 1991, p. A-13; November 29, 1991, p. A-10; December 1, 1991, p. 9; December 4, 1991, p. A-8; February 2, 1992, p. A-8; February 2, 1993, p. A-6; May 4, 2005, p. A-10.

On-line

L'Info en Direct Togo, www.republicoftogo.com/fr/home.asp (June 9, 2005).

"Profile: Faure Gnassingbé," *BBC News*, http://news.bbc.co.uk/2/hi/africa/4242469.stm (May 31, 2005).

—Anne Janette Johnson and Sara Pendergast

Aaron Freeman

1956—

Comedian, commentator, actor

Performer and writer Aaron Freeman has been a fixture of Chicago arts and entertainment ever since he created his satirical *Council Wars* stage show in the early 1980s. He has developed and starred in other one-man shows, including the acclaimed *Do the White Thing,* written commentaries for National Public Radio and the Public Broadcasting System, and released several comedy CDs. Freeman's comedy is based on astute observation and insatiable curiosity rather than on outrageous transgression, and his curiosity has led him into explorations of new religious realms (he is a convert from Catholicism to Judaism) and into a life-long love affair with science and technology, which he has taught to children. As his career has developed, his activities have become more and more diverse.

Freeman was born in 1956 in Chicago but was sent as a baby to live with his paternal grandparents on a farm in downstate Pembroke, near Kankakee. "It was such a small town that I clearly remember it was fun—big fun!—to go down and watch people drive on the new blacktop. We would get dressed up for that," he told the *Chicago Reader*'s Michael G. Glab. When he grew to school age, he was returned Chicago and to his mother Leona, a salon owner, and father James, a factory worker. Freeman was enrolled in St. Jarlath Catholic elementary school after the family was befriended by white Catholic civil rights workers from nearby Mundelein Seminary. He later attended Notre Dame School and St. Michael's High School, which seethed with racial conflict after the assassination of the Rev. Martin Luther King Jr. in 1968.

Not a class clown like other future comedians, the young Freeman was interested in physics in high school and excelled as a student. School was almost too easy. "I had this brilliant idea in my junior year to show my utter contempt for the kids who actually had to study to get anywhere," he told the *Reader.* "I announced to my teachers that I was going to flunk everything in the third quarter. I thought it would be really funny: A, A, F, A." His teachers were not amused, but Freeman did knuckle down in one area: he tried out for a play, won the role, and became more and more interested in theater. Before finishing high school he was admitted to New York University, where he studied with the famed theater teacher Stella Adler. Soon he was appearing in plays in New York and later in London, England, where he spent several years.

Parodied Chicago Council Conflicts

Back in the United States in 1976, Freeman thought of heading for the West Coast. But when he stopped to visit his family in Chicago he auditioned for the famed Second City comedy troupe and won a spot in its Chateau Louise subsidiary. Driving around the city with a Rolls-Royce grille on the front of his Volkswagen, Freeman got noticed by other performers and began building a career. He and two Second City actors made a low-budget video spoof, *Vegetable House,* in the early 1980s and put together a comedy program called *With Sex in the Title.* The Chicago political scene was even wilder than usual at the time as the city's first black mayor, Harold Washington, battled with the

At a Glance . . .

Born in 1956 in Chicago, IL; raised partly in Pembroke, IL, near Kankakee; son of James (a factory worker) and Leona (a salon owner) Freeman; children: twin daughters. *Education:* Studied acting at New York University. *Religion:* Raised Baptist and Roman Catholic; converted to Judaism.

Career: Comedian and journalist, late 1970s–; Chateau Louise troupe (associated with Second City comedy theater), member, late 1970s; *Talking with Aaron Freeman,* WPWR television, Chicago, host, 1980s-1990s; Columbia College, Chicago, adjunct professor of telecommunications, mid-1990s; *All Things Considered* (National Public Radio), *The MacNeil-Lehrer News Hour* (Public Broadcasting System), and *Eight Forty-Eight* (Chicago Public Radio), writer, early 1990s–.

Addresses: *Office*—Chicago Public Radio, Navy Pier, 848 East Grand Avenue, Chicago, IL 60611-3462; *Web*—www.aaronfreeman.com.

white-dominated city council led by alderman Edward Vrdolyak. Freeman devised a pair of characters named Harold Skytalker and Lord Darth Vrdolyak, using the popular *Star Wars* films to parody the two main antagonists.

The resulting *Council Wars* sketches were a local smash. The term "council wars" became part of Chicago's political lexicon. Most adult Chicagoans knew about them and could identify Freeman as their creator, and Freeman, newly married to an actress named Wandachristine in 1984, found his doings chronicled by the city's peripatetic gossip columnists. In 1986 Freeman joined the main Second City troupe, and the following year he issued a book called *Confessions of a Lottery Ball*—in a television commercial he had appeared as a ball that bounced around inside a lottery random-drawing machine. He also wrote articles for *Playboy* and numerous editorial commentaries for the Chicago's daily newspapers, and he produced a television documentary, *Do What You Love,* that told the stories of three teenagers who had turned hobbies into businesses. A strong believer in self-reliance, Freeman was a supporter of both President Ronald Reagan and Nation of Islam leader Louis Farrakhan. As a performer he was partly inspired by the edgy comedy of actress Whoopi Goldberg.

After his early successes, Freeman once again considered heading for Los Angeles when his career hit a slow stretch. But Chicago ties once again kept him in place; he spent several months caring for a friend, Chicago news anchor Max Robinson, in the later stages of Robinson's fatal AIDS infection. In 1989 Freeman and collaborator Rob Kolson began working on sketches for a new show, *Do the White Thing.* The title, although it was a takeoff on that of director Spike Lee's controversial *Do the Right Thing,* did not refer to race. Indeed, Freeman's material often didn't emphasize racial themes. "Been there, done that. Unfortunately I'm not that interested in ethnic stuff," he told the *Chicago Sun-Times.*

Instead, *Do the White Thing* (which did include a segment in which Freeman portrayed a crazed African consumed with hatred for whites) took its title from its tragicomic central monologue, which dealt with the death of Freeman's brother Julius from lung cancer in 1989. The "white thing" was the blending of all colors into white light that is thought to be experienced by the dying. In the intensely competitive world of Chicago theater, *Do the White Thing* lasted for several years and became the city's longest-running revue. Freeman and Kolson followed it up with another show with a financial theme, *Gentlemen Prefer Bonds, or Girls Just Wanna Have Funds.*

Converted to Judaism

During the run of *Do the White Thing,* Freeman announced his conversion to Judaism. Some wondered whether the conversion was a kind of experiment or stunt on the part of the unpredictable performer, but his seriousness emerged over time as he took courses at Chicago's Spertus College of Judaica and began appearing before Jewish groups. Asked by the *Reader* if he had believed in Jesus Christ when he was younger, Freeman responded: "As long as I didn't think about it, I did. The point about Judaism is it's a way cool tribe....I like the traditions of the tribe. I like what it stands for. It's less a matter of theology."

Living with partner Rhonda Steakley, who became the mother of his twin daughters, Freeman branched out into new areas in the 1990s. His high-school enthusiasm for science resurfaced. "When Rhonda and I go out, we go to lectures at [the] I[llinois] I[nstitute of] T[echnology]," he told the *Reader.* "We're science groupies." His interests also included polo, and he worked on a film script about the sport at one point. An Internet enthusiast as early as 1994, Freeman taught a computer course at Chicago's Columbia College. He hosted a talk show called *Metropolis* on Chicago's National Public Radio affiliate WBEZ and later began writing commentaries for the network's national evening news program, *All Things Considered* and for the *MacNeil/Lehrer NewsHour,* where he became the show's first African-American essayist. Freeman was also the host, for ten years, of *Talking with Aaron Freeman* on Chicago television station WPWR.

On the performance front, Freeman premiered a new revue, *Disguised as a Grownup,* in 1993. He took on his first dramatic role the following year, playing a political prisoner in a play called *Someone Who'll Watch Over Me.* He appeared in a Chicago Symphony Orchestra children's concert, and he merged his scientific and broadcast interests as chief science correspondent for the Chicago Public Television technology program *Chicago Tomorrow.* His Chicago-themed comedy CD *312 4 Ever* became a perennial strong seller.

Made Directorial Debut

Freeman continued to perform with Second City, and in 1998 he spearheaded a new company comedy production, *An Evening with the Second City,* that was mounted on Chicago's predominantly African-American South Side. The company's casts had grown more diverse over the years, but black audiences had mostly stayed away. Freeman made his debut as a director for the new revue, which had some material with African-American themes but also reprised some of the company's tried-and-true skits. "There's nothing inherently North Side or pale about sketch comedy," Freeman pointed out to Chris Jones of the *Chicago Tribune.* "The human condition hasn't changed much in the last 6,000 years."

The early 2000s saw Freeman as busy as ever. Continuing to step into the director's chair on occasion, he retained his knack for wringing comedy from tense situations when he brought together a Palestinian Arab and a Jewish Israeli comedian in a show called *The Arab/Israeli Comedy Hour* in 2003; years earlier, he had included a sketch called "West Bank Story" in *Do the White Thing.* His website included links to those of both the Israeli daily newspaper *Ha'aretz* and the Palestinian militant organization Hamas.

In the early 2000s, Freeman was active in the broadcast field as a writer and correspondent for the Chicago Public Radio newsmagazine program *Eight Forty-Eight.* Freeman also kept up his solo performing career, developing a diverse clientele by appearing before business, campus, and Jewish groups all over the U.S., and he developed new one-man show, *The Joy of News,* in 2004. *Chicago Tribune* reviewer Nina Metz complained that in that show, the "most interesting subject," Freeman's status as an African-American Jew, "remains untouched." But Freeman prepared to address that topic with the release of a new CD, *Confessions of a Hebro,* in 2005.

Selected works

Council Wars (political satire), 1984.
Confessions of a Lottery Ball (book), 1986.
(With Rob Kolson) *Do the White Thing* (comedy program with serious monologues), 1989.
(With Rob Kolson) *Gentlemen Prefer Bonds* (comedy program), 2000.
The Arab/Israeli Comedy Hour (comedy revue), 2003.
The Joy of News (one-man comedy program), 2004.
312 4 Ever (CD), 2004.
Confessions of a Hebro (CD), 2005.

Sources

Periodicals

Chicago Reader, April 23, 1993, sec. 1.
Chicago Sun-Times, September 19, 1986, p. 10; October 9, 1987, p. 20; December 22, 1989, p. 5; March 12, 1993, Weekend Plus sec., p. 10; April 30, 1993, Weekend Plus sec., p. 25; April 17, 1994, Show sec., p. 2; May 20, 1994, Weekend Plus sec., p. 3; August 2, 1994, p. 16.
Chicago Tribune, April 10, 1998, p. 4; April 11, 2003, p. 2; December 23, 2004, p. 8.
Reason, August 1994, p. 51.

On-line

Aaron Freeman, www.aaronfreeman.com (March 3, 2005).

—James M. Manheim

David Harewood

1965—

Actor

British actor David Harewood starred in *Babyfather,* a hit British Broadcasting Corporation (BBC) television series that followed the exploits of a quartet of black men and their struggles with romance, fidelity, and parenthood. Harewood played Augustus "Gus" Pottinger across eight episodes in 2001 and 2002 in a performance that garnered excellent reviews and made him one of Britain's newest leading men. After struggling for a number of years earlier in his career because of the "black actor" tag usually appended to his name, Harewood was thrilled that *Babyfather* seemed to be breaking new ground. "It challenges a lot of stereotypes and shows a side of the black male that we just haven't seen before," he told Graham Keal of Liverpool's *Daily Post.* "A side that's a lot more sensitive, a lot more understanding, a lot more humorous."

Harewood, David, photograph. Will Conran/Getty Images.

Born in 1965, Harewood was the last of four children born to parents who were originally from Barbados, the West Indian island nation, and had settled in Birmingham, a major city located in the central part of England known as the Midlands. His father was a long-distance truck driver, while his mother worked as a caterer, but they separated when Harewood was in his

early teens. Birmingham was a hotbed of racial tensions during those years, with a large skinhead population and frequent skirmishes between blacks and whites. As he recalled in an interview with Nina Myskow for London's *Mirror* newspaper, there were definitely "no-go areas for black people. There was quite a lot of racism. I remember being chased, gangs and rottweilers. You'd wait for the screech of [tires], and find yourself half laughing and running for your life, clambering over fences. It was just part of life."

Though Harewood was an admittedly indifferent student at Washwood Heath comprehensive school, he was a talented mimic and the unofficial class clown. His career ambitions seemed dim at this point, and he imagined that if he would be able to get a job after leaving school at all, it would be in one of the nearby factories. But his English teacher suggested that he might try acting, and though Harewood's parents scoffed at the idea, he was able to earn a place in a six-week course at the Britain's prestigious National Youth Theatre. "I had the most brilliant time," he told a writer for London's *Independent,* Andrew G. Marshall. "There were three other black guys, but two of

At a Glance . . .

Born in 1965 in Birmingham, England; son of a Romeo (a truck driver) and Malene (a caterer) Harewood. *Education:* Attended London's Royal Academy of Dramatic Art.

Career: Actor, 1991–.

Memberships: Royal Academy of Dramatic Art, associate.

Addresses: *Office*—c/o Royal Academy of Dramatic Art, 62-64 Gower St., London WC1E 6ED, United Kingdom.

them completely ignored me. It was the first time I got a taste of what it would be like to be in competition in the business."

Trained as Shakespearean Actor

From this starting point, Harewood won a coveted spot at the Royal Academy of Dramatic Art (RADA), where he shed his distinctive "Brummie," or Birmingham, accent. Not long after he finished, he was cast in a production of *Romeo and Juliet* as the male lead in the doomed romantic tragedy from Shakespeare, and his skin color occasioned much press for the unknown actor. Further articles also seemed to emphasize his race, and within two years of leaving school Harewood suffered a nervous breakdown, caused in part by overwork but also due to intense media scrutiny. He recalled that he began speaking in a variety of character voices, and at one point believed he was actually a secret agent. "I'd literally wake up on Oxford Street at four in the afternoon and think 'What am I doing here? Dressed as a clown, in a pair of shorts and a pair of boots. I'd better get home,'" he told Myskow in the *Mirror* interview. "I'd start walking home and the next thing I knew, I'd find myself in Islington at 3am. I kept waking up in various places in London."

Harewood was temporarily committed to a hospital for treatment, which involved a heavy dose of stabilizing drugs, but thankfully his RADA professors and theater colleagues stepped in, along with "incredibly supportive friends and family who rang up the institution and said, 'Look, he's not mad, he's an actor and just stressed,'" he told Rebecca Fletcher in another *Mirror* article. "I was lucky. If I'd been an anonymous black guy in another city, I'd probably have disappeared into the system."

After some months of rest, Harewood resumed his career, and began to win an increasing number of roles

in British-made television series and films. In 1995, Vanessa Redgrave cast him in the lead in another Shakespearean romantic tragedy, *Antony and Cleopatra,* opposite herself in a production staged by her repertory theater company. They reprised the roles on a lengthy two-year tour, and their on-stage chemistry was so apparent that rumors arose they were romantically involved in real life as well. Redgrave, scion of a British acting family and known for her outspoken political views, was nearly 30 years Harewood's senior, and the pair did live together for a time in Redgrave's suburban London home. But Harewood maintains that theirs was a platonic relationship, and the two remain close friends.

Impressed Critics in London, New York

Harewood's career was boosted by his appearance in the title role of yet another Shakespearean tragedy, *Othello,* at the Royal National Theatre beginning in 1997. He was cast in the part by theater director Sam Mendes, who would go on to earn an Academy Award for the 1999 film, *American Beauty.* Harewood's performance earned excellent reviews, with the *Financial Times* critic Alastair Macaulay noting that he "so fully inhabits the role of Othello that he carries the play's later acts. His rapport with Desdemona and Iago is full of superb detail." Macaulay concluded by musing, "sometimes I think that the best experience of all is to encounter a familiar play as if for the first time. So with this superb Othello." Robert L. Daniels, a critic for the entertainment-industry trade journal *Variety,* saw the play at the Brooklyn Academy of Music in April of 1998 and also gave Harewood's stage talents some high marks. "The actor makes the transition from dignified general to tormented pawn with a startling and pitiful descent into festering fury," Daniels asserted.

Harewood won a role in a British police-drama series, *The Vice,* in 1999 as Sergeant Joe Robinson. He also began another job in a medical drama, *Always and Everyone,* that also went on the air in Britain that same year. In the latter drama, which ran until 2002, he played a hospital physician, Dr. Mike Gregson. In 2001, he began appearing in *Babyfather,* a BBC2 series based on a book of the same name. He played Augustus "Gus" Pottinger, a successful jeweler who carries on romantic dalliances with two women, but Pottinger was one of just four men on the series, each with their own set of relationship troubles. The series ran into a second season and scored high ratings.

Harewood has also appeared in the film version of *The Merchant of Venice,* a 2004 production that featured Al Pacino and Jeremy Irons in the leading roles. He was eager to explore new roles as an actor, perhaps even as the first black James Bond. "My dream role would be to play a villain in *Lord of the Rings*—but there's another movie where they didn't seem to want to cast any black actors," he said in *Independent* interview from 2003. "This country refuses to—or cannot find the energy to—produce a black international film star."

Selected works

Films

The Hawk, 1993.
Mad Dogs and Englishmen, 1995.
The Merchant of Venice, 2004.
Strings, 2004.

Plays

Romeo and Juliet, London.
Antony and Cleopatra (toured), 1995-97.
Othello (toured), 1997-98.
Badnuff, London, 2004.
Henry IV, Parts 1 and 2, London, 2005.

Television

The Vice, BBC-TV, 1999.
Always and Everyone, BBC-TV, 1999-2002.
Babyfather, BBC-TV, 2001-02.

Sources

Periodicals

Back Stage, March 21, 1997, p. 52; April 17, 1998, p. 49.
Daily Post (Liverpool, England), October 6, 2001, p. 2.
Express (London, England), October 28, 2002, p. 32.
Financial Times, May 6, 1998, p. 16.
Independent (London, England), May 12, 1998, p. 14; May 31, 2003, p. 5.
Mirror (London, England), April 6, 2001, p. 32; February 16, 2002, p. 6.
New Statesman, September 19, 1997, p. 40.
Times (London, England), January 20, 2000, p. 38.
Variety, March 17, 1997, p. 62; April 20, 1998, p. 55.

—Carol Brennan

Lenny Henry

1958—

Comedian, actor, "Comic Relief" campaigner

Naming him one of the 50 funniest people in Britain in 2003, the *Observer* newspaper described Lenny Henry as "a comic genius with a highly effective social conscience." Henry is one of the most successful British comedians of the "alternative comedy" generation that emerged in the 1980s, enjoying a 30-year career that spans stand-up live performances, TV comedy shows, TV drama, voiceovers, and movies. Henry became famous for his gentle and affectionate mockery of the Jamaican community in which he grew up, but he has also been a savage critic of jokes that exploit minority groups out of bigotry or ignorance. He had a brief and unsuccessful flirtation with Hollywood in the 1990s, but has since returned to the "character comedy" for which he is best known. In 1999 he was awarded a CBE (meaning Commander of the British Empire, an honor bestowed by the royalty of England), in part for his years of campaign work with the charity Comic Relief.

Lenny Henry was born on August 29, 1958, and grew up in Dudley, a suburb of Birmingham, England. His family was from Jamaica and moved to Birmingham in the 1950s. He attended Bluecoat Secondary Modern School, W.R. Tewson School, and Preston College, but in 1975, aged just 17, his show business career took off when he was a repeat winner on the weekly TV talent show, *New Faces*. His act consisted of impersonating white TV celebrities, and for the next few years he performed in pubs and local clubs around Britain. He also went on tour with the *Black and White Minstrels' Show*—a variety show featuring white performers with blacked-up faces—and endured many

jokes based on his color. On his official Web site he explains: "I think by '79—I'd had enough. The jokes were boring—'And now the only one of 'em who doesn't need make up'…It hurts thinking about it now."

Between 1978 and 1980 he performed on the chaotic British Saturday morning children's TV show *Tiswas*, where he was allowed to improvise and where he invented characters such as Delbert Wilkins, an inept pirate radio DJ from the West Indian London suburb of Brixton, who would later become part of his adult stand-up act. For the next few years he performed in the "summer season" variety shows at English seaside resorts, but continued with *Tiswas* and began to tour colleges and universities in the United Kingdom. Henry notes that performing for students had a liberating effect because it allowed him to swear in front of an audience.

In 1980 he became involved with The Comic Strip, a group of comedy performers from the London "Comedy Store," best known for their anti-establishment sentiment and (for the time) shocking comedy shows produced as *The Comic Strip Presents…* It was through The Comic Strip that he met Dawn French (later known as the Vicar of Dibley), whom he married in 1984, and who steered him towards "alternative" comedy, a style of comedy that was radically different from the "summer season" shows in which he began his career. In 1981 he teamed up with Tracy Ullman and David Copperfield in the sketch show *Three of a Kind*, which ran on BBC TV for three years. He left to perform in his own TV show, *The Lenny Henry Show,* featuring Delbert Wilkins. Other characters

At a Glance . . .

Born Lenworth George Henry on August 29, 1958, in Dudley, near Birmingham, England; married Dawn French, 1984; children: adopted daughter Billie.

Career: Comedian, England, performed in pubs and clubs as well as with the Black and White Minstrels, 1970s; television and film actor, 1980s–; The Comic Strip, comedian group, 1980–; Comic Relief, founder, 1985–; Crucial Films, independent film production company, founder, 1980s(?).

Awards: *New Faces* talent show, winner, 1975; Monte Carlo Television Festival, Monaco Red Cross and the Golden Nymph Award, 1991, for *Alive and Kicking*; Royal Television Society Silver Award; BBC British Personality of the Year Award, 1993; Edric Connor Inspiration to Black People Award; Commander of the Order of the British Empire (CBE), 1999; BFM Awards, Winner of the Inspiration Award, 2002; Black Entertainment Comedy Awards, Winner of Lifetime Achievement Award, 2003; British Comedy Awards, Winner of Lifetime Achievement Award, 2003.

Addresses: *Agent*—PBJ Management, 7 Soho Street, London W1D 3DQ, England; *Web*—www.lennyhenry.com.

Besides his work as a performer Henry is also a founder, frontman, and an important creative force behind the charity Comic Relief, which raises money to fund education, immunization, rebuilding, and community work in the United Kingdom and around the world. Launched at Christmas in 1985 from a refugee camp in Sudan, Comic Relief runs a fundraising effort every two years in the United Kingdom culminating in "Red Nose Day," a day when Britons are encouraged to do silly things to raise money. The centerpiece of the campaign is a mammoth telethon that contrasts comedy routines with documentaries about the various causes. Between 1985 and 2003 the charity raised £337 million; "Red Nose Day" is the United Kingdom's biggest charitable event.

In the 1990s Henry's production company, Crucial Films, involved him in many new projects including a workshop for new writers and performers called Step Forward. He also began to garner a reputation as a television actor. His performance in *Alive and Kicking* alongside Robbie Coltrane won several awards, while his situation comedy *Chef!* ran for three seasons. In 1999 he appeared as school head teacher Ian George in *Hope and Glory*, a TV drama that reflected current fears about the British state school system and brought him personal critical acclaim, though the series itself was not highly rated. In 2001 Henry himself returned to education when he began studying for a degree in English literature part-time at the Open University. Henry has credits as writer, actor, director, and producer of many TV shows, has performed voiceovers for cartoons and documentaries, and continues to tour with his one-man show. In 1999 he was rewarded for his contribution to entertainment and for his work with Comic Relief when he was honored as a Commander of the Order of the British Empire (CBE).

Selected works

Films

Lenny Live and Unleashed, 1989.
True Identity, 1991.
Harry Potter and the Prisoner of Azkhaban, 2004.

Television

The Lenny Henry Show, 1984-93.
Alive and Kicking, 1991.
Chef!, 1993-4, 1996.
Hope and Glory, 1999-2000.
Lenny Henry in Pieces, 1999.

Sources

Books

appearing on the show included Theophilis P. Wildebeest, a parody of black R&B singers in the style of Barry White, and Trevor McDoughnut, based on the black British news anchor, Trevor MacDonald. *The Lenny Henry Show* ran for a decade and was revived as *Lenny Henry in Pieces* in 1999.

Henry became a well-known British TV personality during the 1980s. His humor was gentler than other "alternative comedy" performers and his TV show aired in prime time. But Henry retained his pioneering edge and in 1989 he became the first British comedy performer to make a live stand-up movie, *Lenny Live and Unleashed*. Offers from Hollywood followed and in 1991 he made *True Identity*, which was supposed to be the first of three movies for Disney. Unfortunately the film failed and the remainder of the contract was canceled. In 2004 he returned to the big screen as a shrunken head in *Harry Potter and the Prisoner of Azkaban*.

Margolis, Jonathan, *Lenny Henry: A Biography*, Orion Press, 1995.

Periodicals

Essence, August 1991.
The Independent (UK), March 2002.
The Observer (UK), December 7, 2003.

On-line

Comic Relief, www.comicrelief.com/allaboutus/index .shtml (accessed April 11, 2005).
"Lenny Henry," *100 Great Black Britons*, www.100 greatblackbritons.com/bios/lenny_henry.html (accessed April 11, 2005).
"Lenny Henry," *The Black Presence in Britain*, www. blackpresence.co.uk/pages/entertainment/henry. htm (accessed April 11, 2005).
Lenny Henry, www.lennyhenry.com/home/index. asp?pID=0 (accessed April 11, 2005).

—Chris Routledge

Nathan Irvin Huggins

1927-1989

Scholar

In the *New York Times* obituary of his death, a fellow historian called Nathan Irvin Huggins, "an extraordinary teacher who cared deeply about his students." Huggins not only spent a quarter of a century imparting knowledge to budding American historians, he also helped define the emerging field of African-American studies. Reared and educated against the backdrop of a changing America—World War II, Civil Rights—Huggins witnessed firsthand the impact of history on the present. He turned his critical eye to the study of African slaves in America as a way to understand the social fabric of modern American society. He then distilled that knowledge into a body of work that was literary, passionate, and accessible to the general public.

Early Life Marked by Racial Prejudice

Nathan Irvin Huggins was born on January 14, 1927, in Chicago, Illinois, to Winston J. Huggins, a black waiter and railroad worker, and Marie Warsaw Huggins, a white Jewish immigrant of Polish descent. Huggins's mixed racial heritage gave him up-close, early exposure to the implications of race. When Huggins was 12, his father abandoned the family and Marie moved Huggins and his older sister Kathryn to San Francisco, California. Barely two years later, she died, leaving the two teenagers own their own. Howard Thurman, an African-American minister and scholar of black spirituals, and his wife Sue Bailey Thurman, later adopted them.

Huggins dropped out of high school to work a variety of menial jobs—porter, longshoreman, warehouse worker. At 18, near the end of World War II, Huggins was drafted into the U.S. Army. His experiences in the black corps gave him further insight into the realities of racism. He was assigned a guard post at a German prisoner-of-war facility. Despite his position of authority, Huggins was denied the right to eat in the same mess hall as the prisoners. Though they were the enemy, they were white and therefore accorded privileges that Huggins was not. Historian David Blight, writing in *Reviews in American History,* noted that incidents like this did not make Huggins angry. Known for his good-natured sense of humor, Huggins explored, "the bitterness of racial ironies in America, processed through metaphors of humor."

After earning his high school diploma in the Army, Huggins returned to civilian life with his GI Bill and enrolled in the University of California at Berkeley to study history. He earned a bachelor's degree in 1954 and a master's in 1955. At Berkeley Huggins studied under historian Kenneth Stampp, one of the first scholars to turn the probing light of historical research on the subject of slavery. Prior to the 1950s, slavery had been deemed unworthy of serious study. The research that had been done generally concluded that slavery was a natural system of labor, based on the inferiority of blacks and their need to be controlled by white masters—an arrangement that was both paternalistic and harmless. Huggins recalled that as a schoolboy he was taught a "rather sunny picture of slavery...about darkies sitting on a plantation, eating

College in Illinois, and University of Massachusetts at Boston, Huggins landed a full professorship in the department of history at Columbia University in 1970.

Huggins's academic progress was set against the unfolding civil rightsmovement. Throughout his academic training, Huggins was legally considered a second-class citizen in much of the country. "Whites Only" signs blanketed the American South, and the North, while more liberal, was riddled by racial divisions stemming mainly from economic imbalance. He was an undergraduate when the 1954 Supreme Court case *Brown v. the Board of Education* declared segregated schooling to be unconstitutional. Two years after he earned his doctorate, the Civil Rights Act of 1964 was passed, criminalizing discrimination in education, employment, and public facilities. While activists from Rosa Parks to Martin Luther King, Jr., to Malcolm X, took to the streets spurring sit-ins, protest marches, and boycotts, Huggins and other black historians, turned to the past understand the present plight of African Americans.

Huggins helped build the field of African-American history as it was happening. "Huggins entered the field of Afro-American history with, not before, the crest of revolutions in society and scholarship through which that field found extraordinary new growth," noted Blight. Huggins had a personal, passionate commitment to his field, not just as an African-American scholar, but as an African American. For this reason, much of his published work, though academically grounded, is accessible to the average reader.

Began a Decade of Intense Academic Activity

Starting in 1971 Huggins launched a decade of intense activity. In July he married Brenda Carlita Smith, an actress and writer who in later years would co-author and edit many of Huggins works. That same year he published *Protestants Against Poverty: Boston's Charities,* a reworking of his doctoral thesis which analyzed the social impulses behind late 19th century poverty relief programs aimed at immigrants. The book also highlighted the role of society as a major factor in poverty, a theme that fed the civil rightsmovement, and has continued into the 21st century as a tenant of American social welfare policy.

Later that year, Huggins published *Harlem Renaissance,* a cultural history of the African-American arts scene that emerged in New York City's Harlem during the 1920s. Writers Langston Hughes and Zora Neale Hurston, musicians Bessie Smith and Duke Ellington, and painters Romare Bearden and Jacob Lawrence were all products of the movement. Huggins examined the Renaissance within a greater framework of American history and culture. Thirty years after its publication, *Harlem Renaissance* was still considered essential reading for students of this fascinating era.

During his ten-year tenure at Columbia, Huggins maintained an active life as an academic, becoming a noted

watermelons and singing songs," Blight noted. Stampp refuted that image, calling slavery a highly profitable economic system based on exploitation, cruelty, and fear. Stampp's analyses, coupled with the burgeoning civil rights movement, greatly influenced Huggins own way of thinking about slavery and race in America.

Educated Amidst Civil Rights Strife

In 1957 Huggins older sister Kathryn was killed in a car accident. After this tragedy, Huggins transferred to Harvard University, where three decades later he would establish the Kathryn Huggins Prize to honor outstanding undergraduate work in the field of African-American studies. At Harvard, Huggins earned a second master's degree in 1959 and a doctorate in 1962. After a cross-country maze of brief teaching posts at Long Beach State College in California, Lake Forest

authority in African-American studies. He was awarded several fellowships and grants from prestigious institutions such as the Guggenheim, the Ford Foundation, and the Center for Advanced Studies in Behavioral Sciences. As a Fulbright scholar he was sent to lecture in France. He served on the boards of several educational organizations including the Smithsonian Institution, the New York Council on the Humanities, the Library of America (of which he was also a director), and the Organization of American Historians. During this decade, Huggins also taught history, published scholarly papers, and traveled in Africa.

Published Seminal Work on American Slavery

In 1977 Huggins published his third, and most acclaimed, book. At 250 pages, *Black Odyssey: The Afro-American's Ordeal in Slavery* was a brief tome with an expansive goal—to explain how African Americans rose up from the wreckage of slavery to build their own unique, dynamic culture. "Nowhere are the psychological dynamics of this ordeal and triumph more clearly, gracefully, or economically set forth," than in *Black Odyssey*, wrote Willie Lee Rose for *The New York Review of Books*.

The lingering impact of *Black Odyssey*—still required reading in African-American history courses—was Huggins's recreation of the slave experience, a task he accomplished by blurring the boundaries between academic scholarship and literary art. Though based on solid ethnographic and historical research, *Black Odyssey* was rooted in literature. "The prose is moving and provocative; sometimes it almost sings, and sometimes it is abstract," Blight wrote. By exploring the inner thoughts and emotions of a slave ripped from his land, chained in the dank hull of a creaking ship, and whipped bloody into servitude in a hostile world, Huggins forced readers to face hard questions. Rose noted some of those questions: "What was it really like to have been a slave? What emotions and feelings would *we* have had, had *we* been there?"

Black Odyssey was also notable for its unflinching look at the ugly realities of slavery. He blatantly called the founding of America on the backs of slaves nothing short of tyranny. He also refuted the common opinion that white Europeans were the sole architects of the slave trade, pointing out that Africans were also active participants, capturing and selling members of rival tribes in order to obtain Western luxuries such as guns, pots and pans, and clothing. Even as Huggins pointed out these hard facts of slavery, he made no grand conclusions about them. As Blight noted, "[the book] offers no ultimate resolution or happy ending." Rather it evoked reflection and feeling.

Led African-American Studies at Harvard

In 1980 Huggins published *Slave and Citizen: The Life of Frederick Douglass*, an overview of the 19th century abolitionist's life. That same year, Huggins returned to Harvard as a professor of history and chair of the Afro-American studies department. He was also appointed director of the school's W. E. B. Du Bois Institute for Afro-American Research (since renamed the W. E. B. Du Bois Institute for African and African-American Research). At the time the field of African-American studies was considered more an instrument of activism rather than of academia, and it lacked the scholarly respect of other fields. This was particularly evident at Harvard where the department had been created in reaction to student protests. In the 1970s it was isolated from the rest of the university and had trouble attracting quality professors. Hiring Huggins, with his esteemed background, was a coup for Harvard.

"Huggins opened up the Du Bois Institute to attract more interest from the undergraduate community," a Harvard historian told *The Journal of Blacks in Higher Education*. In 1981 he established the W. E. B. Du Bois Lectureship in Afro-American life, history, and culture. The program brought black scholars from around the world to study at Harvard, including Czech scholar Dr. Josef Jarab who studied there in the late 1980s. Later Jarab helped found the Nathan Irvin Huggins Library for American Studies at Palacky University in Olomouc, Czech Republic.

In addition to running the Harvard programs, Huggins gave lectures, wrote for scholarly and general publications, and served as a consultant to television and radio programs about the black experience. He was also the senior consulting editor for the book series, *Black Americans of Achievement*. He kept up this pace until his untimely death on December 5, 1989, from pancreatic cancer. He left behind him a body of work that not only shaped the course of African-American scholarship but changed the study of American history. "I find in the study of history the special discipline which forces me to consider peoples and ages, not my own," Blight quoted Huggins as saying in 1982. "It is the most humane of disciplines, and in ways the most humbling. For one cannot ignore those historians of the future who will look back on us in the same way." With a Harvard lecture series named after him, the 1995 posthumous publication of his essays as *Revelations: American History, American Myths*, and the continued inclusion of his works on university curriculums, Huggins was poised to fulfill his own prophecy.

Selected writings

Protestants against Poverty: Boston's Charities, 1870-1900, Greenwood Press, 1971.
Harlem Renaissance, Oxford University Press, 1971.
Black Odyssey: The Afro-American Ordeal in Slavery, Pantheon, 1977.
Slave and Citizen: The Life of Frederick Douglass, Little, Brown, 1980.

Revelations: American History, American Myths, Oxford University Press, 1995.

Sources

Periodicals

The Journal of Blacks in Higher Education, September 30, 1995.
The New York Review of Books, January 26, 1978.
New York Times, December 7, 1989.
Reviews in American History, March 1994.

—Candace LaBalle

Etta James

1938—

Singer

Etta James may have surprised herself by living long enough to become a big star. Her singing career, more than 50 years long, has included more highs and lows than her vocal range. For decades she subverted her own success by maintaining a reckless lifestyle that included serious drug abuse and a number of questionable love-life decisions. At various career stages she has been a rhythm-and-blues belter, a blues crooner, and a rock-and-roll screamer. Although her powerful voice has handled each type of material with equal skill, this style-hopping has made it hard for the music industry to categorize her. In the 1990s, James finally gained widespread recognition as one of the most gifted singers of her time, much to the delight of hardcore fans who have remained loyal since she recorded her first hits as a teenager in the 1950s. By the turn of the century, James had become a legend.

James was born Jamesetta Hawkins on January 25, 1938, in Los Angeles, California. Her mother, Dorothy, was only 14 years old when Jamesetta was born, and she never directly revealed the identity of Jamesetta's father. In her 1995 autobiography, *Rage to Survive*, James put forth her belief that pool legend Minnesota Fats was her real father. Because Dorothy Hawkins led a somewhat wild, Bohemian lifestyle, Jamesetta was left in the care of a middle-aged couple named Rogers. Jamesetta became especially close to her foster mother, Lula "Mama Lu" Rogers.

Jamesetta's powerful singing voice began to gain attention when she was still a small child. As early as age five, she was singing solos with her church choir, and soon she was even performing gospel music on local radio. As she got older, she began taking an interest in the smooth doo-wop music that was becoming popular on the streets. When Jamesetta was about 12, Mama Lu died after a series of strokes. She was then taken to San Francisco to live with her biological mother, Dorothy Hawkins.

With the unpredictable Dorothy, Jamesetta's home life was very unhappy. Increasingly, she sought refuge in music. She formed a girl singing group called the Creolettes, which quickly attained a sizable local following. When Jamesetta was 14, the Creolettes were discovered by bandleader and promoter Johnny Otis. Otis took the Creolettes to Los Angeles—with the forged permission of the underage Jamesetta's mother—and put them into his revue. He renamed the group the Peaches, and reversed Jamesetta's name, creating what has remained her stage name ever since: Etta James.

In 1955 James made her first recording with the Peaches on the Modern Records label. Originally titled "Roll with Me Henry," the song was an answer to Hank Ballard and the Midnighters' hit "Work with Me Annie." Since "Roll with Me Henry" was considered too racy a title for radio airplay, the song was renamed "The Wallflower." It eventually made it into the top ten on the R&B charts. Although "The Wallflower" was a hit for James, it made an even bigger splash when it was subsequently recorded as "Dance with Me Henry" by white singer Georgia Gibbs. Although she collected a share of the royalties, James was outraged to see another singer get most of the glory for her song.

At a Glance . . .

Born Jamesetta Hawkins on January 25, 1938, in Los Angeles, CA; daughter of Dorothy Hawkins; married Artis Mills, 1969; children: Donto, Sametto (both sons).

Career: Singer, 1943–; toured with bandleader Johnny Otis, 1954-55; toured with a variety of performers, including Little Richard, Bo Diddley, Marvin Gaye; recording artist for a variety of companies, including Modern, 1955; Chess, 1960-75; Warner Brothers, 1978; Island, 1988-93; Private, 1994–; RCA, 2004–.

Awards: W. C. Handy Award, 1989; NAACP Image Award, 1990; Blues Society Hall of Fame, 1991; Rock and Roll Hall of Fame, 1993; Grammy Award, Best Jazz Vocal, 1995, for *Mystery Lady*; Blues Hall of Fame, 2001; Lifetime Achievement Award, Grammy, 2003; Grammy Award, Best Contemporary Blues Album, 2004, for *Let's Roll*; Grammy Award, Best Traditional Blues Album, 2005, for *Blues to the Bone*.

Addresses: *Web*—www.etta-james.com.

James had one more big hit on Modern in 1955, "Good Rockin' Daddy." She spent the next few years traveling the country at the bottom end of bills that featured stars like Little Richard, Bo Diddley, and zydeco king Clifton Chenier. Though she was still a minor, James grew up on these tours, meeting celebrities, witnessing their sometimes outrageous lifestyles, and receiving treatment that ranged from adulation to racist intimidation to outright theft. Her star faded somewhat from her initial hits of 1955, but she was still performing in front of large and enthusiastic crowds during this period.

As the 1950s drew to a close, James frequently found herself on the road and penniless. Landing in Chicago, she managed to attract the attention of Leonard Chess of the Chicago-based Chess Records, an emerging company that was making a name for itself with artists like Chuck Berry and Bo Diddley. During the early 1960s, James scored a string of major hits for Chess and its subsidiary labels, making her one of the biggest stars on the R&B scene. In 1960, two James songs made the R&B charts. Four more reached the charts the following year, including the soulful ballad "At Last," which peaked at number two. In 1962, James' "Something's Got a Hold on Me" reached the number four spot, the highest of her three hits that year. She also recorded several duets with Harvey Fuqua of the

Moonglows, with whom her relationship was romantic as well as professional. The material that James recorded for Chess exhibited the full range of her stylistic capabilities, from tender love ballads to heavy blues to easy-on-the-ears pop. Although the people at Chess kept her career alive, they also exploited her, as they did many artists, finding ways to withhold royalties and grabbing the publishing rights to musicians' original material. During this time, James lived at the historic—and cheap—Sutherland Hotel along with many other musicians destined for stardom, including Fuqua, Marvin Gaye, and Curtis Mayfield.

Unfortunately, the pressures of constant touring wreaked havoc on her personal life. By the time she was 21 years old, James was addicted to heroin. Her problems with drugs made it all the more difficult for James to sustain her career. She also seemed drawn to violent and abusive men. By the mid-1960s, she had disappeared from the scene again. She rebounded in 1966 to record a widely-acclaimed blues album, *Call My Name*. She also recorded a series of duets with singer Sugar Pie DeSanto, a childhood friend, and those sessions produced a big hit in "In the Basement." In 1967 James began recording at Fame Studios in Alabama, and this period produced the well-received albums *Tell Mama* and *I'd Rather Go Blind*.

Although James remained largely unknown outside of the black community despite her hits, white rockers knew who she was. Many rock stars had become Etta James fans early on, and her no-holds-barred singing style influenced several of them. Janis Joplin and Rolling Stone Keith Richards were among those who were listening to James when she was still toiling on shoestring-budget tours.

By the early 1970s, James' life was very much out of control, although she managed to arrive at the recording studio and at live performances when required. In order to support her growing heroin habit, she found it necessary to become a petty criminal, forging prescriptions and writing bad checks. When things got bad enough, she was not above stealing from friends and acquaintances. In 1973, faced with the prospect of several years in prison, James opted to enter the residential drug rehabilitation program at Tarzana Psychiatric Hospital outside of Los Angeles.

James continued to record during her rehabilitation, producing two more albums in 1974. During the rest of the 1970s and into the early 1980s, she kept busy performing in small clubs and occasionally at big-time blues and jazz festivals, usually bringing down the house. Finally free of her various addictions, James' career suddenly skyrocketed in the mid-1980s. After decades of failing to find a crossover audience, James' albums began to catch on with white listeners. As fans of her early work rose to positions of power in the entertainment industry, James' songs began to find their way into all sorts of unexpected places. She sang at the opening ceremony for the 1984 Olympics, for example. "The Wallflower," her first hit, was used in the soundtrack of the blockbuster movie *Back to the Future*. James also began making occasional spot appearances on television shows.

In 1988, after seven years without a recording contract, James released *Seven Year Itch* on Island Records. She continued to record at a frenzied pace, and as the 1990s unfolded James found herself elevated to the status of R&B legend. She was inducted into the Rock and Roll Hall of Fame in 1993. In 1995 James won her first Grammy award, after several nominations, for *Mystery Lady*, a collection of songs associated with the great Billie Holiday, with whom James had long identified. It is somewhat ironic that James' first Grammy came in the jazz category, after some 40 years spent chasing rhythm-and-blues dreams. Her follow-up album, *Time After Time*, also consisted mainly of jazz standards.

Having reinvented herself as a jazz singer, James seemed to have finally fulfilled the promise that some in the music industry had always seen in her. Perhaps the same demons that haunted and hindered her career for so long have simultaneously fueled her drive to succeed. As James observed in her 1995 autobiography, *Rage to Live*, "I've learned to live with rage. In some ways, it's my rage that keeps me going. Without it, I would have been whipped long ago. With it, I got a lot more songs to sing."

James' demons caught up with her over the years, however. She piled on weight until she had difficulty walking. For years she was helped onto stage in a wheelchair for knee problems exacerbated by her weight. But when she fell on a New York City sidewalk and had trouble getting her nearly 400-pound body back up, James knew she needed help. She had gastric bypass surgery in 2002 and dropped approximately 200 pounds. James told *Ebony* that she credits her doctor for having "saved my life."

More than regaining her mobility, however, James discovered a new voice within herself. She told *Ebony* that after the surgery she was able to sing "lower, higher, and louder." With her "new" voice James embraced both touring and studio sessions, traveling the country to perform and recording new albums. For her contributions to blues music, James was inducted into the Blues Hall of Fame in 2001. In 2003 James was honored with a lifetime achievement Grammy award, her own star on Hollywood's walk of fame, as well as a Grammy for best contemporary blues album the next year for *Let's Roll*. James became especially inspired by Martin Scorsese's documentary *The Blues*, produced by PBS, and recorded a selection of traditional blues songs on her 2004 album *Blues to the Bone,* for which she won a Grammy in 2005. At nearly 70 years old, James—who had long related her love of music and continued to wow audiences with her raucous and enthusiastic concerts—showed no interest retiring any time soon.

Selected works

Albums

At Last, Cadet, 1961.
Etta James Sings for Lovers, Argo, 1962.
Etta James, Argo, 1962.
Etta James Rocks the House, Chess, 1963.
Top Ten, Cadet, 1963.
Queen of Soul, Argo, 1964.
Etta James Sings Funk, Chess, 1965.
Call My Name, Cadet, 1966.
Tell Mama, Cadet, 1967.
Losers Weepers, Cadet, 1970.
Etta James, Chess, 1973.
Come a Little Closer, Chess, 1974.
Peaches, Chess, 1974.
(With Eddie "Cleanhead" Vinson) *Blues in the Night*, Fantasy, 1986.
Seven Year Itch, Island, 1988.
Stickin' to My Guns, Island, 1990.
The Right Time, Rounder, 1992.
How Strong is a Woman, Island, 1993.
Mystery Lady: The Songs of Billie Holiday, Private, 1994.
Etta James Live from San Francisco, Private, 1994.
Time After Time, Private, 1995.
Love's Been Rough on Me, Private, 1997.
Life, Love and the Blues, Private, 1998.
Heart of a Woman, Private, 1999.
Matriarch of the Blues, Private, 2000.
Blue Gardenia, Private, 2001.
Burnin' Down the House, Private, 2002.
Let's Roll, Private, 2003.
Blues to the Bone, RCA, 2004.

Sources

Books

James, Etta (with David Ritz), *Rage to Survive*, Villard, 1995.

Periodicals

Ebony, September 2003, p. 174.
Essence, January 2004, p. 158.
Jet, May 12, 2003, p. 45.
Living Blues, Autumn/Winter 1982, p. 12.
Los Angeles Times, August 2, 1995, p. F1.
Newsweek, November 21, 1994, p. 98.
Rolling Stone, August 10, 1978, p. 22.

On-line

Etta James, www.etta-james.com (May 31, 2005).

—Robert R. Jacobson and Sara Pendergast

Angela Johnson

1961—

Children's writer

With over 40 books to her name Ohio-based Angela Johnson is one of the most prolific and celebrated children's writers. She began working full-time as a writer in 1989 and her work includes award-winning picture books, board books, poetry, stories, and novels for young adults. She has become well known for her realistic characters, many of whom carry over through several books, and for her sensitive depictions of family life, but she has also branched out to explore African-American history. Johnson is famously reclusive, disliking even to have her photograph taken, but she has won many awards, including the prestigious MacArthur Fellowship, a no strings attached "genius award" of $500,000.

Born in Tuskegee, Alabama, on June 18, 1961, Angela Johnson is the daughter of Arthur, an autoworker, and Truzetta (Hall) Johnson, an accountant. The family moved to Ohio when Johnson was 15 months old, and she has lived there ever since. She attended Kent State University where she studied special needs education, but fearing having a degree would push her into teaching rather than allowing her to write she left before graduation.

Stories were an important part of Johnson's childhood. Her father and grandfather were storytellers and she enjoyed listening to stories being read at school. She wrote short stories and "punk poetry" while she was a college student, but she realized that children's writing was where her future lay while working as a nanny for the young son of writer Cynthia Rylant, author of the Henry and Mudge series, in the mid-1980s. Rylant's library of children's books along with her encourage-

ment inspired Johnson to begin working on her first picture books. It was Rylant who submitted Johnson's first book, *Tell Me a Story, Mama*, to her publisher. Johnson subsequently bought Rylant's house when Rylant and her partner, Dav Pilkey, author of the "Captain Underpants" stories, moved away. She told the *Pittsburg Post-Gazette* that her readers love the idea that she lives in Captain Underpants' house. By 1993 when her first novel for young adults, *Toning the Sweep* appeared, she had published seven picture books, including the award-winning *Tell Me a Story, Mama* (1989), and *When I am Old With You* (1990).

Tell Me a Story, Mama was Johnson's first picture book. It won her the *School Library Journal's* "Best Books" award in 1989 and gave her the confidence to write more. By 1991 she had won two further commendations, the Ezra Jack Keats award for new writers, and her first Coretta Scott King award—she won three more Coretta Scott King awards in the 1990s. By then she had also established herself as a writer interested in exploring the relationships within families; between children, between adults, and between children and adults. *When I am Old With You* (1990), for example, is the story of a girl and her grandfather. Although her characters are black, Johnson aims to make her stories non-racial; the themes and issues they cover are rarely specific to the black community.

Johnson continues to produce picture books, but in 1993 she published her first novel for young adults, *Toning the Sweep*, and began to become well known. *Toning the Sweep* tells the story of Emily, a fourteen year-old who videotapes her grandmother during the last days of her life, recording stories, friendships, and family connections. The novel set the tone for many of Johnson's books for young adults, which address issues such as divorce, peer pressure, illness, and death, underpinned with the affection and reassurance the characters show for one another. But while that might sound like Johnson's work is unrealistic and overly sentimental, she is not afraid to confront difficult subjects. In *Heaven* (1998) the main character discovers that the people she thought were her parents are actually her uncle and aunt; and her collection of poems *The Other Side*, published the same year, was inspired by the Alabama town of Shorter, which was flattened by developers in her grandmother's time. Both of these serious works were widely praised by critics. *Heaven* won the 1998 Coretta Scott King Author Award, and *The Other Side* received an honor citation.

Johnson also has a less serious side. *Maniac Monkeys on Magnolia Street* (1999) and *When Mules Flew on Magnolia Street* (2001) celebrate imagination and life, but her picture books for young children are also

light-hearted and playful while consistently supporting Johnson's belief in the power of affection and family ties. *Shoes Like Miss Alice* (1995) for example, centers on a babysitter who has a pair of shoes for every activity. She is often praised for the poetic style and cadences of her prose works.

Johnson's prolific output—two books a year since 1989—her consistency, and the range her work covers make her one of the most celebrated contemporary children's writers. In 2003 Johnson's importance as a writer was recognized with the MacArthur Foundation's "genius award," which presented her with $100,000 each year for five years to allow her to work without outside pressures. The high-profile award came as a surprise to Johnson, who resists interviews and avoids publicity.

Selected writings

Books

Tell Me a Story, Mama, illustrated by David Soman, Orchard Books, 1989.
Do Like Kyla, illustrated by James Ransome, Orchard Books, 1990.
When I Am Old with You, illustrated by David Soman, Orchard Books, 1990.
One of Three, illustrated by David Soman, Orchard Books, 1991.
The Leaving Morning, illustrated by David Soman, Orchard Books, 1992.
The Girl Who Wore Snakes, Orchard Books, 1993.
Julius, illustrated by Dav Pilkey, Orchard Books, 1993.
Toning the Sweep, Orchard Books, 1993.
Joshua by the Sea, illustrated by Rhonda Mitchell, Orchard Books, 1994.
Joshua's Night Whispers, illustrated by Rhonda Mitchell, Orchard Books, 1994.
Mama Bird, Baby Birds, illustrated by Rhonda Mitchell, Orchard Books, 1994.
Rain Feet, illustrated by Rhonda Mitchell, Orchard Books, 1994.
Shoes Like Miss Alice's, illustrated by Ken Page, Orchard Books, 1995.
Humming Whispers, Orchard Books, 1995 .
The Aunt in Our House, illustrated by David Soman, Orchard Books, 1996.
The Rolling Store, illustrated by Peter Catalanotto, Orchard Books, 1997.
Daddy Calls Me Man, illustrated by Rhonda Mitchell, Orchard Books, 1997.
Gone from Home: Short Takes, DK Publishing, 1998.
Songs of Faith, Orchard Books, 1998.
Heaven, Simon & Schuster, 1998.
The Other Side: Shorter Poems, Orchard Books, 1998.
Maniac Monkeys on Magnolia Street, illustrated by John Ward, Random House, 1999.

The Wedding, illustrated by David Soman, Orchard Books, 1999.

Those Building Men, illustrated by Mike Benny, Scholastic, 1999.

Down the Winding Road, illustrated by Shane W. Evans, DK Ink, 2000.

When Mules Flew on Magnolia Street, Alfred A. Knopf, 2001.

Rain Feet, illustrated by Rhonda Mitchell, Orchard Books, 2001.

Running Back to Ludie, Orchard Books, 2002.

Looking for Red, Simon & Schuster, 2002.

I Dream of Trains, illustrated by Loren Long, Simon & Schuster, 2003.

The First Part Last, Simon & Schuster, 2003.

A Cool Moonlight, Dial Books, 2003.

Just Like Josh Gibson, illustrated by Beth Peck, Simon & Schuster, 2003.

Violet's Music, illustrated by Laura Huliska-Beith, Dial Books, 2004.

Bird, Dial Books, 2004.

Sources

Periodicals

Essence, February 2004, p. 34.

Pittsburg Post-Gazette, Saturday, February 21, 2004.

World Literature Today, September-December 2004, p. 75.

Publishers Weekly, January 3, 2005, p. 55.

On-line

"Angela Johnson," *African American Literature Book Club*, http://aalbc.com/authors/angela.htm (April 21, 2005).

"Angela Johnson," *Biography Resource Center*, www.galenet.com/servlet/BioRC (April 21, 2005).

"The Accidental Genius," *Chilren's Lit: Meet Writers and Illustrators*, www.childrenslit.com/f_johnson.htm (April 21, 2005).

"Who Wrote That?" *Patricia M.* Newman, www.patriciamnewman.com/johnsona.html (21 April, 2005).

—Chris Routledge

Clifford "Connie" Johnson

1922-2004

Baseball pitcher

Right-hander Connie Johnson was part of the pitching staff that made the fabled Kansas City Monarchs the most feared team in baseball's Negro Leagues in the 1940s. Later in his career he played for the major-league Chicago White Sox and Baltimore Orioles, having lost the fastball of his youth and learned a repertoire of pinpoint-control pitches in its place. Like many of the other Negro Leaguers who joined the majors as veterans, Johnson inspired baseball observers to wonder what he might have accomplished had desegregation come earlier to baseball. "Connie was a good pitcher in the major leagues," former Monarchs manager Buck O'Neil told Joe Posnanski of the *Kansas City Star.* "He was a great pitcher in the Negro Leagues…. He threw hard for the Monarchs. Hard. He had good control. Could have won 20 games in the big leagues…. Could have won 20 games every year."

Born on December 27, 1922, Clifford Johnson, Jr., was a native of Stone Mountain, Georgia, outside Atlanta. He played softball when he was young, and a few times he tried his hand at sandlot semiprofessional baseball. The first time he took the mound, he told Posnanski, two female fans of the opposing team heckled him, asking "Who's that, Ichabod Crane?" (referring to the geeky schoolmaster in Washington Irving's *The Legend of Sleepy Hollow*). By the game's end, he was attracting more positive attention from women in the stands and had come to see the game of baseball in a whole new light. "Oh man! Now I'm the greatest ballplayer in the world! Girls trying to catch me and kiss me," Johnson recalled, describing his feelings to Kyle McNary of the *Pitch Black Baseball* Web site.

Johnson was still an extremely inexperienced player when the Monarchs came to Atlanta in the summer of 1940 for a series against a ragtag Toledo Crawfords squad. The Toledo team, short of pitchers, hoped to find a local player to take the mound, and Johnson's neighbor Joe Greene, who had played for the Monarchs, suggested the 17-year-old Johnson. Despite his protestations that he wasn't a "hardball" player, Johnson was put in a jersey several sizes too large—he was a lanky six-feet, four-inches tall—and sent out on the field. He kept the Monarchs' hitters at bay with his blazing fastball.

Hired by Jesse Owens

The following Monday, Johnson returned to work at a rock quarry. He was already in a mood to see the world; his brother, a chauffeur, had traveled around the country, and Johnson dreamed of visiting the big cities and of seeing California. The Crawfords' part-owner, former Olympic track star Jesse Owens, showed up at the quarry with the team's manager and offered him a contract. After being assured that the team would make stops in Chicago, New York, and New Orleans, and after asking and being given his mother's permission, Johnson signed with the Toledo team. At the end of the 1940 season, Johnson appeared in the Negro Leagues' East-West All-Star Game, becoming the youngest player ever to do so. At the time, he told interviewer Eric Enders, "I didn't even know what the East-West Game *was!*," according to Eric Enders' Web site.

The Crawfords soon disbanded and moved on to Indianapolis, Indiana, and Johnson was asked to join the Monarchs themselves. The Kansas City squad ruled the Negro Leagues through much of the 1940s, with pitchers like Hilton Smith, Lefty LaMarque, and the crowd-pleasing and verbally ingenious Satchel Paige forming the backbone of the roster and drawing white as well as black baseball fans to the team's games. At first, Johnson was intimidated by the company of baseball stars. He didn't know the names of the players, so he used the nickname "Connie" to address any player whose name he couldn't remember. The Monarchs in turn bestowed that nickname on Johnson, and it stuck.

One high point of Johnson's first career was a trip to the 1942 Negro World Series with the victorious Monarchs. After the series was over, Johnson enlisted in the United States Army. He remained in the service, serving part of his stint in the European theater, until the end of World War II, pitching in intra-military contests and often racking up more than 15 strikeouts per game against the less-than-major-league batters he faced. The heavy work took its toll on Johnson's pitching arm, but he resumed his career with the Monarchs in 1946 after returning to the United States.

The following year brought news of Jackie Robinson's epochal debut with the Brooklyn Dodgers, breaking the barrier of segregation in the formerly all-white National and American leagues. Friends told Johnson that he had the stuff to follow quickly in Robinson's footsteps, but the pitcher showed no enthusiasm for that prospect. When his sister pointed out that he might soon be pitching against the best players in the game, Johnson replied: "I've been doing that for ten years," as he recalled to Posnanski.

Notched All-Star Game Win

Johnson remained with the Monarchs through the 1950 season, during which he notched what was probably a personal-best record of 11 wins and 2 losses (record-keeping in the Negro Leagues was spotty). He made his second appearance in the Negro Leagues All-Star game that year, allowing one run in three innings, striking out three batters, and helping his own cause with a triple. He was credited as the winning pitcher. After that season Johnson was drafted by the Chicago White Sox, and with the Negro Leagues on the decline he was sold by the Monarchs to the White Sox organization for $1,000 after asking the Monarchs' owner for a raise in salary.

Playing for a team in Saint-Hyacinthe, Quebec in 1951, Johnson led the Canadian Provincial League in strikeouts and at one point won 11 games in row. By this time, Johnson's fabled fastball was a shadow of its former self. Years of injuries and rough treatment had damaged his arm to a point where he could barely raise it over his head. But Johnson retooled his pitching game, partly at the suggestion of the St.-Hyacinthe club's general manager. Quoted on the *True Baseball* Web site, Johnson recalled the manager's advice: "Connie, if you are ever gonna win 20 games in a season you are gonna have to beat 'em when you got no stuff." Johnson developed a curveball and slider to go with his fastball. "I couldn't break glass," he once said of his curveball, as quoted in the Toronto *Globe and Mail* newspaper, "but I knew just where it was going."

In 1952 Johnson moved up to the Colorado Sky Sox of the Western League, once again leading the league in strikeouts and winning, by his own recollection, 18 or 19 games. He bounced between the White Sox and their Charleston, West Virginia American Association affiliate in 1953, making his American League debut with the White Sox on April 17 of that year and giving up two hits to the Boston Red Sox hitting ace Ted Williams. Johnson amassed a record of 4 wins and 4 losses before showing control problems and being sent down to the Charleston squad. He spent 1954 and part of 1955 with the Toronto Maple Leafs, then a minor-league team affiliated with the White Sox. In 1954, with future New York Yankees star Elston Howard as his catcher, Johnson notched a 17-8 record with 145 strikeouts.

Traded to Orioles

Johnson returned to the White Sox midway through the 1955 season after going 12-2 in Toronto. For Chicago he pitched 99 innings, finishing with a 7-4 record. In May of 1956 he was sent to the Baltimore Orioles as part of a complex trade, and in his first game with his new team he beat the White Sox 3-2, pitching a five-hit complete game. His best year came with the Orioles in 1957, as he won 14 games with 177 strikeouts, both top marks on the squad that year.

After a 6-9 record in Baltimore the following year, the aging pitcher spent a year with the Vancouver Mounties in Canada, notching an 8-4 record even at this late date. Several times during the 1950s he had played for Latin American teams during the off-season, and he played in Puebla, Mexico in 1960 before retiring for good. Over the course of his five-year major-league career his won-lost record was 40-39, with 497 strikeouts and 257 bases on balls in 716 innings pitched.

Johnson continued to make his home in Kansas City, living there into his old age. In later years he often answered interviewers' questions about Satchel Paige and recalled his Monarchs teammate's speed in a segment of the Ken Burns television documentary *Baseball.* But details of his own career emerged only slowly. "I had a good time," Johnson told interviewer Eric Enders. "… I have no regrets. The world owes me nothing. If anything, I might owe the world." He lived in a nursing home at the end of his life, and sources disagree as to the exact date of his death. According to Joe Posnanski, the writer who followed his career most closely, Johnson died on Saturday, November 27, 2004. He was buried in Leavenworth National Cemetery in Kansas. The *Pitch Black Baseball* Web site posthumously named him Negro Leaguer of the Month in January of 2005.

Sources

Periodicals

Globe and Mail (Toronto, Canada), January 25, 2005.
Kansas City Star, December 1, 2004.

On-line

"An Interview with Connie Johnson," *Eric E. Enders.* www.ericenders.com/conniejohnson.htm (April 28, 2005).
"Connie Johnson," *Baseball-Reference,* www.baseball-reference.com/j/johnsco.shtml (April 28, 2005).
"Connie Johnson," *True Baseball,* www.truebaseball.com/cj1940.htm (April 28, 2005).
"Negro Leaguer of the Month: January, 2005," *Pitch Black Baseball,* www.pitchblackbaseball.com/nlotmedconniejohnson.html (April 28, 2005).

—James M. Manheim

Absalom Jones

1746-1818

Minister

The transformation of Absalom Jones from slave into one of the founders of the black Episcopal church in America and a leading figure among Philadelphia's African-American community shows the great strides made by blacks during this eventful period of early American history. Jones bought his own freedom as well as that of his wife's through years of hard work, and went on to lead the African Church of St. Thomas in Philadelphia, the first black Episcopal church in the United States. He was also a respected community leader who put his own life in danger to help those afflicted by a yellow-fever epidemic during a terrible few months of 1793.

Jones was born into servitude in Sussex County, Delaware, on November 6, 1746. His master was Benjamin Wynkoop, a merchant and planter, and Jones's siblings and mother were property of Wynkoop as well. As a youngster, Jones held a coveted position inside the Wynkoop house, where he was able to earn small tips, which he saved up to buy a primer, a book that taught children the basics of reading and writing; reportedly he would ask everyone whose paths crossed his to help him learn how to read. Other prized possessions he managed to acquire through his earnings included a spelling book—though his abilities in this remained poor throughout his life—and a New Testament bible.

When Jones was around 16 years old, Wynkoop sold off Jones's mother and six siblings, but retained the teenager and took him with him to Philadelphia, where Wynkoop had a store. Jones worked in the business, and even went to a school set up for African Americans

for a time. In 1770, he married a slave woman named Mary King, and began seeking donations in order to purchase her freedom. But he also worked overtime to fund this goal, and finally in 1778 was able to begin saving money to buy his own freedom. He was manumitted, or released from slavery, on October 1, 1784, but remained in Wynkoop's employ as a wage-earner.

Philadelphia was home to a large number of freed blacks like Jones during the era. Some were members of St. George's Methodist Episcopal Church, which was notable in that it welcomed black as well as white members into its congregation. It is known that around 1786 Jones became a licensed Methodist lay preacher, and the following year founded the Free African Society with Richard Allen, another recently freed slave. This society, which may have been the first independent black organization in the United States, provided economic and medical aid to African Americans transitioning from slavery to freedom. It also sought to further ties between blacks in America and those in Africa.

Told to Rise from Pew

On a Sunday in November of 1787, Jones and Allen kneeled for prayer in a newly constructed gallery of St. George's. Some white members of the congregation, however, felt that the black members should be confined to the balcony, and the sexton, or church officer, collared Jones and tried to pull him to his feet during opening prayers. Appalled, Jones and Allen walked out, and set to work on forming their own group with

At a Glance . . .

Born on November 6, 1746, in Sussex, DE; died on February 13, 1818, Philadelphia, PA; married Mary King, 1770. *Religion:* African Episcopal.

Career: Sussex, DE, and Philadelphia, PA, slave; manumitted October 1, 1784; Methodist lay preacher, licensed, 1786; Free African Society, co-founder, 1787; African Church of St. Thomas, co-founder, 1794; Episcopal church, ordained deacon, 1795; Episcopal church, priest, 1804.

Memberships: Grand Master of the Black Masonic lodge of Philadelphia.

others who had also left St. George's in disgust. On January 1, 1791, the Free African Society held religious services for the first time, and the congregation that grew out of that began to raise funds to build their own church.

The mission of Jones and Allen to establish their own black Protestant church was supported by William White, the esteemed bishop of the Philadelphia Episcopal diocese and a leading figure in the formation of the American Episcopal creed as an offshoot of the Church of England. They were also supported by whites among Philadelphia's devout, liberal-minded Quaker community, and Jones's and Allen's reputation in the city was boosted immensely when they courageously worked to aid the sick and bury the dead felled by a three-month yellow fever epidemic in 1793, when the city was the seat of the U.S. government.

Benjamin Rush, a signer of the Declaration of Independence and prominent Philadelphia physician and abolitionist, believed that blacks were immune from the epidemic, and Jones and others took on the task in order to enhance the reputation of Philadelphia's black community. Many blacks died anyway, though Jones and his colleagues were spared, and for their role they were attacked in a pamphlet that attempted to discredit them. He and Allen penned a response, *A Narrative of the Proceedings of the Black People, During the Late Awful Calamity in Philadelphia, In the Year 1793*, that defended their service to the city during a time when many whites, including the highest-ranking members of the federal government, had fled.

Founded Black Episcopal Church

Despite such setbacks, the church Jones co-founded, the African Church of St. Thomas, was formally dedicated on July 17, 1794. It was affiliated with the white

Episcopal church in order to be granted official recognition by the state, and Jones served as its first lay reader. On August 6, 1795, he was ordained a deacon in the Episcopal church. Rules required that Episcopalian deacons must to know some Greek and Latin, but this requirement was waived for him. Nine years later, in 1804, he became an ordained priest, and he and Allen would become the first black Americans to be formally ordained in any denomination.

Jones led St. Thomas for many years, and it became a center of social and religious life for Philadelphia's African-American community. At the pulpit, his sermons advocated the abolition of slavery, and he also organized petition drives—one of them the first ever from an African-American group—that pleaded with government to end slavery in the United States. Jones was also active in education, both as a teacher and the founder of a school for blacks, and in the Black Masonic lodge in Philadelphia, of which he served as a Grand Master. In 1809, he co-founded the Society for the Suppression of Vice and Immorality with Allen and James Forten, an affluent sail-maker. The group campaigned against the sale of alcoholic beverages, and was also active in civil defense efforts in Philadelphia during the War of 1812.

Richard Allen eventually formed a Methodist congregation that became the African Methodist Episcopal (AME) Church, and was ordained the first bishop of that church on April 11, 1816, with his longtime colleague likely there that historic day. Jones was also known to have been present at large meeting of African Americans in January of 1817, at which some formal opposition was organized in response to the American Colonization Society, which had offered to provide passage for free blacks to Africa. A year before he died, Jones founded a literary organization, the Augustine Society. He died on February 13, 1818, and was buried in the St. Thomas churchyard.

Honored with Portrait

Jones's prominent role in early Philadelphia history is confirmed by the existence of a formal portrait of him, in ecclesiastical robes and holding a bible, that was painted by Raphaelle Peale, son of well-known Philadelphia portrait artist Charles Willson Peale. For a black to be depicted in a portrait that honored his status in life was still a rarity at the time, and the work hangs in the Delaware Art Museum. Jones's legacy also survived in the church he founded. "For decades, Saint Thomas's was emblematic of the striving for dignity, self-improvement, and autonomy of a generation of African Americans released or self-released from bondage," noted Gary B. Nash in the *Encyclopedia of African-American Culture and History*. "In his first sermon at the African Church of Philadelphia, Jones put out the call to his fellow African Americans to 'arise out of the dust and shake ourselves, and throw off that servile fear, that the habit of oppression and bondage trained us up in.'"

Selected writings

Books

(With Richard Allen) *A Narrative of the Proceedings of the Black People, During the Late Awful Calamity in Philadelphia, In the Year 1793,* privately printed, (Philadelphia), 1794.

Sources

Books

African American Almanac, edited by Jeffrey Lehman, 9th edition, Charles Scribner's Sons, 2003, pp. 417-433.
Encyclopedia of African-American Culture and History, 5 vols., Macmillan, 1996.
Notable Black American Men, Gale, 1998.

Periodicals

Christian History, May 1999, p. 38.

—Carol Brennan

Gibson Kente

1932-2004

Playwright

South African writer Gibson Kente single-handedly made the "township musical," a form of popular theater in black South African culture during the repressive apartheid era, into a dominant means of expression and exuberance. He died of acquired immune-deficiency syndrome (AIDS) in 2004 after a career that spanned nearly 50 years, and his impact on South African culture was impressive. "He wrote and performed plays which reflected township life," noted a *Guardian* tribute by Liz McGregor, "and trained and inspired hundreds of black actors and singers at a time when black creativity was viewed as a threat and suppressed by the apartheid state. Using the limited resources available in townships, he created musicals and plays that reflected the fears, hopes, joys and tribulations of black urban communities."

Born in 1932, Kente grew up in Duncan Village, the black township outside the city of East London in South Africa's Eastern Cape. He was schooled at a Seventh-Day Adventist college in Butterworth, and around 1956 moved to Johannesburg to enroll at the Jan Hofmeyer School of Social Work. He formed a gospel jazz group called the Kente Choristers while there, and eventually abandoned his studies altogether after joining a black theater group called the Union Artists. The township drama was born out of a 1959 musical, *King Kong,* which had been written by whites but proved a hit with black audiences. In apartheid-era South Africa, the term "township" denoted a place that was anything but pastoral or idyllic. The townships were blacks-only suburbs, with shanties and cinder-block homes among the better-constructed residences, situated near large cities like Johannesburg. There were schools and churches, but very little in the way of organized entertainment.

Endured Arduous Tours

Kente founded a theater business in the early 1960s and asked his friends to submit scripts. Few that met his requirements were forthcoming, so he began writing his own plays. The first of these was *Manana, the Jazz Prophet,* which premiered in 1963. His next was *Sikalo,* which was a great success and even played to white audiences in the city of Witwatersrand in 1965 and 1966. Its story features a young man who tries to avoid the gangs in his township, but winds up in jail anyway. These and subsequent township musicals had several common features: much of the action took place in the quasi-legal *shebeens,* or taverns, where black South Africans could drink. Such establishments were usually run by a formidable woman, and populated by *tsotsis,* or thugs, dancing girls, and ordinary workers. There was usually a pompous police officer to provide comic relief, as well as dissolute priests and a Zulu boy who delivered his lines in broken English. Song and dance were also key elements of the township musical, and Kente wrote his own scores, which were heavy on jazz and African gospel.

Kente's musicals proved a great success, and he and his actors were determined to bring them to a wider audience outside of Soweto, the Johannesburg township that was his home. Government restrictions, however, usually granted them a performance permit

At a Glance . . .

Born Gibson Mthuthuzeli Kente on July 25 (some sources say July 23), 1932, in Duncan Village, Eastern Cape, South Africa; died November 7, 2004, in Soweto, South Africa, of complications from AIDS; children: sons Feza and Mzwandile. *Education:* Attended a Seventh-Day Adventist college in Butterworth, South Africa, early 1950s, and Jan Hofmeyer School of Social Work, mid-1950s.

Career: Playwright, theater director, and theater manager. Formed a gospel jazz group, the Kente Choristers, in Johannesburg in the late 1950s; became a member of a black theatre group, the Union Artists; wrote and directed his first musical, *Manana, the Jazz Prophet,* in 1963; established his own theater group, G. K. Productions.

for one night only, and so they were constantly en route from one community hall to another. His group, G. K. Productions, trained an entire generation of black South African performers, some of whom would attain stardom on the international stage—among them Mbongeni Ngema, the writer, composer, and director of the musical *Sarafina!*

In the early 1970s, as South Africa's detested apartheid laws neared their quarter-century mark, Kente's writings for the stage began to reflect his dissent against white rule. *How Long,* first produced in Soweto in December of 1973, recounts the story of a humble dustman who is determined to provide his son, named "Africa," with the necessary funds to stay in school. At the time, educational opportunities for South Africa's black majority were severely restricted, and the government was even about to implement a new education policy that made Afrikaans, the language of the white South African, the only language of instruction in secondary schools for blacks. There was much resentment against this 1974 law, and it eventually led to a dramatic and bloody uprising in Soweto in 1976 that garnered international attention.

I Believe, produced in April of 1974, was Kente's next work, and one that took to task the different ethnic tensions in the black townships and the divisiveness that resulted. Its protagonist is Zwelithsa, a Xhosa, who falls in love with young woman from a different tribe. *Too Late,* which opened in Soweto in February of 1975, is usually deemed to be Kente's finest work. Its story centers around an orphan, Saduwa, who comes to Soweto to live with his aunt, who runs a shebeen. Though his cousin, Ntanana, he meets a young woman named Totozi and romance blossoms. Desperate to

find work in Johannesburg, Saduwa must first obtain an all-important "pass," without which he cannot leave the township to get to his job. His attempts to do so bring a priest and then a police officer into his life, and in the end his aunt is arrested. When authorities try to arrest Saduwa as well, his cousin Ntanana, who is disabled, attempts to help, and is slain. The work had a relatively happy ending, but Kente's *Times* of London obituary found that *Too Late, I Believe,* and *How Long* seemed to be works "which, with the benefit of hindsight, have come to be seen as prophetic in their warnings that violence would soon come to South Africa if circumstances did not change," the newspaper noted. "The authorities received these plays with overt hostility, and some theatres banned them."

Retreated from the Political Message

Kente was arrested during the making of a film version of *How Long* in 1976, which went by the longer title *How Long Must We Suffer…?* It was filmed during the historic Soweto uprising, and was the first black-made film in South African cinema history. Kente spent six months in jail, and after his release in 1977 returned to writing musicals, though the political content was virtually nonexistent. His later works include *Can You Take It?, Lobola,* and *Mama and the Load,* but the rest of the 1980s saw the rise of a formal protest theater movement emerging in South Africa. Kente distanced himself from this and even criticized it for fomenting racial hatred. "Kente came under pressure from activists to be more political," explained Chris Barron in an Africa News Service report. "On at least one occasion they tried to disrupt a show, but Kente aficionados in the audience outnumbered them and they were silenced."

In 1988 Kente touched upon political themes once again with *Sekunjao,* whose message seemed a warning to South Africa's black elite not to abuse their power should they attain it in the future. Government authorities stepped in and arrested the entire cast—a somewhat ironic move, for they seemed to have missed *Sekunjao's* message entirely, which hinted that a black-run government might treat its own even worse than an apartheid-centered one. "Presumably someone got the message at last," noted Barron in the Africa News Service article, "because the play was then unbanned, and Kente was invited by the government-sponsored Performing Arts Council of the Transvaal to stage it at the State Theatre in Pretoria." Because of that, however, his house was firebombed by black extremists in 1989.

With the end of apartheid and the first free and democratic elections in South Africa in 1994, Kente's plays finally began to receive official support and funding. By then, however, he was on the fringes of the South African cultural scene. A 13-part television project in 1995 titled *Mama's Love* earned such scathing reviews that it was nearly cancelled after just two episodes, and Kente's critics called him a disgrace to black theater. Despite the initial bad press, the project did remain on the air in its entirety, and one of its lines even entered the vernacular and became a popular soccer stadium chant.

"Let's Hold Hands. Let's Not Hide."

Kente struggled financially over the years. He never earned royalties from his earlier works, and was mired in debt by the time he announced, in late 2003, that he had tested positive for the human immunodeficiency virus (HIV) that causes AIDS. He made his announcement with two of South Africa's most famous musical stars, Hugh Masekela and Miriam Makeba, at his side, in what many hailed as an extremely courageous move. There was still an enormous taboo associated with the disease in South Africa, where even prominent members of the African National Congress had asserted that AIDS deaths were due to poverty, not HIV infection. Five years earlier, a South African woman named Gugu Dlamini had publicly disclosed she had the disease and was beaten to death by a mob. Kente was one of four million South Africans thought to be HIV-positive, and he told the nation that day that "my HIV status is going to let me live longer," his *Times* of London obituary quoted him as saying, "because I've got a challenge, because I know that I've got a duty to the people out there to inspire them that, 'Folks, the fight is on! Let's hold hands. Let's not hide.'"

Kente died on November 7, 2004, in Soweto. Though his township musicals passed out of popular favor as relics of a distant and painful past, they remain important in the history of South Africa's struggle toward majority rule. "One theme that runs through Kente's plays," noted an essay on his life and work in *Contemporary Dramatists,* "is the idea of human interest and hope in times of trouble, with family and community always being there to support the individual."

Selected writings

Plays

Manana, the Jazz Prophet, 1963.
Sikalo, produced by Union Artists at The Great Hall of Witwatersrand University, 1965-66.

Life, produced 1967-70.
Zwi, produced 1967-70.
How Long, produced in Soweto, 1973.
I Believe, produced 1974.
Too Late, produced in Soweto, February 1975.
Can You Take It?, produced 1977.
Hard Road, produced 1978.
Lobola, produced 1980.
Mama and the Load, produced 1981.
Sekunjao, produced 1988.

Television

Mama's Love, 1995.

Sources

Books

Contemporary Dramatists, 6th ed., St. James Press, 1999.
Solberg, Rolf, *Alternative Theatre in South Africa: Talks with Prime Movers Since the 1970s,* Hadeda Books, 1999.
South African People's Plays: Ons Phoba Hi, Heinemann, 1981.

Periodicals

Africa News Service, November 15, 2004.
Guardian (London, England), November 10, 2004, p. 33.
Independent (London, England), November 15, 2004, p. 35.
Times (London, England), November 11, 2004, p. 81.

On-line

"Gibson Kente," *National Arts Council of South Africa,* www.nac.org.za/showcase_G_Kente.htm (June 9, 2005).

—Carol Brennan

Cynthia Ann McKinney

1955—

Legislator

The first black woman from the state of Georgia ever to fill a Congressional seat, Cynthia McKinney has proven a maverick presence on Capitol Hill. A liberal Democrat, McKinney first represented Georgia's 11th district, which encompassed 22 counties and parts of suburban Atlanta, Augusta, and Savannah, before redistricting moved her to the 4th district. McKinney's trademark gold running shoes and braided hair became symbols of her challenge to the mostly white, mostly male U.S. Congress. A divorced working mother who grew up during the civil rights era, she appreciates the needs of the poor, of blacks, and of women. Though McKinney was defeated in her reelection bid of 2002, after controversy over her criticisms of President Bush's foreign policy. she won reelection in 2004 and returned to Congress determined to continue her fight.

Brought New Face to Washington

In an *Atlanta Journal/Constitution* profile, McKinney reflected that her ability to win a seat in Congress is nothing less than a mandate from common Americans for more sensitive representation in the national government. "Now we have people in Congress who are like the rest of America," she said. "It's wonderful to have ordinary people making decisions about the lives of ordinary Americans. It brings a level of sensitivity that has not been there." Asked about the role black female legislators hope to play in Congress, McKinney declared in the *Washington Post*: "We're shaking up the place. If one of the godfathers says you can't do

this, my next question is: 'Why not? And, who are you to say we can't?'"

McKinney first joined Congress in 1992 as a member of "an energetic and aggressive coterie of black female lawmakers," to quote *Washington Post* correspondent Kevin Merida. Since then she has proven to be an independent thinker who challenges conservative colleagues on such issues as abortion rights, welfare reform, and accepting gifts and services from lobbyists. In *Newsweek*, Bill Turque noted that from her first entree into the "kingdom ruled by an aging white patriarchy of Brooks Brothers pinstripes," McKinney "stood in bold relief: a divorced, black, single mother with gold canvas tennis shoes, flowing, brightly patterned skirts and hair braided in elaborate cornrows."

The congresswoman from Georgia has never let anyone intimidate her, from the president to the parking attendants in the House garage: she feels a powerful call to be an example not only to her own constituents but also to other black women. "My father cries every time he sees me on C-SPAN because people like me don't get this far," she told *The Hill*. "Especially black politicians like me." She paused and then added: "Especially black politicians from the South like me."

Learned from Her Father

One of Cynthia McKinney's earliest memories is that of following her father to a sit-in at the segregated Sheraton Biltmore Hotel in Atlanta. Born in 1955, she was only four years old when the civil rights movement

At a Glance . . .

Born on March 17, 1955, in Atlanta, GA; daughter of Billy (a state legislator) and Leola (a retired nurse) McKinney; married Coy Grandison, c. 1983 (divorced); children: Coy Grandison, Jr. *Education*: University of Southern California, BA, 1978; Tufts University, MA in law and diplomacy; University of California, Berkeley, pursuing a PhD, 2000–.

Career: Spelman College, Atlanta, GA, diplomatic fellow, 1984; professor of political science at Clark Atlanta University and Agnes Scott College, c. 1986-88; Georgia State House of Representatives, Augusta, representative, 1988-92; congresswoman from Georgia's 11th district, 1992-2002, 2004–.

Memberships: National Council of Negro Women; National Association for the Advancement of Colored People (NAACP); Sierra Club; Congressional Black Caucus; Progressive Caucus; Women's Caucus (secretary, 1994-96).

Addresses: *Office*—320 Cannon House Office Building, Washington, DC 20515; North DeKalb Mall, 2050 Lawrenceville Highway, Suite D-46, Decatur, GA 30033; 3523 Buford Highway NE, Suite 201, Atlanta, GA 30329.

gained momentum, largely through the efforts of people like her father, Billy, a retired police officer and Georgia state legislator. Billy and his second wife Leola McKinney were determined to give their daughter opportunities that they had been denied as youngsters. Concerned about her education, they sent Cynthia to Catholic school, a decision that has had lasting ramifications in the congresswoman's life. At first the young McKinney was so taken with Catholic school that she announced her intention of becoming a nun. "The nuns wear the ring, and they say that they're married to God," she explained in the *Atlanta Journal/Constitution*. "I just thought that was what you wanted to be in life." Later she chose other career paths, but remained a member of the Catholic Church despite her parents being Baptists.

McKinney attended Catholic schools through high school graduation and then decided to leave her native Atlanta to study at the University of Southern California. She was not particularly happy there, but her parents encouraged her to stay, and she earned a bachelor's degree in 1978. The following year found

her back on the civil rights path with her father. They traveled together to Alabama to protest the conviction of Tommy Lee Hines, a retarded black man accused of raping a white woman. For the first time since her earliest childhood, McKinney encountered the full force of racism at the protest.

Awakened to Racism

McKinney was threatened by Ku Klux Klansmen in full regalia. Eventually the National Guard had to be called to the event, and four people were wounded by gunfire. "That was probably my day of awakening," McKinney recalled in the *Washington Post*. "That day, I experienced hatred for the first time. I learned that there really are people who hate me without even knowing me…. Prior to that day, everything was theory. On that day, I saw fact. That was when I knew that politics was going to be something I would do."

Entering graduate school to study international relations, McKinney began to pursue a doctorate at the Fletcher School of Law and Diplomacy of Tufts University. She worked on a thesis about the satellite states of the former Soviet Union. In 1984 she became a diplomatic fellow at Spelman College in Atlanta, and she has also taught political science at Clark Atlanta University and Agnes Scott College. Her short-lived marriage to a Jamaican politician, Coy Grandison, ended in the mid-1980s. McKinney says little in the press about her former husband, with whom she had one son. "Suffice it to say, he was no prince in shining armor," she commented in the *Washington Post*. "My radar just went down."

McKinney was still living in Jamaica in 1986 when, unbeknownst to her, her father put her name on the ballot for the Georgia state legislature. By that time Billy McKinney had become a respected state politician himself and was a leader among black lawmakers in the Georgia State House of Representatives. His daughter thought her inclusion on the ballot was just a joke— until she earned 20 percent of the vote in that district without any effort. She returned to Atlanta with her young son, sought a divorce, and entered state politics in earnest in 1987.

Became State Legislator

McKinney easily won her first election to the Georgia State House of Representatives in 1988. She joined her father in the legislature–becoming the only father-daughter lawmaker team in the country–and immediately began to prove that she would set her own course. "[My father] thought he was going to have another vote, but once I got in there, we disagreed on everything and I ended up voting against him all the time," McKinney remembered in *Cosmopolitan*. "I was a chip off the old block, a maverick."

Never was that more apparent than the day Cynthia McKinney stood in the Georgia legislature to condemn

George Bush's decision to send troops to fight in the Persian Gulf. Declaring that President Bush "should be ashamed of himself," McKinney earned hisses from her colleagues, and quite a number of them walked out of the chamber. She was stunned by that reaction. "Those guys treated me like dirt. They were so nasty and mean," she said in the *Atlanta Journal/Constitution*. "Everything I did after that was suspect." Opponents, reveling in her troubles, took to calling her "Hanoi Cynthia."

In the late 1980s Cynthia McKinney joined a group of state legislators who were pressing Georgia's Justice Department to ensure proportional representation for blacks in the U.S. Congress. McKinney and her colleagues were successful in winning the right to draw three new congressional districts in such a way that they would have large populations of blacks. The 11th was one of the new districts. Its boundaries stretched 250 miles—roughly the same area as the whole state of New Jersey—through rural, suburban, and urban areas of 22 counties and three major Georgia cities. Predominantly Democratic, and 60 percent black, the district elected McKinney to Congress in an easy victory in 1992.

Joined U.S. Congress

American voters elected 110 new members—or "freshmen"—to Congress in 1992. McKinney was among them and, very quickly, she established herself as a leader and innovator. She was named secretary of the Democratic freshman class, and she lobbied—unsuccessfully—for a place on the prestigious House Rules Committee. After new assignments had been made, McKinney found herself on the Agriculture Committee and the International Relations Committee. She also found that life in Washington would present its own set of problems. As Bill Turque put it, "Months after most freshmen were recognizable figures on Capitol Hill, McKinney still found herself treated like a wayward tourist."

In February 1993, a House elevator operator tried to order McKinney off a members-only car. In April, a Capitol garage attendant confronted her and two staff members and asked edgily: "Who you folks supposed to be with?" She had assumed that over time such institutional slights would cease. But in early August, after a Capitol Hill police officer grabbed her by the arm at a metal detector that members are allowed to bypass, McKinney complained to House Sergeant-at-Arms Werner Brandt. "There's not that many people here who look like me," she told him.

The "institutional slights" have declined since many members of Congress have come to recognize McKinney. The gold tennis shoes and cornrow braids have actually helped to establish her visibility and individuality on the House floor. According to the congresswoman in the *Atlanta Journal/Constitution*, the gold shoes were not meant to become a trademark item. "My feet were hurting, and I was complaining to my mother about these floors [in Washington]," she recalled. "My mom looks in a magazine, sees these gold tennis shoes, orders them and told me that I could wear those shoes. I wore them on the House floor, and the men loved it. They would come by and see if I had on my tennis shoes."

The braids were a simple timesaving expedient that McKinney absolutely refused to change, even if they might cost her an election. "A lot of people judge me based on a stereotype," McKinney explained. "They look at me, they see a black woman, they say, She's got to be another Maxine Waters (a fiery liberal from Los Angeles). Well, heck, I don't mind being another Maxine Waters when it comes to the strength and force of advocacy. But to judge me in my entirety by what I look like is quite base."

Working in Washington, D.C., and trying to be a presence in a far-flung district has proven a challenge both for McKinney and for her young son, Coy. At first McKinney thought she might be able to cover all of her Capitol Hill business in just three days out of each week. That quickly proved impossible, and she soon found herself juggling a full congressional schedule, weekend visits to her state offices, and quality time with her son, who lives in Atlanta with his grandparents. The adjustment was difficult, but Coy has had the benefits of summer vacations in Washington and the opportunity to meet the president and numerous visiting dignitaries.

McKinney reflected on the difficulties of single parenting in a 1994 *Ebony* profile. "While on the one hand, my commitment to the public good and public service is a part of what I stand for politically, I can't do that at the expense of raising my child," she said. "I've tried to expose my son to that public expectation and I think he rolls with the punches much better than I do." She added: "Even with its difficulties, the fact that I'm a member of Congress allows me to expose my son to all of the diversity of American life and to the world. It's been a positive experience for me and for him."

Promoted Liberal Interests

An acknowledged liberal who sometimes votes against liberal interests if they collide with those of her constituents, McKinney established a vocal presence on Capitol Hill. She supported President Clinton's legislative agenda on numerous occasions, but despite much presidential prodding, she voted against the controversial North American Free Trade Agreement in 1993. On behalf of her district, she enlisted the Environmental Protection Agency to help clean up an Augusta neighborhood tainted with industrial pollution, and she obtained federal money to pave some of the rural roads. At the same time, she challenged the powerful kaolin companies in her district and urged the Justice

Department to investigate antitrust violations among the kaolin mines. She has also been a presence on the Congressional Black Caucus, the Progressive Caucus, and the Women's Caucus.

In the middle of her second term in Congress, McKinney faced a potentially devastating blow in 1995 when the United States Supreme Court ruled that the boundaries of her 11th district were unconstitutional, as they had been drawn solely on the basis of race. Overnight McKinney became the symbol of a new sort of civil rights struggle as politicians fought to redraw Georgia's congressional districts to suit their interests. Before the redrawing, McKinney's 11th district had been 60 percent black; after the redrawing, the new 4th district was just 32 percent black. In a heated 1996 election contest that saw her father discharged from her campaign for accusing her opponent of being a "racist Jew," McKinney pulled off a major surprise, winning the seat with 59 percent of the vote and becoming the first black woman elected to represent a Congressional district with a white majority.

Not only did McKinney win her seat, she kept it, winning reelection in 1998 and 2000. Her growing seniority allowed her access to more prestigious committee assignments, including posts on the National Security Committee and the International Relations Committee (as a member of the latter's International Operations and Human Rights Subcommittee). She became increasingly interested in foreign policy, offering support to new governments in the African countries of Liberia and the Democratic Republic of Congo. She also became a vocal supporter of the idea of creating a Palestinian state in Israeli-occupied territory, a stance that won her the support of Arabs and Muslims throughout the world. It was this latter stance, however, that brought McKinney into her greatest controversy in office.

Courted Controversy

Even before the terrorist attacks of September 11, 2001, McKinney was a vocal critic of American policy in the Middle East, especially in Iraq. She openly criticized President Bush's pre-9/11 policies on Iraq, and her criticisms became even more vocal after the attacks. She lambasted New York mayor Rudolph Giuliani when he refused an offer of $10 million in aid from a Saudi Arabian prince. Then, she indicated that President Bush may have known about the 9/11 attacks before they occurred and that his business associates had profited from the war of terror that followed the attack. McKinney's comments—often misquoted or misrepresented by a media eager for sensation—soon sparked a firestorm of controversy. A

fellow legislator from her home state, Senator Zell Miller, called her "loony" and the *National Review* called her a "race-baiting conspiracy theorist." She was labeled as pro-terrorist by her political enemies, and it didn't help that she received campaign donations from Arab groups, including some who were linked to terrorism. In the election of 2002, McKinney could not overcome the negative associations she had earned in the last several years and she was defeated by another black female candidate, Denise Majette.

Despite the catastrophe of the 2002 election, McKinney ran for and was reelected to Congress in 2004. According to her campaign Web site, she intends to direct her "maximum effort into redirecting America's spending priorities to our children, seniors, neighborhoods, environment, veterans, and for peace." It remains to be seen whether McKinney will return to her role as a lighting rod for controversy, or whether she will be better known for her consistent efforts to work on behalf of her constituents.

Sources

Periodicals

Atlanta Constitution, November 4, 1992, p. 1A; November 27, 1992, p. 1A; July 1, 1995, p. 12A.
Atlanta Journal/Constitution, November 4, 1992, p. 8B; December 13, 1992, p. 10A; April 25, 1993, p. 2D; July 30, 1995, p. 3M.
Cosmopolitan, October 1994, pp. 220-21.
Ebony, September 1994, pp. 127-30.
Economist, July 24, 2004, p. 28.
Jet, November 22, 2004.
National Review, August 23, 2004, p. 12.
New African, May 2004, p. 66.
Newsweek, November 30, 1993, pp. 32-38.
The Hill, March 8, 1995, p. 38.
Time, December 5, 1994, p. 59.
U.S. News and World Report, December 28, 1992, p. 86; August 27, 2002.
Washington Post, August 2, 1993, p. 1A; July 5, 1995, p. 1C.
Washington Report on Middle East Affairs, July-August 2004.
Weekly Standard, January 3, 2005.

On-line

Cynthia McKinney for Congress 2004, www.cynthiaforcongress.com/ (June 8, 2005).
Representative McKinney Home Page, www.house.gov/mckinney/ (June 8, 2005).

—Ann Janette Johnson and Tom Pendergast

Haydain Neale

1970—

Singer

Haydain Neale, charismatic lead singer of Canadian super group jacksoul, has made a name for himself with intelligent lyrics served up with a deep side of soul. His songs exalt love, kindness, and joy—decidedly un-cool traits in an urban music market defined by guns, gangstas, and gratuitous sex. Neale is unrepentant. "This is the world that I bought into and this is the world I'm selling," he told the *Toronto Sun*. "Other people can push whatever images they want and go on about types of shoes and cars. I'm in your face and I'm not going away."

Born into Music, Not Money

Haydain Neale was born on September 3, 1970, in Hamilton, Ontario, Canada, and raised in that city's poorest neighborhood. "We had no cash. We were in government housing for years," Neale recalled to the *FFWD Weekly* Web site. "But the nice thing about having no money in Canada is you never feel like you're being hung out to dry. You have access to what everybody else has access to. You go to the same schools, you do the same things. You end up with a pretty middle-class attitude."

One thing never lacking in the Neale home was music. "My mom brought all the music into the house when I was little…. classical, the best of opera, the best of reggae, the best of calypso," he continued with *FFWD Weekly*. "She helped me appreciate loving melody for melody's sake." Neale spiced up his mother's musical mix with a steady diet of radio pop, old school R&B, and classical jazz. The jangled soundtrack seeped into Neale's late-night dreams. "I would get these melodies that I would want to remember," he told *Maclean's*. "I'd find really strange ways to graft them on paper so maybe in the morning I'd remember enough to recapture it."

Despite his nocturnal musical musings, Neale headed off to the University of Guelph with the intention of earning a degree in biology. However, the music inside him would not be denied, and Neale soon started thinking about pursuing a career in the music industry. In 1994 he dropped his studies altogether and formed jacksoul (with a lowercase 'j') with Davide Direnzo, Ron Lopata, Adrian Eccleston, and Dave Murray, four white musicians who have earned the nickname "funk brothers of Canada."

Infused Music with Dose of Intellectualism

Neale's vision of new soul music drove jacksoul. He wrote most of the songs and provided the band with its characteristic vocal sound—part R&B crooner, part funky playboy, but mostly soul slinger. He's been compared to classic wailers like Al Green and Barry White, as well as modern masters like Seal, and even a male version of Macy Gray. Fans are forgiven for thinking that Neale is jacksoul. "There's always been an impetus to just call it 'Haydain' on a pragmatic level," Neale said in a biography on his agent Chris Smith's Web site. "But I've always been most excited by the live presentation of music. That's what got me hooked in the first place."

At a Glance . . .

Born on September 3, 1970, in Hamilton, Ontario, Canada; married Michaela; children: Yasmin. *Education*: University of Guelph, Canada, degree in biology.

Career: jacksoul, singer, 1994–; Québécité (opera), Guelph Jazz Festival, performer, 2003; Megawatt Studios, Toronto, Ontario, Canada, proprietor, 2004–.

Memberships: Songwriters Association of Canada, board of directors.

Awards: Juno Awards, Best R&B/Soul Recording, 2001, for *Absolute*; Canadian Urban Music Awards, Songwriter of the Year, 2004, for *Resurrected*.

Addresses: *Office*—Megawatt Studios, 190 Liberty Street, Suite 100, Toronto, Ontario, Canada, M6K 3L5. *Record company*—BMG Music Canada, 150 John Street, 6th Floor, Toronto, Ontario, Canada, M5V 3C3.

jacksoul began rehearsing in a refurbished chicken coop in Kitchener, Ontario, and soon had a roster of songs which they performed wherever they could get a gig—from dive bars to small-town jazz festivals. They recorded a demo tape at the live shows and began shopping it around. The demo highlighted Neale's activist approach to song writing. "We should speak but not just from a ghetto mentality," he told *Gay Guide Toronto*. "I may be black but, you know what? I also know there's terrorism, problems in the Middle East, and Jewish gravestones being vandalized here at home. It's good to sing about the world *and* throw in a good tune about getting it on."

After a representative from a major U.S. record label told the band that although he loved the music, it was too intellectual for American release, Viking, a Canadian wing of international mega-label BMG picked up the group. In 1996 the label released jacksoul's debut album, *ABsolute*. A funked-up blend of R&B, soul, and pop with just a hint of rap, *ABsolute*'s 11 tracks shook up Canada's urban music normal offerings of sexual innuendos and x-rated lyrics. "I hope that we transcend any kind of bump'n grind, wanna-get-freaky-with you-tune, and really hit you on a different level that's not even really sexual," Neale told *Octopus Media Ink*. Songs like the soul-stewed "Eastbound," the unapologetic romance of "Unconditional," and the thudding-funk of "Indigo," helped earn *ABsolute* a nomination for Best R&B/Soul Recording of the Year at the 1996 Juno Awards, Canada's version of the Grammys.

Topped Canadian Record Charts

Following *ABsolute's* release, jacksoul toured extensively, amassing a diverse fan base. Neale recalled a performance given on the back of a flatbed truck during Canada Day celebrations in Kitchener. "I remember seeing so many kids running around the stage," he told *Octopus Media Ink*. "We were playing in front of a couple of hundred people, and I remember watching everyone—from young to old, most who hadn't heard us before—grooving to the beats."

After relocating to Toronto, jacksoul released *Sleepless*. With the addition of pianist Jon Levine, from the Toronto funk-outfit Philosopher King, the album was another savory mix of old soul and new funk, acid jazz and trip-hop, all against the roiling R&B flow of Neale's vocals. "[*Sleepless*] allows me to be as much of an artist as I can be," Neale said on Chris Smith's web site. "Not just the frontman or singer or the interview guy with the sound-bytes, but, when all is said and done, what I stand for...strong music, taking everything I think is great about music and adding a little something." He added, "I think what you have here is a perfect example of someone who appreciates music and tried to surround himself with good musicians and learn from those people, putting together something that's totally funky for the new millennium."

"Can't Stop," the first single from the album hit the top ten on Canada's radio charts and clocked in as the most-played pop song on Canadian radio in 2000. The song was driven by a chorus of vocals and a pop beat—a label Neale embraced. "You're a human being and I'm trying to hit you on an emotional level," he told *FFWD Weekly*. "[Music] is about trying to communicate. That's pop. Pop is the umbrella under which music that just hits you lives, whether it's soul or whatever." That "whatever" helped jacksoul snag the 2001 Juno award for Best R&B/Soul Recording.

Resurrected Soul's Old-School Sound

In 2004 jacksoul released their third album, *Resurrected*, an homage to soul music. In preparation for recording, Neale spent months listening to and reading about his soul music idols from Marvin Gaye to Motown producer Berry Gordy. "I didn't want to hide my love for that music and pretend it was all ours," Neale said in an article reprinted on the *Canoe* Web site. "We called the album *Resurrected* in the first place because we're bringing back great melodies, irresistible grooves and stories that you can really vibe to. It's music that paints pictures in the brain."

To capture the authentic sound of soul classics, jacksoul recorded the album in an old-fashioned, bare-bones rehearsal studio. "Pristine recording environments make for great pop songs, but soul is about a certain amount of dirt...the magic is in the imperfection," Neale said on jacksoul's web site. Featuring a cover photo of Neale locked in a loving embrace with his wife of ten years, Michaela, *Resurrected* served up love songs, pure and sweet. "I think honesty is sexy and I think love is sexy, and if you're not willing to brag about it then that's too bad for you," he told the *Toronto Sun*. However, true to his worldly awareness, some of the songs blatantly confronted the mayhem of war, the futility of violence, and the need for spirituality.

Led by the Al Green-inspired single "Still Believe in Love," *Resurrected* earned immediate critical acclaim. Neale's voice, which Toronto's *Globe & Mail* called "the album's best part" was repeatedly compared to Green, as well Luther Vandross and Sam Cooke. *Resurrected* won jacksoul several award nominations and scored Neale the Canadian Urban Music Awards Songwriter of the Year nod. It also caught the attention of soul legend James Brown, who invited jacksoul to open for him during his 2004 Canadian tour. "When we first started we thought it would be wicked to play with James Brown and now we're doing it," Neale gushed to the *Coast*. "Our goal is to play great music for cool people and I'm pretty sure we'll pick up the James Brown fans. It's like preaching to the choir."

Selected discography

Albums (with jacksoul)

Absolute, 1996.
Sleepless, BMG, 2000.
Resurrected, V.I.K., 2004.

Sources

Periodicals

Globe & Mail, (Toronto), March 25, 2004.
Maclean's, December 4, 2000.

On-line

"Jacksoul," *FFWD Weekly,* www.ffwdweekly.com/Issues/2000/0622/mus4.htm (April 5, 2005).
"Jacksoul, ABsolute," *Octopus Media Ink,* www.octopusmediaink.com/jacksoul.html (April 5, 2005).
"Jacksoul Biography," Chris Smith Management, www.chrissmithmanagement.com/bio_jacksoul_1.html (April 5, 2005).
"Jacksoul, Biography," *Vik Recordings: Jacksoul,* www.vikrecordings.com/jacksoul/index.html (April 5, 2005).
"Jacksoul: Every Song Tells a Story," *North Shore News,* www.nsnews.com/issues00/w041700/jacksoul.html (April 5, 2005).
"Neale Taps into R&B to Break Out of Funk," *Canoe,* http://jam.canoe.ca/Music/Artists/J/Jacksoul/2004/07/15/746246.html (April 5, 2005).
"Shaun Proulx Talks to Haydain Neale," *Gay Guide Toronto,* www.gayguidetoronto.com/1_shaun/april_2004.html (April 5, 2005).
"Soul Proprietor," *Toronto Sun,* www.canoe.ca/NewsStand/TorontoSun/Entertainment/2004/03/25/394817.html (April 5, 2005).
"Sure Things: Jacksoul w/ James Brown," *The Coast* www.thecoast.ca/archives/112504/surethings.html (April 5, 2005).

—Candace LaBalle

Winston Ntshona

1941—

Actor

Ntshona, Winston, photograph. Evening Standard/Getty Images.

One of the most widely acclaimed plays internationally during the last decades of the twentieth century was *The Island,* which began its theatrical life in secret performances held in apartheid-era South Africa in 1973. The play was partly the creation of Winston Ntshona, one of the actors who appeared in it. *The Island* was a pointed and partly humorous protest against the conditions at South Africa's infamous Robben Island prison, where the country's future president, Nelson Mandela, had been serving a life sentence since 1964. But the play proved to have universal appeal, maintaining its popularity after apartheid was dismantled. It has been translated into more than 30 languages.

The Island and its companion piece *Sizwe Bansi Is Dead* have been staged in London, on Broadway in New York (where Ntshona and his co-star John Kani won Tony Awards in 1975), in Orlando, Florida, where *The Island* was performed by incarcerated teenage drug offenders, and in many other cities and countries, including Russia and Israel, where the main characters of *The Island* were played by Palestinian actors. These successes launched a long acting career for Ntshona, who starred in the key anti-apartheid film *A Dry White*

Season and became a leading figure of the South African arts scene.

Worked at Ford Plant

Winston Ntshona was born on October 6, 1941, in Cape Elizabeth, in South Africa's Eastern Cape region. His remarkable stage chemistry with John Kani began to take shape as the two performed in plays together in high school. Staying on in Port Elizabeth and working in a lab at a Ford Motor Company plant, Ntshona was introduced by Kani to the Serpent Players, a theater group founded by the anti-apartheid white South African playwright Athol Fugard and so named because its stage lay above what had once been a snake pit.

Fugard aided the careers of Ntshona and Kani in various ways. At a time when black South African adults were required by law to carry a passbook whose contents dictated where they could and could not travel within the country, he invented a fictitious employment status for Ntshona as his chauffeur (Kani became a gardener). Ntshona thus was able to perform with the company for white theater enthusiasts, even if he and

At a Glance . . .

Born on October 6, 1941 in Port Elizabeth, Eastern Cape region, South Africa.

Career: Ford Motor Company plant, early 1960s; Serpent Players, actor, 1967-72; stage and film actor, and playwright, 1970s–; Eastern Cape Cultural Units, South Africa, chairman, 2000(?)–.

Selected awards: Tony award, 1975, for *The Island*; National Arts Council of South Africa, Living Treasure awards.

Addresses: *Home*—Port Elizabeth, South Africa. *Office*—National Arts Council of South Africa, P.O. Box 500, Newtown 2113, Johannesburg, South Africa.

Kani faced brushes with South Africa's Special Branch security service as they traveled to performances. But when Ntshona first joined the Serpent Players, in the mid-1960s, the group's productions did not reflect the dehumanizing reality of black South African life. Instead, they tended to perform European theatrical classics and other imported productions.

That changed after the company's members demanded plays that connected with what their black audiences were experiencing and striving for outside the theater. Where no plays existed, the troupe members worked to improvise new ones. And as the movement for black South African equality began to rise in the late 1960s and 1970s, it was theater that took the lead in circulating new ideas among progressive South Africans. After all, a play was much harder for white South African authorities to censor than a publication was; if Ntshona and Kani memorized their lines, a play could be staged anywhere, with minimal sets, on short notice. Ntshona appeared in about 20 Serpent Players productions between 1967 and 1972.

Shaped Plays in Workshops

All these developments set the stage for first *Sizwe Bansi Is Dead* and then *The Island*. Both plays were developed by Ntshona and Kani in improvisatory Serpent Players workshop sessions in the early 1970s, with the two actors drawing on their experiences of apartheid. Although the plays were initially credited to Fugard, they were in large part the work of the two actors, with Fugard serving as director. *Sizwe Bansi Is Dead*, a darkly comic fable about a black migrant worker who debates ways of assuming a new identity in order to obtain a travel pass, broke new ground in

South African theater. And *The Island*, which depicted two Robben Island cellmates who decide to stage an in-prison production of the ancient Greek classic *Antigone* as one of them is given a life sentence, took direct aim at the apartheid system. The character Antigone herself, who defies orders so that she can see her brother properly buried, held strong meaning for black South Africans.

By even mentioning Nelson Mandela's name, which Ntshona and Kani did, they were breaking the law. *The Island* kept a low profile at first, quickly moving from place to place among homes and community centers in segregated black areas when it was first performed in 1973. When it moved to the larger Space Theater in Cape Town, the South African government tried to ban it without success. The play moved to the Royal Court theater in London, England in 1974 and was soon an international hit, winning critical waves and an unusual dual Tony Award for Ntshona and Kani after its Broadway run in 1975. The two were in fact arrested after a 1976 performance of the play in South Africa. They were released, but they did not perform *The Island* again in South Africa until 1995. They were also arrested after performing in a third collaboration with Fugard, *Statements after an Arrest under the Immorality Act.*

Part of the success Ntshona and Kani achieved was due to the way they blended comedy into profoundly serious subject matter. Ntshona delighted audiences as the Greek princess Antigone, complaining as he donned a mop wig and fake breasts to take on the role. Even the white police officers assigned to keep tabs on Ntshona ended up enjoying his performances. "One time we were doing *Sizwe* in Natal [province]," he told *Newsweek,* "and just before I walked on I saw two or three policemen walking into the theater. I thought they were coming to [arrest us]. Then the first guy left and more came in. By the time we finished there was a good percentage of policemen [in the audience]. As it turned out, the first guy that came in to see the show, a white police captain, enjoyed it, and…called his colleagues to come and enjoy themselves and they sure did—laughed themselves sick."

Appeared in Films

While *The Island*, in the words of the *Times* of London, "unleashed a revolution in S[outh] A[frican] theatre," Ntshona's success in New York led to a series of film roles in the 1980s and 1990s. He made his debut with a small role in *The Wild Geese* (1978) and was reunited with Kani and Fugard in the 1984 drama *Marigolds in August*. That film explored the conflicts among blacks that apartheid engendered, featuring Ntshona as a gardener protecting his employment turf from a still poorer interloper (Kani). "Ntshona and Kani are, as always, irresistible. They never play for sympathy: they play two men who are sympathetic," wrote *New Republic* reviewer Stanley Kauffmann.

Ntshona's most substantial film role came in 1989's *A Dry White Season,* a hard-hitting anti-apartheid film in which his character enlists the help of a white South African, played by Donald Sutherland, in finding out what became of his missing son. Ntshona also appeared in other theatrical productions, including a London run of Edward Albee's *The Death of Bessie Smith* and a production of Samuel Beckett's *Waiting for Godot,* a play that had influenced the two-man format of *The Island.* In London in 2002 he directed a new play, *Ghetto Goats,* which was collaboratively created by three young actors from Port Elizabeth, working in much the same way as he himself had 30 years earlier.

Ntshona and Kani reunited several times for productions of *The Island,* announcing after a 2003 tour that it would be their last. By that time the play had taken on a life of its own. Ntshona continued to live in South Africa, taking a post as chairman of the Eastern Cape Cultural Units arts agency in later life and working to interest young South Africans in theater. He was famous enough to appear in television commercials, and he was honored with a Living Treasures award from South Africa's National Arts Council. Although he had played a large part in creating theater pieces that changed the world, his name was mostly absent from theatrical histories and reference books.

Selected works

Films

The Wild Geese, 1978.
Gandhi, 1982.
Marigolds in August, 1984.
A Dry White Season, 1989.
The Air Up There, 1993.
Tarzan and the Lost City, 1998.

Plays

Sizwe Bansi Is Dead (performer, co-author, with John Kani and Athol Fugard), 1972.
The Island (performer, co-author, with John Kani and Athol Fugard), 1973.
The Death of Bessie Smith, 1979.
Waiting for Godot, 1980-81.

Sources

Books

Kennedy, Dennis, ed., *Oxford Encyclopedia of Theatre and Performance,* Oxford, 2003.

Periodicals

Atlanta Journal-Constitution, July 17, 2003, p. P22.
New Republic, July 2, 1984, p. 24.
New York Times, June 20, 1984, p. C21.
Newsweek (International ed.), March 27, 2000, p. 32.
Orlando Sentinel, June 21, 1993, p. D1.
Time, September 25, 1989, p. 78.
Times (London, England), February 6, 2000.
Washington Post, November 4, 2001, p. G1; November 9, 2001, p. C1.

On-line

"Ghetto Goats," *Young Vic Theatre* (London, England), www.youngvic.org/htmlonly/play25.html (March 1, 2005).
"Top Actors Headline Coega Ad Drive," *Coega Development Corporation,* www.coega.co.za/NewsView.asp?NewsID=488 (March 1, 2004).
"Winston Ntshona," *All Movie Guide,* www.allmovie.com (March 1, 2005).
"Winston Ntshona," *National Arts Council of South Africa: Living Treasures Awards,* www.nac.org.za/showcase_W_Ntshona.html (March 1, 2005).

—James M. Manheim

Ol' Dirty Bastard

1968-2004

Rapper

After rapper Ol' Dirty Bastard died of cardiac arrest in a Manhattan recording studio in 2004, an autopsy revealed a dangerous mixture of cocaine and prescription drugs in his system. To some who had followed career the career of a man often known as ODB, his death seemed an unsurprising outcome to a notorious spree of criminal behavior that spanned most of a decade. While he was alive ODB's drug-fueled crimes tended to overshadow his considerable musical creativity. As a member of the innovative hip-hop act the Wu-Tang Clan and later as a solo artist, ODB forged a humorous, often obscene, ragged-edged, but subtle style that evoked hip-hop's roots in older funk music. What *Salon* writer Pete L'Official described as ODB's "gold-toothed, marble-mouthed, free-associative nonsense raps" seemed to emerge after his death as his most important contributions to hip-hop musical culture.

Ol' Dirty Bastard, photograph. AP/Wide World Photos.

Ol' Dirty Bastard, whose given name was Russell Tyrone Jones, was born in Brooklyn, New York, on November 15, 1968, and grew up in the tough Fort Greene neighborhood. His mother Cherry Jones called him Rusty and after his death described him to the New York *Daily News* as "the kindest and most generous soul on earth." Over his short life, he would have many names. The most famous of them, Ol' Dirty Bastard, took shape after he began to spend time on Staten Island with his cousins Robert Diggs and Gary Grice and put together a hip-hop group partially inspired by the Asian kung-fu films they all liked. That group, first called All in Together Now in the late 1980s, became the Wu-Tang Clan after Diggs read books on Eastern philosophy during a prison stint. Diggs and Grice became RZA and GZA, and Russell Jones became Ol' Dirty Bastard—because, as the Wu-Tang Clan put it on their 1993 album *Enter the Wu-Tang: 36 Chambers,* "there ain't no father to his style."

Arrived at Welfare Office in Limousine

The Wu-Tang Clan issued a limited-edition single called "Protect Ya Neck" in 1992, and news of their innovative style spread from college radio stations to major labels. *Enter the Wu-Tang: 36 Chambers* appeared the following year, with ODB preparing the way for the group's contract with the Loud label by offering an out-of-control version of "Somewhere Over the Rainbow" before a group of executives from Loud's conglomerate distributor, RCA/BMG. ODB showed a flair for attracting attention to the group; he once drove to a welfare office in a limousine to collect food stamps, trailed by invited camera operators from the cable-television music channel MTV.

By the early 1990s, ODB had already begun to run afoul of the law; he drew a second-degree assault conviction in 1993 and was shot in the stomach during a street dispute the following year. His injuries were minor and did not prevent him from finishing work, with RZA as producer, on his album *Return to the 36 Chambers: The Dirty Version,* released early in 1995. Kelefa Sanneh of the *New York Times* later termed it "a wildly entertaining collection of low-down jokes and memorable rhymes." The album cracked *Billboard* magazine's top 10, and two of its singles, "Shimmy Shimmy Ya" and "Brooklyn Zoo," became hits. "Shimmy Shimmy Ya," though less raunchy than many other ODB numbers, was typical of his style musically: its refrain of "Baby, I like it raw" was mostly rapped but was subtly structured so that it landed on sung pitches from time to time.

ODB continued to experience success in 1996 and 1997, contributing a guest rap to vocal diva Mariah Carey's "Fantasy" and a piece called "Dog S–t" to the top-selling *Wu-Tang Forever* album. In November of 1997 he was arrested for nonpayment of child support; he had three children with his wife Icelene Jones, and there were reports that he fathered as many as ten other children (though only four out-of-wedlock children were located after his death). The Wu-Tang Clan took hip-hop cross-marketing to new levels, and ODB launched his own clothing line, My Dirty Wear, early in 1998. Around the same time, he helped rescue a four-year-old girl who was trapped under a car that had hit her. He also grabbed headlines that year by grabbing the microphone from singer Shawn Colvin at the Grammy awards ceremony in Los Angeles and ranting

about the Wu-Tang Clan's loss to Sean "Puffy" Combs for the best rap album award.

Arrested Repeatedly

After that bizarre incident, ODB's life fell apart. Over the course of the next year, he pleaded guilty to charges of assaulting Icelene Jones; was charged with threatening an ex-girlfriend; was arrested for shoplifting in Virginia Beach, Virginia; was robbed and shot in an apartment in Brooklyn; was arrested at a hotel in Berlin, Germany, for lying nude on a balcony; threatened to kill a security guard at the House of Blues club in Los Angeles; was charged with attempted murder after allegedly shooting at police in Brooklyn (a charge that was eventually dismissed); and became the first person arrested under a new California law barring convicted felons from wearing bulletproof vests.

The bad news continued in 1999 despite help from former O.J. Simpson defense attorney Robert Shapiro. ODB was jailed for a bond violation in connection with the House of Blues threats, and in New York officers found marijuana and 20 vials of crack cocaine in his car after he ran a red light. Between court-mandated stints in a pair of drug-rehabilitation centers, he teamed with rapper Pras on the hit "Ghetto Supastar (That Is What You Are)" and recorded the album *Nigga Please,* another top-ten smash that landed the rapper on the radio once again with "Got Your Money." That single featured future stars, including "Milkshake" rapper Kelis and the production duo the Neptunes. The album also included a version of the Billie Holiday jazz standard "Good Morning Heartache" that, Sanneh noted, "should have sounded like a joke but somehow didn't. You could hear the sorrow that lurked beneath the surface of so many other ODB songs and stunts."

In 2000, ODB walked out of a rehabilitation facility in California and officially became a fugitive. He recorded music for the new Wu-Tang Clan album *The W,* but only one track, "Conditioner," was coherent enough to be included. The ODB mystique grew as he eluded arrest at the album's record-release party in November of 2000, but he was picked up at a Philadelphia McDonald's restaurant a few days later by a police officer who recognized him because her son was an ODB fan. Faced with a blizzard of charges, ODB pleaded guilty to cocaine possession in April of 2001 and was sentenced to two to four years in a New York state prison. He was placed under a suicide watch.

New ODB Albums Cobbled Together

Various levels of the music industry responded to the temporary lack of new ODB product by repackaging material he had already recorded: the Elektra label released *Dirty Story: The Best of Ol' Dirty Bastard,* and a small company called D-3 gathered the material

ODB had recorded while on the run from police, added a largely random group of contributions by other musicians, and released the whole under the title *The Trials and Tribulations of Russell Jones* in 2002. Despite the slapdash quality of the album, it rose to the top ten of *Billboard*'s R&B/Hip-Hop album chart.

Released from prison in 2003, ODB was signed to the hot Roc-a-Fella label, owned by rapper Jay-Z. He announced a name change to Dirt McGirt and began working with the Neptunes and other producers on a new album. The album's eventual title, *Osirus*, referred to another of ODB's numerous aliases, which also included Joe Bannanas, Dirt Dog, Big Baby Jesus, as well as yet other variants. "I created all those worlds," he once said (according to London's *Independent*). The album was essentially completed, and reports indicated that ODB had gotten his life in order as its release date approached. The *Hartford Courant* termed it "the rapper's strongest work in years," pointing out that "'Dirty Dirty' features the same sort of manic raps that made him the comic relief in Wu-Tang."

On November 13, 2004, however, paramedics were called to a Manhattan studio after ODB, putting the finishing touches on *Osirus,* complained of chest pains and collapsed. His death was ruled accidental after an autopsy revealed that he had taken cocaine and the powerful prescription painkiller Tramadol. The surviving members of the Wu-Tang Clan recorded a tribute track, "I Go Through Life," that was posthumously included on *Osirus.* After his death, ODB's sister Lamarenae Jones mused to the New York *Daily News* that the rapper would have wanted his memorial service held at the Coney Island amusement park. "He was a big kid," she said. "He loved riding the Cyclone."

Selected discography

(With the Wu-Tang Clan) *Enter the Wu-Tang: 36 Chambers,* Loud, 1993.
Return to the 36 Chambers: The Dirty Version, Elektra, 1995.

(With the Wu-Tang Clan) *Wu-Tang Forever,* Loud, 1997.
Nigga Please, Elektra, 1999.
(With the Wu-Tang Clan) *The W,* Loud, 2000.
The Dirty Story: The Best of Ol' Dirty Bastard, Elektra, 2001.
The Trials and Tribulations of Russell Jones, D3, 2002.
Osirus: The Official Mixtape, Sure Shot, 2005.

Sources

Books

Contemporary Musicians, volume 42, Gale, 2005.

Periodicals

Daily News (New York), November 14, 2004, p. 5; November 16, 2004, Entertainment section.
Hartford Courant, January 6, 2005, Calendar section, p. 6.
Houston Chronicle, November 16, 2004, Star section, p. 1.
Independent (London, England), November 15, 2004, p. 34.
New York Times, November 17, 2004, p. E1.
Toronto Sun, February 11, 2005, p. E15.

On-line

"Ode to an Ol' Dirty Bastard," *Salon* (November 16, 2004), www.salon.com (May 7, 2005).
"Ol' Dirty Bastard," *All Music Guide,* www.allmusic.com (May 7, 2005).
"Ol' Dirty Bastard," *Atlantic Records,* www.atlanticrecords.com/olddirtybastard/ (May 19, 2005).
"Ol' Dirty Bastard," *Biography Resource Center,* www.galenet.com/servlet/BioRC (May 19, 2005).

—James M. Manheim

David Ortiz

1975—

Baseball player

Lots of baseball players shine early, struggle a bit as they make the transition to the majors, then blossom and lead their teams to World Series glory. Few, however, do it with the charisma and drama of David Ortiz. Known almost as much for his appealing personality as for his lethal bat, Ortiz played a key role in helping the Boston Red Sox win their first World Series in 86 years, ending a reign of futility that had reached mythic proportions.

David Americo Ortiz Arias was born on November 18, 1975, in Santa Domingo, the capital of the Dominican Republic. Ortiz, the oldest of parents Enrique and Angela Rosa's four children, was born with an easygoing personality that allowed him to make friends readily. Baseball was big in the household. Enrique, who went by the nickname Leo, was a baseball player himself, having played professional and semi-professional ball in the Dominican leagues for years. David's heroes were the Martinez brothers, Ramon and Pedro, local boys who had made good in the major leagues.

At Estudia Espallat High School Ortiz excelled in basketball as well as baseball. The major league Seattle

Ortiz, David, photograph. AP/Wide World Photos.

Mariners saw enough promise in Ortiz to sign him to a free agent contract in 1992, shortly after his 17th birthday. He spent one season with the Mariners' Dominican Summer League team before moving on to the club's Peoria, Arizona-based rookie league squad. Initially, Ortiz struggled with the bat, hitting only .246 that year. However, he showed flashes of skill in the field. The following year, things started to click offensively. In 1995 he batted .332 and led the Arizona League in doubles and runs batted in (RBIs).

That performance earned Ortiz a promotion to the Wisconsin Timber Rattlers of the Class A Midwest League, where he quickly established himself as one of the Mariners' top prospects. For 1996, he batted .322 with 18 home runs and 93 RBIs, earning him honors as a Midwest league All-Star. During the off-season that followed, Ortiz—who had gone by the name David Arias up to this time—was traded to the Minnesota Twins organization. From a career standpoint, the trade was good new for Ortiz. The Mariners already had established starters at both of his likely positions, first base and designated hitter, while the Twins had question marks at both positions. Ortiz started the

the field too, finishing the season with only one error in 223 chances.

2001 was a pivotal year for the Twins. After managing to win only 69 games the previous season, they recorded a respectable 85 victories in 2001. Unfortunately, Ortiz's role in that turnaround was diminished by another wrist fracture, which kept him out of the lineup for several weeks. Ortiz struggled with injuries—this time a knee–for the first half of 2002 as well. During the second half of that season, however, he began to show the hitting wizardry that has marked his career since. He caught fire after the All-Star break, finishing the season with 20 home runs and 75 RBIs in only 125 games, and helping Minnesota capture its first division title in more than a decade.

Of course, one consequence of success for a baseball player is that his price tag goes up, and Ortiz became too expensive for the financially struggling Twins. They attempted to find a trade for him but, failing to do so, ended up releasing him during the off-season. Fellow Dominican Pedro Martinez of the Boston Red Sox, who had been something of a mentor to Ortiz, lobbied Red Sox management to sign Ortiz. Red Sox management listened. They soon signed Ortiz to a one-year contract. With the Red Sox, Ortiz eventually beat out a number of competitors for the role of full-time designated hitter. In the last 97 games along of the 2003 season, he batted .293 and socked 29 home runs, helping his team to a spot in the playoffs. In the postseason, Ortiz had several key hits, but the Red Sox came up short in the American League Championship Series against their archrivals the Yankees.

The Red Sox rewarded Ortiz for his contribution in 2003 with a two-year contract worth more than $12 million. Not only did he did not disappoint in 2004; he emerged as one of the top players in the league. He was chosen to play in the Major League All-Star Game for the first time in his career. More importantly, Ortiz helped lead the team to 98 wins and another playoff berth. He recorded new personal bests in a number of categories: 41 home runs, 47 doubles, and 139 RBIs; and his batting average was a solid .301. Above all, he helped the Red Sox win their first World Series title since 1918, breaking the so-called "Curse of the Bambino"—a championship drought said to have been brought on by the Red Sox's foolish sale of Babe Ruth to the Yankees before the 1920 season.

By all accounts, Ortiz's contributions in the clubhouse are as important to the Red Sox as his production on the field. He is widely regarded as a team leader, and his easygoing personality is appreciated by teammates, fans and journalists alike. While comparisons to Babe Ruth's legendary performance are at best premature, Ortiz will go down in history as one of the players most responsible for terminating once and for all the Bambino's legendary Beantown hex.

At a Glance . . .

Born David Americo Ortiz Arias on November 18, 1975 in Santa Domingo, Dominican Republic; married Tiffany Ortiz; children: Yessica, Alexandra and D'Angelo.

Career: Professional baseball player, 1992–. Seattle Mariners, free agent, 1992; Mariners' Peoria, AZ Rookie League team, 1994-95; Wisconsin Timber Rattlers (Mariners' Class A affiliate), 1996; Fort Myers (Minnesota Twins Class A affiliate), 1997; New Britain (Twins Class AA affiliate), 1997; Salt Lake City (Twins AAA affiliate), 1997-99; Minnesota Twins major league club, parts of 1997, 1998 and 1999, and full seasons 2000-02; Boston Red Sox, 2003–.

Awards: *Baseball America,* Best Defensive First Baseman, 1997; American League All-Star Team, 2004; Most Valuable Player, American League Championship Series, 2004.

Address: *Office*—c/o Boston Red Sox, 4 Yawkey Way, Boston, MA 02215-3496.

1997 season with the Class A Fort Myers Miracle, the Twins' Florida State league affiliate. It was here that he started going by the name Ortiz. It didn't take long for him to make his mark there; he got hits in his first 11 games with Fort Myers. In June he was promoted to the Class AA New Britain Rock Cats. Again Ortiz wasted no time destroying pitchers at his new level. After only a month in Class AA, he moved up again, this time to Salt Lake City in the AAA Pacific Coast League. While his numbers in AAA ball were not as impressive right away as they had been at his two previous minor league stops, Ortiz was still called up to the parent team in September, where he batted an impressive .327 in 15 games for the Twins.

On the strength of that performance, Ortiz started the 1998 campaign in the majors. Early in the season, however, he broke a bone in his wrist and was rendered inactive until late June. Once he was back in action, he quickly returned to form, batting .277 with nine home runs and 46 RBIs in 86 games. In spite of his success, Ortiz spent the entire 1999 season back in the minors at Salt Lake City, much to his chagrin, with the exception of a few games in the majors at the end of the season. 2000 was another story. By June, Ortiz had established himself as an every-day player. He batted .282 for the season. He acquitted himself well in

Sources

Periodicals

New York Times, June 29, 2004, p. D1; October 9, 2004, p. D3; October 19, 2004, p. D2.
Sports Illustrated, August 2, 2004, p. 149.
The Sporting News, November 1, 2004, p. 17.
USA Today, October 26, 2004, p. 1C.

On-line

"David Ortiz," *JockBio.com*, www.jockbio.com/Bios/ Ortiz/Ortiz_bio.html (March 1, 2005).
"David Ortiz Biography and Career Highlights," *Boston Red Sox,* http://boston.redsox.mlb.com/NASA pp/mlb/team/player_career.jsp?player_id=120074 (March 11, 2005).

—Bob Jacobson

Nicole Ari Parker

1970—

Actor

Parker, Nicole Ari, photograph. AP/Wide World Photos.

Stage and screen veteran Nicole Ari Parker is best known for her role as the icy attorney Teri on the acclaimed Showtime original series *Soul Food.* She and her real-life partner, fellow actor and *Soul Food* alumnus Boris Kodjoe, landed their own sitcom, *Second Time Around,* which made its debut on the UPN in the fall of 2004. Their tempestuous pairing on *Soul Food* had helped make the show a winner with viewers, and Parker told *Ebony* writer Zondra Hughes, "that's the great thing about *Second Time Around*—this show is fulfilling for the fans who loved Teri and Damon's relationship. They finally get to see Damon and Teri happy."

Born in 1970, Parker grew up in the Baltimore, Maryland, area, where her father was a dentist and her mother a health-care professional; they later divorced. She attended an all-female private school, where for a time she was the sole African-American student. Still, Parker's natural exuberance shone during her formative years, and her class-clown persona naturally led her into the high school drama club. She won top prize for best actress in a statewide student drama competition, and appeared in productions at the Baltimore Actors

Theatre and the Washington Ballet Company.

Broadway-Bound, Despite Parents

Parker's parents, however, were wary about the performing arts as an appropriate career for her, and she failed to tell them that she applied to New York University when college-application time came around. After she was accepted, she moved to New York City at age 17 and originally agreed to study English and journalism at NYU. She later switched to performing arts after winning a spot at NYU's Tisch School of the Arts. Eventually she landed roles in off-Broadway productions, and her stage credits grew to include *House Arrest: First Edition,* a play by Anna Deveare Smith, and the Signature Theatre Company's production of *Chicago.* She also had roles in *Romeo and Juliet* with the Metropolitan Playhouse and in *The Flattened Fifth* with the New Group.

Parker's feature film debut came in a little-seen independent feature film from 1995, *The Incredibly True Adventure of Two Girls in Love.* The romantic comedy chronicled the burgeoning affair between two young women from vastly different socio-economic

At a Glance . . .

Born on October 7, 1970, in Baltimore, MD; daughter of Donald (a dentist) and Susan (a health care professional) Parker; married Boris Kodjoe (an actor), 2005; children: one. *Education:* Attended New York University's Tisch School of the Arts.

Career: Baltimore Actors Theatre, Washington Ballet Company, Signature Theatre Company, Metropolitan Playhouse, and the New Group, stage actor, 1990s–; film actor, 1995–; television actor, 2000–.

Addresses: *Office*—c/o *Second Time Around,* 11800 Wilshire Blvd., Los Angeles, CA 90025.

backgrounds. Parker played Evie Roy, the high-schooler from a well-to-do family who loves literature and the opera. Other roles were slow to come, however, and Parker had some lean years in the Big Apple. "One of the things that really took a toll on me was the waiting," she recalled in an interview with Lori Talley for *Back Stage West.* "You hustle, hustle, and hustle, and then you wait."

Parker's break came in 1997 when she joined an outstanding supporting cast in *Boogie Nights,* the behind-the-scenes look at the porn-film industry in southern California in the 1970s. She played Becky Barnet, a star of X-rated films and one of the characters who manages to escape the exploitative industry unscathed. From there, Parker began to appear in other feature films, landing a starring role alongside Terrence Howard in *Spark,* a 1998 thriller in which they portrayed a Chicago couple stranded in a menacing desert town in the American West. She had roles in several films in 1999, including *200 Cigarettes, Loving Jezebel, A Map of the World,* and *Blue Streak.*

Won Kudos for
Entertainment-Exec Role

Parker's next major project was as the lead an original HBO movie, *Dancing in September.* She played television producer as Tomasina "Tommy" Crawford, who is determined to force onto the airwaves series that she believes more accurately portray, and perhaps even inspire, African-American viewers. After signing on with a new network with what she believes is a credible, well-written show, Tommy begins a romance with a network executive; when her show tanks in the ratings game, she is forced to make some distasteful changes. "In the end, the film's greatest pleasure is the opportunity it affords to watch Nicole Ari Parker sustain a

serious lead performance," noted *Variety* critic Todd McCarthy. "One of the sexiest young actresses on the scene today, she compellingly projects headstrong confidence as well as a certain vulnerable wariness as her character picks up speed on her way to crashing into a glass wall."

While delving into the world of television and how shows are written, Parker was stunned to find that it wasn't a cadre of white television executives deciding how minorities were portrayed on the small screen. "A lot of black women are writing the shucking and jiving, and the booty jokes," she told *Essence* in 2001. "That blew my mind!" For herself, she sought out more balanced roles as an actress, and indeed won some coveted ones: as Denzel Washington's wife in *Remember the Titans,* and as the fiancé of Taye Diggs's character in 2002's *Brown Sugar.*

But Parker's most significant role came on the Showtime series *Soul Food,* which debuted in 2000, three years after an acclaimed feature film of the same name upon which it was based. Parker played the eldest of a family of three sisters, the hardheaded attorney Teri Joseph. Vanessa Williams was cast as the next sister, a wife and mother, and the youngest, a hairdresser, was played by Malinda Williams. Each represented a different socio-economic milieu and domestic-partnership situation, with the larger supporting cast bringing other topical matters into the plotlines. The series, perhaps because it appeared on a commercial-free pay television channel, was allowed to grow, and seemed to hit its stride after the first season. In 2002, it became first African-American-centered drama on television to make it past a second season. "What makes 'Soul Food' so different is that it focuses on traditional family issues without sanding down the details of regular black life," remarked *Newsweek* writer Allison Samuels. "The producers cast African-Americans of all hues and then dig deep into a family full of love, disagreements and its fair amount of drama."

Soul Food's fans were entranced by Teri's on-again, off-again romance with Damon, a man whom she met when he was a delivery-person at her office. Damon, who would go on to a career as a translator, was played by bilingual actor Boris Kodjoe, of Ghanaian-German heritage. Parker was initially frosty when she first met the man who would become her real-life partner, she admitted to Hughes in the *Ebony* interview. "When he walked into the room, I thought, with some dismay 'Oh great, they've got a supermodel to play my boyfriend.' I mean he's obviously beautiful, but I was an actress from New York who wanted an established actor from New York to walk through the door."

Scored Hit with UPN Series

Life seemed to mimic art for Parker and Kodjoe when they began a real-life romance. *Soul Food* ran through 2004, and the pair found a new home on UPN as the stars of their own sitcom, *Second Time Around,* which debuted that fall. Parker played Ryan, an artist, while Kodjoe was cast as her architect-husband, Jackson. The pair have remarried, after a brief, earlier union that ended in divorce, and the show's plotlines revolved around the "opposites-attract" premise, with Parker's carefree, spirited Ryan often butting heads with her more earnest spouse. Its stars, noted a critic for *Entertainment Weekly,* possess a "rare on-screen chemistry that real-life acting couples so often lack."

During *Second Time Around's* first season, Parker announced that she and Kodjoe were about to become parents. Fans of *Soul Food* were thrilled to see her back on-screen with Kodjoe after a rocky five seasons of romantic ups and downs. That aforementioned chemistry had been apparent then, and it was to a producer of the new show as well. "I developed a deep admiration for their relationship while shooting the pilot and seeing that connection between the two of them, how they supported each other," Ralph Farquhar told *Jet.* "In one scene where Ryan tells Jackson: 'I love you' and as he says it back to her, you cannot pay for that chemistry. It would take a season or more to work up to that with actors who weren't connected."

Parker and Kodjoe were married in the spring of 2005, around the same time her next feature film, *King's Ransom,* was slated for release. Still keenly interested in shaping new and exciting roles for African-American actors, Parker was writing three separate film scripts. She still loves theater, though she has not appeared on stage in a few years. "It's the closest to real-life experiences," she enthused to Talley in the *Back Stage West* interview. "It's almost like you have to surrender to a higher power when you're onstage. The zipper on your dress could break, a light could fall, someone could miss their cue, and you just have to keep going. It's beautiful that way. It's like life."

Selected works

Films

The Incredibly True Adventure of Two Girls in Love, 1995.
Boogie Nights, 1997.
The End of Violence, 1997.
Spark, 1998.
The Adventures of Sebastian Cole, 1998.
200 Cigarettes, 1999.
Loving Jezebel, 1999.
A Map of the World, 1999.
Blue Streak, 1999.
Remember the Titans, 2000.
Brown Sugar, 2002.
King's Ransom, 2005.

Television

Soul Food, 2000-2004. ·
Second Time Around, 2004—.

Sources

Periodicals

Back Stage West, February 1, 2001, p. 13.
Cineaste, fall 1995, p. 46.
Ebony, October 2004, p. 168.
Entertainment Weekly, September 24, 2004, p. 99.
Essence, January 2001, p. 53.
Jet, September 27, 2004, p. 60.
Newsweek, July 8, 2002, p. 56.
Variety, March 2, 1998, p. 93; February 5, 2001, p. 43.

—Carol Brennan

Oscar Peterson

1925—

Jazz pianist

Peterson, Oscar, photograph. AP/Wide World Photos.

Canadian-born Oscar Peterson is generally acclaimed as one of the most spectacularly talented musicians ever to play the piano in the jazz genre. In the words of Scott Yanow of the *All Music Guide,* Peterson "plays 100 notes where other pianists might use ten"—and, Yanow contended in response to critics who accused Peterson of empty virtuosity, "all 100 usually fit." Peterson made hundreds of recordings over his 65-year career, and even a 1993 stroke that disabled his left hand did not really slow him down.

Peterson was born in Montreal, Quebec, Canada, on August 15, 1925. His father Daniel Peterson was a Canadian National railroad porter, born in the Virgin Islands, who loved classical music and jazz; his mother was of Caribbean background. Peterson started playing the piano at age five, taught at first by his sister Daisy. His older brother Fred introduced him to jazz, and Peterson later remembered Fred's skills as superior to his own. Fred Peterson died of tuberculosis when he was 16, but his younger brother picked up the torch. Oscar Peterson studied classical music with Paul de Marky, a Hungarian-born teacher who had studied with

an apprentice of the nineteenth-century virtuoso Franz Liszt. When he was about 14, Peterson took home first prize on a radio talent show and landed a weekly program on Montreal station CKAC.

Challenged by Tatum Disc

That led to appearances on nationally broadcast Canadian shows like "The Light Up and Listen Hour," and by 1942 he was performing with one of Canada's leading big bands, the Johnny Holmes Orchestra. But Peterson's father still knew how to cut his son down to size and challenge him further: he brought home a record by jazz pianist Art Tatum. "He said, 'You think you're so great. Why don't you put it on?' So I did," Peterson recalled to *Smithsonian* writer Marya Hornbacher. "And of course I was just about flattened.... I swear, I didn't play piano for two months afterward, I was so intimidated." When the two men met later on, Tatum correctly pegged Peterson as a likely successor to his own reign as king of jazz pianists. Another early admirer was bandleader Count Basie, who said in 1945 that Peterson "plays the best ivory

At a Glance . . .

Born on August 15, 1925, in Montreal, Quebec, Canada; son of Daniel (a train porter) and Kathleen Olivia John Peterson; married Lillie Fraser, 1944 (divorced); married Sandra King, 1966 (divorced 1976); married Charlotte Huber, 1977 (divorced); married wife Kelly, 1987(?); children: (first marriage) Lyn, Sharon, Gay, Oscar Jr., Norman; (third marriage) Joel; (fourth marriage) Celine. *Education:* Studied with classical pianist Paul de Marky, 1939(?).

Career: CKAC radio station, Montreal, regular performer, early 1940s; Johnny Holmes orchestra, toured Canada, orchestra member, 1942-47; formed first trio, 1947; Carnegie Hall, Philharmonic concert, performed, 1949; Jazz at the Philharmonic, toured United States and Europe, orchestra member, early 1950s; formed trio, with guitarist Herb Ellis and bassist Ray Brown, 1953; Ellis replaced by drummer Ed Thigpen, 1958; toured widely with own trios, early 1960s; performed as solo artist and with other top jazz figures, 1970s–.

Selected awards: Seven Grammy awards; numerous citations for best jazz pianist from *Contemporary Keyboard* and *Down Beat*; Order of Canada, 1972; Genie film award for best film score, 1978, for *The Silent Partner*; officer of the Order of Arts and Letters, France, 1989; named honorary chancellor, York University, Toronto, 1991.

Addresses: *Home*—Mississauga, Ontario, Canada. *Label*—Universal Music Group/Verve, 1755 Broadway, New York, NY 10019.

box I've ever heard," as quoted in the Canadian magazine *Maclean's.*

Peterson's breakthrough in the United States came in 1949, when jazz promoter Norman Granz heard him playing as part of a trio at Montreal's Alberta Lounge and invited him to perform at Carnegie Hall in New York with an all-star Jazz at the Philharmonic lineup. One widely told story holds that Granz was in taxi on the way to the airport in Montreal, heard a live Peterson broadcast on the radio, and insisted that the cab driver turn around and drive him to the club where the broadcast originated. Peterson had a similar impact on the audience that gathered at Carnegie Hall; on a

bill crowded with top-level jazz talent, including bebop saxophone pioneer Charlie Parker, Peterson (according to a *Down Beat* report quoted in *Maclean's*) "stopped the concert dead cold in its tracks."

Granz took the Jazz at the Philharmonic concept on the road in the early 1950s, and Peterson went along, visiting Japan, Hong Kong, Australia, and the Philippines in addition to 41 North American cities. Peterson formed a trio in 1953 with guitarist Herb Ellis and bassist Ray Brown. In 1956 the trio made one of Peterson's bestselling recordings, *At the Stratford Shakespearean Festival.* Ellis left the band in 1958 and was replaced by drummer Ed Thigpen. Jazz fans never tire of debating which of these classic ensembles was the better one; in the earlier group, each of the three members showed an uncanny awareness for the next move another might make, while the later combo, with its basically percussive sound, showed off Peterson's still-growing talent.

Founded School in Toronto

Despite his success in the United States, Peterson retained his ties to Canada for the rest of his life. He moved to Toronto in 1958 and with several other musicians founded the Advanced School of Contemporary Music, one of the earliest educational institutions devoted to jazz, two years later. The school lasted three years but eventually fell victim to the unflagging demand for Peterson's performances and recordings. The pianist gained fans all over the world, and he even appeared behind the Communist Iron Curtain in the Slovenian city of Ljubljana, then part of Yugoslavia, in 1964. That year, Peterson first made his mark as a composer with his "Canadiana Suite." Peterson branched out into the vocal realm in 1965 with the album *With Respect to Nat*—revealing a voice startlingly similar to that of the great pop singer.

Peterson had been recording for 20 years by that time, beginning with waxings made for the RCA Victor Canada label in the mid-1940s, and his catalog was vast. A few critics asserted that Peterson's playing lacked, in the words of a French reviewer quoted in *Smithsonian*, a "profound sense of the blues," but jazz fans continued to snap up the five or six recordings Peterson might issue in the course of a single year, many of them on the Verve label. He would eventually make more than 400 recordings. In the late 1960s he began recording for MPS, and he made the first of many recordings as a soloist in 1968. Many Peterson dates in the 1970s and 1980s featured him playing solo, at the peak of his powers. He formed another classic piano-guitar-bass trio in the 1970s with guitarist Joe Pass and Danish-born bassist Niels Pederson. Peterson composed film and television scored in the 1970s, and he built a recording studio in his home so that he could experiment with electronic keyboard and sound equipment. He reunited with Ellis and Brown in 1990, recording four CDs over two days. In addition to seven Grammy awards, Peterson could boast an array of other honors including the Order of Canada. He was the subject of two biographies and wrote an autobiography of his own, *A Jazz Odyssey: The Life of Oscar Peterson.*

Suffered Stroke

One of the sources of Peterson's dazzling, full sound was the vigorous activity of his left hand while he played. He is reputed to have reached down during one concert and lit a cigarette for a patron in the front row with his right hand, keeping up the flow of music all the while with his left. But in 1993, while performing at the Blue Note club in New York, Peterson noticed a numbness in his left hand, and by the end of the show he could hardly move it. Doctors diagnosed a stroke, and Peterson, depressed, stopped playing for two years. "The first day I sat at the piano with my therapist, I had tears in my eyes," he told Michael Anthony of the Minneapolis *Star Tribune.* But his fellow musicians proved a strong source of encouragement. Playing with a group, he told Anthony, was "the best therapy of all."

Peterson gradually resumed a full schedule of touring and recording, finding eager audiences among fans who wanted to witness a true jazz legend. Most of those fans didn't realize that Peterson was using his left hand only sparingly. Between engagements, he spent time at his home in suburban Toronto with his wife Kelly and daughter Celine, keeping in touch with six children from two of his three earlier marriages. A square in the heart of Toronto's financial district was named for Peterson in 2004. January of the year 2005 saw Peterson performing at the Canada for Asia concert in Toronto, with proceeds going toward the rebuilding of communities devastated by the Indian Ocean tsunami of the previous year.

Selected works

Albums

I Got Rhythm, RCA, recorded 1947-49.
Norman Granz Jam Session, Verve, 1952.
At the Stratford Shakespearean Festival, Verve, 1956 (reissued 1992).
On the Town, Verve, 1958.
The Trio (live), Verve, 1961.
Affinity, Verve, 1962.
Canadiana Suite, Mercury, 1964.
With Respect to Nat, Limelight, 1965.
The Way I Really Play, MPS, 1968.
My Favorite Instrument, MPS, 1980.
Saturday Night at the Blue Note, Telarc, reissued 1990.
A Jazz Odyssey, Verve, 2002 (issued in conjunction with autobiography of same title).
Solo: Live, Pablo, 2002.

Books

(With Richard Palmer as editor and consultant) *A Jazz Odyssey: The Life of Oscar Peterson,* Continuum, 2002.

Sources

Books

Contemporary Musicians, volume 11, Gale, 1994.
Palmer, Richard, *Oscar Peterson,* Spellmount, 1984.
Lees, Gene, *The Will to Swing,* Prima, 1990.

Periodicals

Maclean's, September 13, 1999, p. 48; September 4, 2000, p. 36.
Seattle Post-Intelligencer, June 30, 2004, p. D6.
Smithsonian, January 2005, p. 56.
Star Tribune (Minneapolis), February 16, 1999, p. E1.

On-line

"Oscar Peterson," *All Music Guide,* http://www.all music.com (May 4, 2005).

—James M. Manheim

Linda A. Randolph

1941—

Physician, public health official, president and CEO of the D.C. Developing Families Center

When Linda Randolph was only three years old, she turned to her mother as they left her pediatrician's office and announced that someday she, too, would become a doctor. Brought up in a family that valued education and creativity, Randolph grew to love learning and to believe in herself. She also developed a deep affection for the African-American community where she grew up, and she has devoted much of her career to helping solve the health problems of that community. In both New York and Washington, D.C., the two cities she considers home, Randolph has worked tirelessly at a multitude of influential jobs in the field of public health, making connections between race, class, education, childcare, and health that have broken new ground in improving community strength and well-being.

Randolph was born on March 9, 1941 in Washington, D.C. Her parents Oscar Horace Randolph and Marie Louise Fernandez had met in New Haven, Connecticut, before moving to Washington, where they married and had two daughters. Oscar Randolph's father had not believed in sending his children to school, but Oscar's older sister was determined that her younger brother would get an education. She took young Oscar

to live in New Haven, where he not only finished high school, but attended college for two years at Washington's Howard University. After leaving college he worked for many years as headwaiter at the Westchester Apartments, home to many influential Washingtonians and foreign diplomats.

Marie Fernandez Randolph also attended college for two years, then worked for four years in the personnel department of the Pentagon, the headquarters of the Department of Defense. After the birth of her daughters, she worked at home caring for her family.

Family Valued Education

For the first eleven years of young Linda's life, her family of four lived in a one-room apartment in the black section of the Adams Morgan neighborhood, which was still segregated during the 1940s and 1950s. One of the characteristics of black neighborhoods during segregation was that African Americans of all classes lived together, creating a community that included rich and poor alike.

At a Glance . . .

Born Linda Ann Randolph on March 9, 1941, in Washington, DC. *Education:* Howard University, BS, zoology, 1962; Howard University, College of Medicine, MD, 1967; Harlem Hospital Center, internal medicine and pediatrics internship, 1967-8; Harlem Hospital Center, pediatric residency, 1968-1970; University of California at Berkeley, MPH, maternal and child health, 1971; University of California at San Diego, certificate, perinatology, 1972; Harvard Business School, certificate, health systems management, 1974.

Career: Department of Health and Human Services, Project Head Start, director of Health Services, 1972-79; New York State Department of Health, Associate State Health Commissioner for New York City Affairs 1980-83; New York State Department of Health, Office of Public Health, director, 1983-91; Carnegie Corporation of New York, Task Force on Meeting the Needs of Young Children, executive director (on assignment from Mount Sinai School of Medicine), 1991-94; National Women's Resource Center for Substance Abuse and Mental Health, director, 1995-99; District of Columbia Developing Families Center (DCDFC), co-chief executive officer, 1999-2002; DCDFC, president and chief executive officer, 2003–.

Memberships: New York Academy of Medicine; AOA Medical Honor Society.

Awards: Public Health Association of New York City, Haven Emerson Award for Distinguished Service to Public Health, 1983; Westchester Black Women's Political Caucus, Leadership Award, 1987; New York State Federation of Professional Health Educators, Distinguished Service Award, 1988; Greater Harlem Chamber of Commerce, Community Service Award, 1994; American Public Health Association, Martha May Eliot Award for exceptional health services to mothers and children, 2001.

Address: *Office*—D.C. Developing Families Center, 801 17th Street, N.E., Washington, DC 20002.

Though the Randolphs were not wealthy, they thought little about being poor. Marie Randolph taught her children to be considerate of the downstairs neighbors by removing their shoes when they came in the door, because they had no rugs to soften their footsteps on the hardwood floors. Along with his work as a waiter, Oscar Randolph was an accomplished artist who painted and sculpted during his off hours. He worked six days a week, and on the seventh day he gave Marie a rest by taking the children to parks and museums where he spent hours teaching them about their city and the world.

In this atmosphere, young Linda grew to love school, reading, and writing poetry. She attended Morgan Elementary School, a "training school" where young teachers went to learn how to teach. As a result, the school was filled with energetic and inventive instructors who made learning fun and interesting. The school also had an extensive arts and drama program. Her presentations on stage in elementary school would prepare Linda Randolph for a lifetime of public speaking.

Along with her studies, Randolph also volunteered with the Junior Red Cross throughout her school years, helping with that organization's annual blood drive. Her attraction to a medical career was so apparent that her class prophecies in elementary, junior, and senior high school all foretold that she would become a doctor.

Though her experiences in elementary and junior high school were mainly positive and inspiring, Randolph's high school years were filled with the tension of a changing society. She entered high school in 1955, just after the U.S. Supreme Court ruled that public schools must be integrated. Previously, in Washington, D.C., and many other places, blacks had not been allowed to attend school with white students, and black schools often received less money and fewer supplies than white schools. Though integration of the schools was a more fair solution, it was not easy to achieve. Black and white students were not comfortable with each other, and many whites had racist attitudes towards blacks. Many whites who did not agree with integration simply took their children out of public schools. In 1955, when Linda Randolph started high school, her class was fifty percent black and fifty percent white. The teaching staff was ninety percent white and ten percent black. By 1958, when Randolph graduated, the class which followed her was ninety percent black, and fifty percent of the white faculty had resigned.

Upon graduation from high school, Randolph received a scholarship to nearby Howard University. She took pre-medical classes and worked evenings and Saturdays selling socks at Woolworth's, a local discount chain store. Even there she was surrounded by the rapidly growing civil rights movement, as Woolworth's "whites only" lunch counters were the focus of early demonstrations.

After her graduation from college, Randolph took a year off school and went to work full time for the federal government in the U.S. Patent Office. There she worked with some of the first computers, hand-coding data for entry into the system. After a year, she was ready to continue her education, this time in medical school.

Entered Medical School

Although Randolph was accepted into Howard's College of Medicine, there was no scholarship money available for first term students. She received help from her godmother, who privately gave Randolph money for her first semester. Even then, she had to use borrowed books to study. She worked hard to obtain loans and scholarships to finance the rest of her medical school career.

As Randolph was finishing medical school at Howard, New York's Harlem Hospital Center began recruiting graduates of traditionally black medical schools for their internship program. Eleven graduating doctors from Howard went to work in Harlem, and Linda Randolph was among them. She liked New York City and loved the feeling of contributing to the community that she got from her work with poor families at Harlem Hospital. It was in Harlem that her perspective deepened about the connections between the conditions of people's lives and their health problems. Throughout the rest of her career, Randolph would insist on the importance of viewing a patient as part of a family, a family as part of a community, and a community as part of a society.

After her internship and residency program was completed, one of Randolph's professors and mentors suggested to her that she might enjoy working in the field of public health. Public health is a part of health service which studies and works to improve the health of the community as a whole. At that time, the School of Public Health at the University of California at Berkeley was trying to recruit minority students. Randolph applied for and received a fellowship to study public health in California. After receiving her masters in public health, she decided to stay in California and work in the community there. She went to San Diego, where she worked in clinics and earned her certificate in perinatology. Perinatology is the branch of medicine which studies the biological, medical, and social issues which surround childbirth. In San Diego, Randolph studied and worked on issues such as infant intensive care and teen pregnancy.

Began Work in Public Health

After completing her training in California, Randolph had hoped to return to her work in Harlem. However, she received a tempting job offer in her hometown:

national medical director for Project Headstart, a program of the Department of Health and Human Services. Headstart was designed to help very young children from poor backgrounds and their parents by providing food, classes, and other support services. Randolph was reluctant to change her plans to return to Harlem. She was also hesitant to give up working directly with patients to take an administrative job. However, the directorship with Project Headstart was a very good job and a remarkable opportunity for a young doctor. She agreed to take the job for two years.

Randolph stayed at Project Headstart for seven years. She discovered she was very good at coordinating the many different health and social service programs nationwide that needed to work together to make the program effective. She made Project Headstart a better and more complete program by combining medical services with other health services, such as dental, nutrition, and mental health programs.

In 1980 Randolph began another important job in the public health field when she went to work for the New York State Department of Health as the Associate State Health Commissioner for New York City Affairs. There she was very successful at improving the often-difficult relations between the state and its largest city. Again, she planned to keep the job for only two years, and again she stayed longer. She worked as Associate State Health Commissioner for New York City Affairs for four years.

In 1983, the New York Commissioner of Health asked Randolph to come to the state capitol of Albany to take the job of Director of the Office of Public Health for the state of New York. Though she was reluctant to move from her beloved New York City to the smaller upstate town, she agreed to go to Albany, keeping her New York apartment for her frequent return trips to the city.

Randolph worked as Director of the Office of Public Health until 1991, when she was recruited to return to New York City full time to work at Mount Sinai Hospital in the Department of Community Medicine. At the same time she served as the director of the Carnegie Corporation of New York's Task Force on Meeting the Needs of Young Children. Her work with the Task Force was a continuation of what Randolph had done to solve the health problems of children, parents, and the community. To help young children, the Task Force developed a policy document called "Starting Points," which emphasized the importance of child health, childcare, responsible parenthood, and community support.

Returned to Washington

In 1995, Randolph returned to her childhood home of Washington, D.C., to be closer to her aging parents. She took a job as director of the National Women's Resource Center for Substance Abuse and Mental

Health (NWRC). Under Randolph's leadership, the Center trained teams of community members to recognize and help women with drug and alcohol addiction and mental health issues. As always, Randolph's approach was "holistic," that is, she taught those who worked for her to consider the patient's whole life experience when trying to identify and solve substance abuse or mental health problems.

In 1999, Randolph began her involvement with the District of Columbia Developing Families Center (DCDFC). The center had originally been the idea of Dr. Ruth Lubic, a New York City nurse-midwife who had envisioned a center which would meet the needs of both parents and children who had few resources. Traditionally, birth centers had mainly served middle-income and wealthy families. With the help of two local community organizations, Lubic renovated an old grocery store and set up a center that offered support for the entire family. The only center of its kind in the United States, DCDFC includes an out-of-hospital birth center, parenting support, and social services for families. The center places special emphasis on pregnant and parenting teens and maintains a child development program for infants and toddlers.

After leaving the National Women's Resource Center for Substance Abuse and Mental Health, Randolph had worked with the Georgetown University National Center for Education in Maternal and Child Health. As she grew more involved with the DCDFC, she gradually left her job at Georgetown and became, with Lubic, co-chief executive officer of the Developing Families Center. The values of the center seemed to include all of the issues that had been important to Randolph throughout her career, the health of mothers and children, the necessity of dealing with the entire family unit, and the need for community involvement.

Her job at DCDFC took Randolph back into the community, where she had always wanted to work.

The Developing Families Center hoped to change the idea that the birth of a baby is a medical procedure. Instead, Randolph and her co-workers have attempted to return childbirth to the family, as an empowering life experience. The goal of DCDFC is to follow families from birth to adulthood, offering services through which patients can take control of their own health care. In 2003, Randolph took over as president and CEO of DCDFC.

In addition to her work in the field of public health, Randolph has also worked to create better funding for community heath related projects. Part of this work was her founding in 2000 of the Fund for Greater Harlem, a fund-raising and grant-making organization through which Randolph hoped to make a contribution to the community where she received her training to be a doctor.

Sources

Periodicals

The Nation's Health, August 1994, pp. 6-7; October 2001, pp. 19-21.
Social Policy, Summer 1994, pp. 25-31.

On-line

"National Advisory Committee Members," *Community Health Scholars Program,* www.sph.umich.edu/chsp/program/nac.shtml (April 1, 2005)

Other

Information for this profile was obtained through an interview with Linda A. Randolph on April 1, 2005.

—Tina Gianoulis

Charles Rangel

1930—

Politician, activist

Congressman Charles Rangel of New York is one of the most influential and respected men in Washington, D.C. Since his legislative career began in 1970, he has been recognized as a dedicated, hardworking individual with a personality that is uniquely suited to political productivity. He expresses his opinions forcefully and stands by them steadfastly, but he is also flexible enough to compromise in order to effect change. His genial personality has helped him to form alliances with people whose philosophies are vastly different from his, and his overall competence has won him the support of many Republicans as well as that of his fellow Democrats.

Left Harlem for Military Service

Rangel was born in Harlem on June 11, 1930, the second of his parents' three children, and was raised by his mother and her father. He grew up amid the drugs and street crime that would later become his main concerns as an elected official. Rangel attended DeWitt Clinton High School in the Bronx but dropped out during his junior year. After working a few low-paying jobs that offered little in the way of satisfaction or potential, he enlisted in the U.S. Army in 1948. Sent to Korea, he took part in heavy combat there. After rescuing some forty soldiers from behind enemy lines, he was decorated with both the Purple Heart and the Bronze Star for valor.

Army life opened new doors for Rangel. He felt no desire to become a career soldier, and he found dis-

crimination in the service, as elsewhere. In fact, years later, during the Gulf War of 1991, he demanded that General Colin L. Powell, chairman of the Joint Chiefs of Staff, investigate claims by black National Guardsmen from Harlem that they had been treated disrespectfully and thrust into combat without proper training. But even though the Army was no haven of equal opportunity, Rangel's tour of duty was a pivotal life experience. For the first time he saw alternatives to the poverty that was the norm in Harlem, and he knew he would never go back to that way of life.

Discharged honorably as a staff sergeant in 1952, Rangel immediately began work on completion of his high school education. In one year's time he went through two years' worth of study and earned his diploma in 1953. By 1957 he had graduated from New York University's School of Commerce, becoming the first person in his family to get a college degree. His academic performance was stellar and won him a full scholarship to St. John's University, the largest Roman Catholic university in the United States.

In 1960 Rangel graduated from St. John's Law School and was admitted to the bar. His first year of practice wasn't particularly lucrative, but he did begin attracting a following among black civil rights activists, who appreciated his willingness to take on their cases. After a year in private practice, Rangel was appointed U.S. attorney in the Southern District of New York by Attorney General Robert F. Kennedy. Over the next few years he served in a variety of posts that deepened his insight into legal matters on both state and local

At a Glance . . .

Born Charles Bernard Rangel on June 11, 1930, in New York, NY; son of Ralph and Blanche (a seamstress; maiden name, Wharton) Rangel; married Alma Carter, July 26, 1964; children: Steven, Alicia. *Education*: New York University, BS, 1957; St. John's University, JD, 1960. *Politics*: Democrat.

Career: Admitted to the Bar of New York State, 1960; private law practice in New York City, 1960-61; assistant U.S. attorney in the Southern District of New York, 1961-62; served as legal counsel to various organizations and officials, 1963-66; New York State Assembly, state representative for the 72nd District of New York, 1966-70; U.S. House of Representatives, Washington, DC, congressman from the 16th District of New York, 1970–.

Memberships: Congressional Black Caucus, founding member, 1974; House Judiciary Committee during impeachment proceedings against President Richard M. Nixon; House Ways and Means Committee, 1975–; Select Committee on Narcotics Abuse and Control, 1976-(?); House Ways and Means Committee's Health Subcommittee, chairman, 1978-early 1980s; Democratic Steering and Policy Committee, member, 1979; Oversight Subcommittee, chairman; House deputy whip, 1983; Joint Committee on Taxation, 1980s–.

Awards: Jackie Robinson Foundation, Lifetime Achievement Award, 2005.

Addresses: *Office*—2354 Rayburn House, Washington, DC 20515; 163 W. 125th Street £737, New York, NY 10027. *Web*—www.house.gov/rangel.

levels. He was legal counsel to New York City's Housing and Redevelopment Board, associate counsel to the speaker of the New York State Assembly, legal assistant to Judge James L. Watson of New York, and general counsel to the National Advisory Commission on Selective Service.

Committed Himself to Public Service

In 1966 he was elected to the New York State Assembly as the representative for the 72nd District in Central Harlem. Before long he was the acknowledged leader on issues affecting working class and lower income people, yet he had also cultivated an alliance with the state's Republican governor, Nelson A. Rockefeller. Rockefeller was even able to get Republican support for Rangel during the representative's 1968 reelection campaign, which he won.

By 1970 Rangel was ready to make his bid for a seat in the national legislature. To do so, he had to challenge the longtime favorite of New York State's 16th Congressional District, Adam Clayton Powell. Powell, another Harlem native, was a high-profile, charismatic leader. Rangel expressed admiration for his opponent's past work but said that he felt compelled to run because the incumbent seemed to be growing lax in his duties. Rangel pointed to Powell's poor congressional attendance record as evidence that the people were not being well served.

Many former supporters of Powell agreed that he was becoming unpredictable and some even speculated that he had grown politically dangerous. Rangel's excellent performance on the state level gave rise to hopes that a fresh, competent congressman could bring about positive changes for Harlem and New York State. But Powell still had many loyal followers, and the primary race was extremely close. Out of 25,000 votes cast for the five men running, Rangel beat Powell by just 150. Compared to the primary, the general election later that year was a walkover—Rangel took 80 percent of the vote.

Rangel's first term as congressman was an active one. He was appointed to the Select Committee on Crime and was a key player in the passage of a 1971 amendment to existing drug laws that gave the president authority to reduce military and financial aid to any country failing to cooperate with U.S. efforts to stop international drug trafficking. His performance fulfilled his supporters' confidence in him, but his reelection in 1972 was by no means assured. The boundaries of the 16th District had been redrawn, and while it still included much of Rangel's core of support in Harlem, the redefined district also took in many white, middle-class streets on New York City's West Side. Rangel had to prove that his appeal was not limited to blacks.

The situation was further complicated by a primary challenge from Livingston Wingate, who, as the former director of a Harlem antipoverty organization, had grass-roots appeal. Furthermore, he had the backing of certain black nationalist groups Rangel had openly denounced, as well as support from many former followers of Powell. In the end, however, Rangel won the primary by a three-to-one margin. Since then, he has faced no serious challengers and has enjoyed the support of both Democratic and Republican voters.

Became Established in his Government Career

Throughout the 1970s, Rangel built up a solid reputation in the House of Representatives. In 1974 he was named chairman of the Congressional Black Caucus. He was in the public eye during 1974 and 1975 as a member of the House Judiciary Committee during the impeachment hearings against former U.S. president Richard Nixon; in that capacity he earned respect for his obvious grasp of the issues and his thoughtful questioning of the witnesses. In 1975 he became the first black appointed to the House Ways and Means Committee, which makes key decisions regarding tax and welfare legislation. In 1976 he was appointed to the Select Committee on Narcotics Abuse and Control; his fellow representatives from New York chose him as their majority regional whip in 1977; the next year he became chairman of the Health Subcommittee of the Ways and Means Committee; and by the end of the decade he was a member of the Democratic Steering and Policy Committee, a powerful group that guides the course of the Democratic party.

The late 1970s also saw Rangel become entangled in tensions between New York City's black communities and the mayor at that time, Ed Koch. In 1977 Rangel had backed Koch over Mario Cuomo (who later became the governor of New York) in the mayoral primary. Koch won the primary and the general election, but during his first term as mayor, many black leaders and voters became convinced that he was indifferent to their concerns. Rangel criticized the mayor for certain budget cuts affecting low-income neighborhoods, but he still supported Koch in 1981. Koch was reelected, but over the next two years he lost Rangel's backing. By 1983 Rangel's criticism of Koch had intensified, and rumor developed that Rangel might run for mayor in 1985. Other such rumors have circulated from time to time, but it now appears that Rangel is unlikely to leave Congress, where he has become so well established. He has stated that becoming House Speaker or chairing the Ways and Means Committee are his real political dreams.

Rangel's commitment to improving social conditions has remained strong throughout his years in office, and he continued to move into increasingly influential positions to help him further his goals. As the Reagan era dawned in the 1980s, Rangel gave up his chairmanship of the important Ways and Means Health Subcommittee to take over the Oversight Subcommittee. In that capacity, he was able to initiate probes into financial cuts to social programs such as welfare, Social Security, and Medicare. By 1983 he was one of the highest-ranking members of the Ways and Means Committee, and in that year House Speaker Thomas "Tip" O'Neill named him deputy whip of the House, bringing Rangel into the inner sanctum of Congress. Rangel continued his strong presence in the House into 2005 as a ranking member of the Ways and Means Committee.

Throughout his career, Rangel has taken an unabashedly liberal stance on most issues, even after the word "liberal" fell out of favor. As early as 1969, he endorsed the first national protest against the war in Vietnam. His voting record is consistently against interventionist foreign policies and excessive military spending, and included vehement opposition to the war in Iraq in the 2000s. He has voted in favor of busing to integrate schools, government funding for abortions, the creation of a consumer protection agency, and the abolishment of a cap on government funding of food stamps. In 2004 Rangel pushed for continued antipoverty funding, warning of the dire straits of the Temporary Assistance for Needy Families (TANF) program and the Child Care and Development Block Grant, among other welfare programs during the administration of President George W. Bush.

Urged Congress to Face Drug Crisis

Having grown up in Harlem, Rangel has a much clearer grasp than many of his political colleagues of how social problems manifest themselves on the street level. As a member of the New York state legislature, he sought to improve poor social conditions in his district without punishing those who suffer from them. For example, he worked to legalize gambling on numbers, knowing that it was already an accepted fact of life on the street. He fought a measure that would have meant longer jail sentences for prostitution, arguing that this would not address the issues that caused women to turn to that life. He has repeatedly denounced anti-drug measures that punish the user instead of the suppliers. When many of his fellow congressmen jumped on the antidrug bandwagon and began calling for harsh sanctions against drug abusers, Rangel protested. "Some of the things that sound rough and mean and antidrug…are really antipeople," he told *Time*.

Congressman Rangel is acknowledged as one of the best informed men in Washington on the subject of drug abuse. He considers the drug problem to be the most serious crisis in the United States. Years before most people came to see drugs as a national threat, Rangel was urging his fellow lawmakers to confront the issue. He contends that even though drug abuse is now a fashionable issue, most politicians are unwilling to dig into the problem. "We need outrage!" he told *Ebony* contributor Lynn Norment. "I don't know what is behind the lackadaisical attitude toward drugs, but I do know that the American people have made it abundantly clear: they are outraged by the indifference of the U.S. government to this problem. Not only is there a lack of commitment, but a feeling that we are not supposed to talk about it."

But Rangel is willing to talk about the problem at length, and he has very definite ideas about what needs to be done. He is vehemently against drug legalization, considering it "moral and political suicide," as he was quoted as saying in *Ebony*. Early in his career he fought a plan by the mayor of New York City to experiment with legalization by giving selected addicts maintenance doses of their drugs. "They just want to go into…Harlem and pick up 500 black and Puerto Rican guinea pigs," he was quoted as saying in the *New York Times* "The philosophy is 'keep them high, write them off.'"

Continued to Address Voters' Concerns

"We have to develop a comprehensive strategy attacking on all fronts," he told *Ebony*. "We could stop drug dealers cold in their tracks, ending sales, if we had effective anti-drug education in every classroom, in every church, out in the shooting galleries, in every community group, and on every radio station, TV station, in every newspaper and magazine." And although he had sharp criticism of President George Bush's military intervention to capture Panamanian strongman Manuel Noriega, Rangel favors a strong anti-drug component in the makeup of U.S. foreign policy. "Not one ounce of opium or coca, which are used to make heroin and cocaine and crack, is grown here on U.S. soil. Ending foreign supplies must become as important to the administration as stopping communism. It's not communists killing our kids; it's drugs," he concluded.

Rangel remained concerned with domestic affairs into the new millennium. He proposed legislation to increase public school funding every year since 1997, and he made national headlines in 2003 railing against Republicans for blocking Democrats from discussions about the future of Medicare. But he did not shy away from broader international challenges, specifically the war in Iraq. As the United States committed more troops to the Iraq war efforts, many, including Rangel, became concerned about America's ability to recruit volunteers to serve in the military. In 2003, Rangel, along with South Carolina Senator Fritz Hollings, proposed a universal draft to spread the burden of war among America's classes and races. Rangel explained in *Time* that the draft would "democratize" the military and "return to the 'citizen soldier' ideal that has served our nation so well." Debate over the draft provoked much discussion and controversy as the U.S. commitments in Iraq continued into 2005. Rangel remained

committed to the idea and renewed his call for a military draft in on May 26, 2005, citing "a 30 percent decline in enlistments, endangering the long-term viability of the U.S. military" as the crisis point in need of a remedy, according to a House press release.

Rangel's characteristic spunk was aptly captured by conservative columnist William F. Buckley Jr. in the *National Review*. Buckley described Rangel as "very bright and very witty and a public figure who rivals Barbara Walters for omnipresence." Although considered a potential vice-presidential candidate during the 2000s, Rangel made clear that he would rather remain focused on his work in the House. In his mid-seventies Rangel signaled no desire to retire, and showed no signs of even slowing down.

Sources

Periodicals

Black Enterprise, October 1983; January 1985; September 1989; July 1990; April 1991.
Ebony, March 1989; August 1989; December 1989.
Economic Opportunity Report, September 13, 2004.
Jet, December 16, 1991; November 24, 2003; August 2, 2004; August 30, 2004; May 9, 2005.
National Review, May 5, 2003.
New York Daily News, June 16, 1971.
New York Post, April 3, 1971.
New York Times, December 12, 1974; April 5, 1987; September 5, 1987; June 6, 1988; July 6, 1988; September 16, 1989; July 24, 1990; August 14, 1990; December 20, 1990; February 28, 1991; August 22, 1991.
Time, September 19, 1988; December 29, 2003.

On-line

Congressman Charles B. Rangel, www.house.gov/rangel (June 10, 2005).
"Press Release: Congressman Charles Rangel Renews Call for Military Draft," *U.S. House of Representatives,* www.house.gov/apps/list/press/ny15_rangel/CBRStatementDraft05262005.html (June 6, 2005).
Rangel for Congress, www.charlierangel.com (June 10, 2005).

—Joan Goldsworthy and Sara Pendergast

Lance Reddick

19??—

Actor

Renowned for his depictions of hard-edged characters on the television crime dramas *Oz* and *The Wire*, Lance Reddick has earned a reputation as a versatile and gifted actor. From his Shakespearean stage performances to his depictions of gritty urban street characters in contemporary television and film, Reddick has brought depth and complexity to an impressive range of roles.

Injury Led to Drama Study

Reddick, Lance, photograph. Peter Kramer/Getty Images.

A native of Baltimore, Maryland, Lance Reddick's year of birth is unknown. Reddick studied composition at the Eastman School of Music in Rochester, New York. He then moved to the Boston area, where he worked at various odd jobs while hoping to establish a career as a pop singer. At one time, he held four different jobs: delivering newspapers, delivering pizza, waiting tables, and working as an artist's model. But he suffered a slipped disc in his back while unloading a particularly heavy shipment of the *Wall Street Journal*, and was forced to quit that job as well as his other work. Reexamining his career prospects, Reddick decided to apply to Yale University's graduate school of drama, where he trained as an actor.

From the beginning, Reddick was involved with reputable and daring productions. His first job in the theater was as an understudy for *Angels in America*, the acclaimed play about AIDS and the Reagan era which was produced on Broadway in 1993-1994 and won that year's Tony Award for best play. Reddick then took a role in Anne Meara's off-Broadway production, *After-Play*. He also appeared in a Shakespeare in the Park production of *Henry V* in New York City's Central Park.

By the late 1990s, Reddick had begun to land small parts on television series, including *Swift Justice*, *The Nanny*, and *The West Wing*. He appeared in several made-for-TV films as well, including *What the Deaf Man Heard*, *Great Expectations*, *The Fixer*, *Witness to the Mob*, and *The Corner*. In 2000 he joined the cast of *Oz*, the HBO dramatic series set in a fictional maximum-security prison. Reddick played the part of Detective John Basil, a cop who goes undercover at the prison as Jamaican drug dealer Desmond Mobay. Already a cult hit, *Oz* was in its fourth season when Reddick came aboard, but he had never actually watched an episode. "I knew it by reputation," he explained in an Internet

At a Glance . . .

Born in 19??, Baltimore, Maryland; children: two. *Education:* Attended Eastman School of Music, Rochester, NY, and Yale Drama School.

Career: Screen, stage, and television actor, 1990s–.

Addresses: *Office*—c/o HBO, 1100 Avenue of the Americas, New York, NY 10036.

chat on *LiveWorld,* "because it has a reputation of being one of the best shows on television."

Oz's unflinching—and often very violent—realism brought the series both controversy and critical respect. Reddick found it "a joy" to play Mobay, he explained to *LiveWorld,* "because I get to play a character that's so real." Indeed, when asked by a *LiveWorld* questioner what he most admired about *Oz,* the actor immediately cited the show's realism. "I don't just mean sex, drugs, and violence," he added. "I also mean the complexity of the characters, the complexity of their relationships with one another, how they constantly change—just as they do in real life." Playing Mobay, he went on, taught him to be a better screen actor because it allowed him for the first time to develop an intense character over an extended period of time.

Played Major Role in HBO Series

Reddick also appeared in several episodes of the detective series *Falcone* and *Law & Order: Special Victims Unit.* In the former, he played Detective Willis Simms in three episodes; in the latter, he played the medical examiner in five episodes. His next major television role came in 2002 when he was cast as Lt. Cedric Daniels in the second season of the HBO series *The Wire.* Like *Oz, The Wire* was acclaimed for its realistic portraits of flawed characters—in this case, the residents of an impoverished Baltimore neighborhood and the police officers who try to keep its drug subculture in check. Daniels, a high-ranking officer with a law degree, has been demoted at the beginning of the season to a dead-end position in the evidence-control unit; the psychological complexity of his character's situation gave Reddick plenty of room to flex his acting skills.

Critics lauded *The Wire* for its boldness and uncompromising vision. Howard Rosenberg in the *Los Angeles Times* hailed it as a "genius series" that offered "provocative, achingly good, high-achieving television" notable for its "complex, densely written characters, first-class acting" and "seductive" storytelling. Every

actor in the "intriguing" series, according to *Boston Globe* critic Matthew Gilbert, was "memorable."

Reddick continued television work with guest appearances in *Law & Order: Criminal Intent* (2003) and *Law & Order* (2004). In 2003, he played Kwame Sekou in an episode of the Emmy-nominated series *100 Centre Street.* Roles in bigger films followed as well. Reddick was cast as Arnie in the thriller *Don't Say a Word,* which starred Michael Douglas, Sean Bean, and Brittany Murphy. He also played Jay Raymond Jones in the made-for-TV movie biopic of the life and career of Congressman Adam Clayton Powell, *Keep the Faith, Baby.* In 2004, Reddick appeared as acclaimed writer James Baldwin in the feature film *Brother to Brother,* about a young man's introduction to the personalities and achievements of the writers and artists who contributed to the artistic blossoming during the 1902s and 1930s known as the Harlem Renaissance.

Busy with television and film roles, Reddick also continued working on the stage. As he said in *LiveWorld,* he enjoys the different challenges that each type of work presents. The theater, he said, is exciting because it provides immediate responses from the audience. Reddick also enjoys "how much you have to use your body to communicate" onstage. "It's scary, and at the same time thrilling every night, because you never know quite what's going to happen," he added. Among his memorable stage roles was his portrayal of Marcus Antonius in the Guthrie Theater production of *Julius Caesar* in Minneapolis in 1999. The production, which critic Peter Ritter described as faithful to the original but set in "a sort of Orwellian netherworld of shadowy cabals and midnight machinations," earned accolades for its acting. In particular, Ritter admired Reddick's performance, noting that the actor "summoned a wiry, red-eyed intensity for his famous 'friends, Romans, countrymen' funeral oration."

Indeed, Reddick enjoyed performing Shakespeare, for which he was trained in graduate school. He noted in *LiveWorld* that he sees a definite connection between programs such as *Oz* and Shakespeare's works, because in both cases the writing defines each character so well. As an actor who welcomes controversial roles that make audiences think, Reddick seems to be cultivating the skills that will nourish a long acting career.

Selected works

Films

What the Deaf Man Heard (TV movie), 1997.
The Fixer (TV movie), 1998.
Great Expectations (TV movie), 1998.
The Siege, 1998.
Witness to the Mob (TV movie), 1998.
The Corner (TV movie), 2000.
I Dreamed of Africa, 2000.

Don't Say a Word, 2001.
Bridget, 2002.
Keep the Faith, Baby (TV movie), 2002.
Brother to Brother, 2004.

Plays

After-Play, New York, NY, 1994.
Henry V, Theater in the Park, New York, NY, 199?.
Julius Caesar, Guthrie Theater, Minneapolis, MN, 1999.

Television

Swift Justice, 1996.
The Nanny, 1997.
The West Wing, 1999.
Law & Order: Special Victims Unit, 2000-01.
Falcone, 2000.
Oz, 2000-2001.
The Wire, 2002.

100 Centre Street, 2002.
Law & Order, 2004.

Sources

Periodicals

Boston Globe, May 31, 2002, p. E14.
Los Angeles Times, May 30, 2002, p. E1.
Variety, November 17, 1997, p. 37.

On-line

"Chat With 'Oz''s Mobay," *LiveWorld,* www.liveworld.com (April 11, 2005).
"Lance Reddick: No Place Like Oz," *E!Online,* www.eonline.com (April 11, 2005).
"Roman Holiday," *City Pages* (Minneapolis and St. Paul), www.citypages.com (April 11, 2005).

—E. M. Shostak

John W. Rogers, Jr.

1958—

Investor, business executive

Once his father gave him shares of stock as a 12th birthday gift, John W. Rogers, Jr., was hooked on Wall Street. He secured the services of his own broker at age 18 and four years later, in 1980, became a broker himself. Raising $180,000 from family and friends, Rogers started his own investment firm, Ariel Capital Management, with one other employee in 1983. By 2004 Ariel had 73 employees, managed nearly $17.5 billion in assets for individuals, corporations, university endowments, and some of the nation's largest public and private pension funds, and was the largest black-owned investment firms in the country. In addition, Rogers created the first two mutual funds in the United States managed by African Americans; the Ariel and Ariel Appreciation Funds both received four-star ratings in 2004. By his mid-40s *Black Enterprise* recognized Rogers as a "master wealth builder."

Rogers was born into a prominent Chicago family in 1958. His mother, Jewel Lafontant, senior partner in a Chicago law firm and longtime figure in national Republican politics, was named ambassador-at-large and U.S. coordinator for refugee affairs by President George Bush in 1989. John Sr., a circuit court judge, instilled early business sense in his son by giving him shares of stock as Christmas and birthday gifts and allowing him a checking account where he could deposit the dividends and his allowance.

Except for one bounced check, John Jr. learned his early financial lessons well. Soon he was following the newspaper stock tables and watching the stock ticker prices race along the bottom of the television screen on Chicago's local business channel. He also spent a lot of time after school in the office of his father's broker, Stacy Adams, one of the first black stockbrokers in Chicago. At the age of 16, Rogers was hawking hot dogs, peanuts, and soft drinks during White Sox games at Comiskey Park, putting the earnings into more stocks and phoning Adams to check on their progress during his work breaks.

Rogers graduated from the highly regarded University of Chicago Laboratory School in 1976, the same year he played on the Illinois Class A, All-State Hall of Fame basketball team. Attending Princeton University as an economics major, he quickly found a local broker whose enthusiasm convinced him that he, too, could be successful in the field. While in college, Rogers flew to the West Coast to appear on the *Wheel of Fortune*, winning $8,600 in prizes that he immediately invested with his broker.

After graduating from Princeton in 1980, Rogers went to work as a stockbroker for William Blair & Company, a Chicago investment banking firm. Besides being the first person hired directly out of college by the company in more than four years, he was the first black professional ever to work at the 400-employee firm.

For Rogers, it was the perfect place to learn his trade. The company had everything under one roof—corporate finance, public finance, trading, money management, mutual funds, and research—and specialized in small-company stocks. With experience and omnivorous reading of financial newsletters, magazines, and investment classics like *Security Analysis* and *A Random Walk Down Wall Street*, Rogers quickly began to develop his value-oriented investment strategy.

Less than three years later, at the age of 25, he left William Blair & Company to form Ariel Capital Management, named after the fleet and nearly extinct African and Asian mountain gazelle. Starting with only one major account—$100,000 worth of Howard University's endowment fund to invest—within six months Rogers and an employee had raised an additional $190,000 in investment capital. From then on Ariel Capital moved nearly as swiftly as its namesake, growing to $45 million in managed assets by 1986.

Family ties helped Rogers's rapid rise in the financial world. His mother was an early investor and remained part-owner of Ariel until her death in 1997. More importantly, her business connections helped open doors. She was a trustee of Howard University, and two other corporations where she served on the board of directors, Revlon and Mobil, later became Ariel clients. The firm also landed such accounts as the retirement funds of city employees in Chicago, Detroit, Los Angeles, and the District of Columbia. But, connections aside, the bottom line is results. "Our private clients can judge us by just one thing," Rogers told *Forbes*, "growth of assets."

To that end, Rogers quickly perfected a creative but conservative investment style best summed up by Ariel's motto, borrowed from Aesop's fable about the tortoise: "Slow and steady wins the race." His overriding philosophy is one of patience, timing, and making the most out of a down market. Unlike many investors, he has no sophisticated computerized trading programs. Rogers avoids buying into the current "hot" stock trends of any given moment, and he does not look for potential takeover targets with share prices that might quickly jump. Instead, he seeks out lesser-known, undervalued companies that produce quality products, then invests long-term in their stock.

Intensive research is the key to finding these companies. Rogers devotes several hours a day to reading five morning newspapers, nine business magazines, and more than 80 newsletters, including his own entitled *The Patient Investor*. He likes to concentrate on smaller companies with market capitalization of $50 million to $1 billion and good earnings records that "do one thing very, very well, and have a well-established niche," he told *Financial World*. Many of these firms are too small to be followed by the bigger Wall Street investors.

Rogers also looks for companies in currently unpopular industries, companies experiencing a temporary setback in earnings, or companies newly created by spinoffs and asset sales, and he aims to find them before they are discovered by other investors. Other criteria are effective and committed management, a clean, simple, and easily-understood balance sheet, good cash flow, and a low debt-to-capital ratio.

"A lot of our work is really tire kicking," he explained in *Black Enterprise*, "going out and visiting the companies, getting to know the employees and management, and talking to the customers, competitors and suppliers. The final judgment is whether there will be long-term demand for that product." Rogers expects the earnings of the companies he invests in to grow at a consistent 12 percent to 15 percent annually.

There are several types of companies, however, that Rogers never invests in. He stays away from cyclical industries like heavy machinery, steel, and automobiles because of their frequent ups and downs. He avoids all start-up companies, regardless of their business, because they have no track record. Commodity stocks like precious metals, gas, and oil are too volatile for his taste, while trucking, airline, banking, and other recently deregulated industries are, in his mind, still working themselves out in their new environments and, therefore, are not good buys. "We don't make exceptions," Rogers said in *Changing Times*. "We're very rigid."

Even more important to Rogers is his strict code of socially conscious investing. He will not buy the stock of any company that does business with South Africa. Nor will he invest in defense contractors, nuclear utilities, cigarette manufacturers, and companies that make weapons or harm the environment.

"The principles just make investment sense," he told *Fortune* magazine. "Many defense companies are too reliant upon big government contracts. This reliance pressures management into doing unethical things to get and keep those contracts," he explained. "I don't own nuclear utilities because I don't like investing in companies that the courts might put out of business. The same goes for cigarette makers: I don't want to invest in a business everyone is trying to outlaw." In fact, when Kraft, one of Rogers's corporate clients, became a part of tobacco manufacturing giant Philip Morris Companies Inc., he terminated business with them.

Rogers's patient, disciplined approach has worked. Some of his earlier successes included investments in companies that manufacture toothbrushes, hospital uniforms, desktop stacking trays, plastic binders, baseball cards, and milk-shake machines. And he has also been known to take advantage of a down market, investing, for instance, $9 million in Caesar's World, the hotel and gambling casino firm, when its stock hit a low of $17 per share during the October 1987 stock market crash. By July of 1992 Caesar's price per share had risen 80 percent. By 2005 Caesar's Entertainment had become the world's largest casino gaming company and remained a part of Ariel's investments.

"Ariel is one of the few managers dealing with the middle-size, unknown, basic-business type of company, and those companies are the ones that have led the [stock market] charge since the crash," Edward G. Lloyd, former senior vice-president of the United Negro College Fund (UNCF), said in *Business Week*. The UNCF was one of Rogers's early clients, joining Ariel in 1984 and seeing its initial investment grow by 140 percent over the next four years. Rogers claims similar results for his other big-money institutional clients, which have included Chrysler, Ford, Procter & Gamble, AT&T, Pillsbury, Sara Lee, and the Stroh Brewing Company. In fact, from 1987 to 1990 Rogers's clients saw their total assets rise more than 53 percent, compared to the nearly 29 percent gain posted by Standard & Poor's index of 500 stocks.

"We were successful during the '80s because we picked some good, reasonably priced small stocks," he told *Black Enterprise*. "We avoided the go-go, glamorous small stocks that soared in 1980 and then plunged by 1985. Instead, we stuck with low-expectation stocks that didn't go up as much, but also didn't suffer as much."

Ariel's institutional clients have average investment accounts of worth tens of millions of dollars. To attract smaller investors, Rogers organized two mutual funds that followed socially responsible investment practices. The Ariel Fund, started in 1986, invests in small companies. From its inception to 2005 the Fund appreciated more than 14 percent annually, growing to $4.5 billion in assets, placing it second among eleven small-company funds followed and ranked by Lipper Analytical Services. His Ariel Appreciation Fund buys stock in mid-sized companies as large as $15 billion. It grew to $3.2 billion in total assets and gained 12.9 percent in value annually from its start in 1989 to 2005. Lipper Analytical Services ranked it eighth out of 51 funds. Ariel also started a money market fund in 1988 and a bond fund in 1995.

But Rogers's very success has caused problems and forced a change in the way he prefers investing. So much new money has flooded his firm and his mutual funds that he can no longer specialize in the small-company stocks that made his reputation. Back in 1986, when he managed only $45 million, Rogers could put 5 to 10 percent of Ariel's total capital in 10 or 20 carefully targeted small companies without disturbing their share price or ending up with too large a percentage of their stock. When their share prices rose, Ariel's total return appreciated accordingly.

However, as a multibillion-dollar money manager since the early 1990s, Rogers can no longer operate this way. His total assets are too large to permit such a concentrated investment strategy among selected small firms without severely jolting their share price. As a result, he must either scatter his investment portfolio among hundreds of small companies, diluting his overall return, or focus on much larger firms. Rogers has tried to steer a middle course. Telling *Forbes* in 1991, "We can't take on any more new cash and still preserve our focus," he stopped seeking institutional clients and closed the Calvert-Ariel Growth Fund to new investors. This has allowed him to continue pursuing small companies while simultaneously investing in larger, more well-known firms like Clorox, Hasbro, and the Fleming Companies. In 2004, Rogers reported to *Forbes* that his original business plan still fit his company.

But he wasn't surprised by his success. "This is what I thought could happen if we did it right," Rogers told *Forbes*. "I used to talk about this with my mom all the time; everyone knows about the brands EBONY and Jet. I wanted people to believe that Ariel Mutual Funds could be that kind of brand where African-Americans all around the country, as well as White Americans, would know that when it comes to mutual funds, you think about Ariel. And that you understand that our long-term investing approach could work for you too...Well, we're getting there. I think what has helped, too, is the [tortoise] and the patience."

Rogers continues his workaholic six-day weeks to find the necessary time to keep up with all his managerial duties and research responsibilities and to write his regular column for *Forbes*. Yet people continue to underestimate him, Justin F. Beckett, senior vice president of NCM Capital Management in Durham, North Carolina, told *Black Enterprise*. "They see a mild-mannered, soft-spoken person, but he is a pure competitor who is out to win." As Ariel President Mellody Hobson put it to *Ebony*, Rogers "is respected and adored by people...nobody doesn't like John Rogers. People want him to succeed."

Sources

Periodicals

Black Enterprise, April 1992; June 2002; January 2005.
Business Week, July 11, 1988.
Changing Times, September 1990.
Ebony, August 2004.
Financial World, April 18, 1989.
Forbes, September 2, 1991.
Fortune, July 16, 1990.
Jet, April 8, 2002.
Pensions and Investments, October 27, 2003.
World Press Review, May 1989.

On-line

Ariel Mutual Funds, www.arielmutualfunds.com/frames/fs_contact.htm (May 31, 2005).

Other

Additional information was obtained from John Rogers's office on October 14, 1992.

—James J. Podesta and Sara Pendergast

Brenda Russell

1944(?)—

Vocalist, composer, keyboardist, producer

Russell, Brenda, photograph. Wenn/Landov.

Singer, songwriter Brenda Russell's talent has earned her new fans and the respect of industry peers since she sang her way through the Age of Aquarius in the rock musical *Hair.* During this time of the Beatles, hippies, campus unrest, love-ins, and the Vietnam War, youth culture took its music seriously, and Russell began to make a name for herself. Russell sang smooth R&B and pop sounds with sensitive and timeless lyrics that are still being covered by artists today. Through the years Russell composed many hits that have earned her and other industry greats the industry's top awards. Her projects have taken her to the movies, writing lyrics with Stevie Wonder for Denzel Washington's movie *John Q.* In 2004 she co-wrote the score for the stage version of Alice Walker's *The Color Purple.* New fans have discovered a gem and fans who came of age with Russell understand her staying power. Her voice remains strong and her beauty endures.

Brenda Gordon (Russell) was born in the 1940s (some sources say April 8, 1944) in Brooklyn, New York. It was evident at a very early age that she could sing, as the story goes: There she was, eyes closed, no older than three, standing at the radio crooning note for note

to a popular jazz tune. "My mother just froze," Russell said in an interview with *Contemporary Black Biography* (*CBB*). "She couldn't believe it." That's how they knew Russell had talent. How could she not? It was all around her. As a kid, Russell would listen at the window as doo-woppers sang on the street corners. "I was thrilled," Russell said. "It was just riveting to see that music could travel so far and touch someone." Talent also runs in the family. Her father, Gus Gordon, was one of the Ink Spots, a popular singing group from the 1930s and 1940s. He later became a member of the Bill Johnson Quartet. Russell's mother, Cinnamon Sharpe, sang and wrote songs, occasionally calling on young Russell for help singing harmony as she rehearsed.

Found Lucky Breaks in Canada

When Russell was twelve, she moved to the little town of Hamilton, Ontario, south of Toronto where her father had settled. It was culture shock moving from a black neighborhood in Brooklyn to a predominantly white area in Canada, but Russell made the adjustment.

Although she later "felt ostracized by the whole dating thing" because of the shortage of black boys at school, Russell made a plan for herself. "I decided if I couldn't get a date for the dances, I'll be the band," Russell told *CBB*. And she's been the band, the singer, and the songwriter ever since.

Two days after graduation, Russell and some friends hung around back stage at a local event in Burlington, Ontario, hoping to get free tickets when they were approached by the manager of the Tiaras, the group performing that night. He wanted to know if Russell was a singer; they needed one. That night they all got in free and Russell became a member of the group; it was her first professional gig. Russell's dreams were coming true. "I knew I wanted to make my income doing music," Russell said to *CBB*. "I used to pray that I would never have to work a nine-to-five job."

In 1969 *Hair—The American Tribal Love/Rock Musical* opened its Canadian run in Toronto with Russell as a cast member. The show, with its themes of love, peace, war and hippies, along with a catchy score and a little bit of nudity, would become a symbol of the times, and ran in the city until 1971. "Those were liberating, heady days," Russell told *CBB*. "It was a training ground for me although I didn't realize it at the time. I learned everything developing as an artist in Toronto. There were so many hippies walking around. We would stop traffic and they would let us perform to the crowds. There was all this different music in a one block area, jazz, country, everything." *Hair* helped kick start the careers of many besides Russell: Ben Vereen, Donna Summer, Melba Moore, Nell Carter, and Meatloaf were just a few.

Learned to Write a Good Song

After the rock musical's run ended, Russell, with several *Hair* cast members, joined a musical group called Dr. Music in 1972. "It was the hippest group around at the time and we toured the country," said Russell. But Russell had learned more than how to be a part of a group in *Hair*. She left Dr. Music within a year and began her own career. "I planted my roots, learning how to write a good song and we did a lot of covers and commercials," she said. Russell had discovered her songwriting talent while teaching herself to play the piano during the *Hair* run. "I used to practice in the lobby of the theater but the owner heard about it and locked the piano." Not to be deterred, Russell soon found another piano—with the help of the musical director—and she continued to develop her own songs. Talking about her desire to learn more about music, Russell revealed a powerful inner drive. "I knew I wanted to be big," Russell remembered to *CBB* about her early ambitions. But her talents surprised her. She knew she could sing, but "It was the writing thing that I didn't know would be so powerful," Russell told *CBB*.

In the early 1970s Russell married Brian Russell and the two moved to Los Angeles where they found work as session singers and sang background for several Neil Sedaka performances. Elton John happened to be watching and liked what he heard; the couple joined John's Rocket label in 1976 and recorded two albums. Their songs were now being recorded by Jermaine Jackson, Tata Vega, Paulette McWilliams, and Rufus. In 1978 the couple separated, but it didn't slow Russell down. She released her debut album *Brenda Russell* the following year, which peaked at 26 on the Black Albums chart. In 1981 Russell released *Love Life* and in 1983 the album *Two Eyes*. Next Russell did a guest solo singing lead for Herb Alpert's *Wild Romance* album in 1985. She then spent some time in Stockholm, Sweden, where she wrote and recorded the song "Get Here."

Russell returned to the states, and in 1987 penned "Dinner with Gershwin" for her fellow cast member from *Hair*, Donna Summer. Russell released *Get Here* as an album in 1988, which included her very popular single "Piano in the Dark." The album peaked at 20 on the Top R&B/Hip-Hop Albums chart. The title single from the album earned the 37th spot on the chart that same year. "Piano in the Dark" peaked in the top ten on the Adult Contemporary, the Hot R&B/Hip-Hop Singles & Tracks, and the Billboard Hot 100 charts. "Piano in the Dark" earned a Grammy nomination for Song of the Year and Best Pop Duo Performance; "Get Here" was nominated for best Pop Female Vocal. "Get Here" was later recorded by Oleta Adams placing the single in the top ten on several charts and becoming an anthem of sorts for soldiers returning from the Gulf War.

Gained Enduring Respect from Her Industry

In 1990 Russell produced a track for a Marilyn Scott album and recorded duets with Gerald Alston and Cart

Anderson. She also released *Kiss Me With the Wind,* her fifth album. Russell's next creation, *Soul Talking,* released in 1991; *Paris Rain* came along in 2000, which Russell also co-produced. Russell's album *So Good So Right,* a retrospective compilation, was released in 2003 featuring the single "It's a Jazz Day." In 2004 Dome Records released her ninth album, *Between the Sun and the Moon.*

Russell's talents were acknowledged by the number of top artists who covered her tunes: Luther Vandross sang "If Only For One Night;" Roberta Flack did "My Love For You;" Earth, Wind & Fire performed "I've Had Enough" and "You." Other of her compositions have been recorded by the likes of Peabo Bryson, Solomon Burke, Ray Charles, Joe Cocker, Rita Coolidge, Al Jarreau, Chaka Khan, Patti LaBelle, Ramsey Lewis, Johnny Mathis, Ann Murray, Phil Perry, Diana Ross, Patrice Rushen, Tavares, Tina Turner, Dionne Warwick, Nancy Wilson, and many others. Collaborating with Brazilian composer Ivan Lins, Russell penned "She Walks This Earth," which won Sting a Grammy award in 2001 for the Best Pop Vocal Performance category. When Russell partnered with Stevie Wonder for the film *John Q,* co-writing lyrics to Wonder's song—"Justice of the Heart," it was clear that he understood the value of collaboration with Russell. Russell told Dale Kawashima in an interview with *Songwriters Universe Magazine* that when she first heard about the project and contacted Wonder, he responded with a return call saying "Sure Brenda, I'll win an Oscar with you." In 2004 Russell joined with Steven Bray and Allee Willis to write the music, lyrics, and score for the stage production of the Pulitzer Prize-winning novel *The Color Purple.* The show opened in Atlanta to standing ovations and sold-out performances and will open on Broadway in 2005.

Inspired by the Beatles

Considering the talents of other songwriters, those who might be called "genius," and the artists who influenced her most, Russell confided to *CBB* that John Lennon and Paul McCartney and the music of the Beatles "heavily influenced" her early years, as did Motown music. "That's what helped me learn how to write songs," she said of her early influences. "But the Beatles were more interesting on one level because they explored territories outside the boundaries of basic song structure. They went over here and back here and you never knew what was coming. And that was exciting to me, that they broke the traditional song structure for pop music." She also found inspiration in other women, especially "the women who played their own songs like Carol King, Nina Simone and Joni Mitchell, who played piano and sang," she told *CBB.* Russell didn't limit herself to rock and roll and pop music. She relished the songs of the thirties and forties. "I'm a big Gershwin fan," she said. Still Russell listed

McCartney, Lennon, Stevie Wonder, and Elton John "at the top of my list."

Though Russell could pinpoint several inspirations for her musical tastes, she found the inspiration for her compositions difficult to explain. "The only thing I can tell you is once I relaxed I was a channel for the music and it got a lot better. It wasn't all about me. I just had a desire and I put it out there until I learned how to play piano and how to write songs. I have this incredible desire to write songs and to do it with all my heart and my passion and my truth, and because of that, beautiful melodies come to me in exchange for that desire, that's how I see it."

Russell recognized that her success was nurtured by several fountains of inspiration. For new artists in the industry who hope for success and fame Russell offered the following advice: "Stay true to yourself; it's the most nurturing thing you can do. Learn from others but don't' lose yourself. If you've got a great gift that's what people understand, and sometimes people try to make you into something that you are not. That is what kills an artist. Remember you can always keep doing who you are." Certainly her long career is proof of her convictions.

Selected discography

Albums

Brenda Russell, A & M, 1979.
Love Life, A & M, 1981.
Two Eyes, Warners, 1983.
Get Here, A & M, 1988.
Kiss Me with the Wind, A & M, 1990.
Soul Talking, EMI, 1991.
Greatest Hits, A&M, 1992.
Paris Rain, Hidden Beach Recordings, 2000.
Ultimate Collection, Hip-O/Universal, 2001.
So Good, So Right, Dome Records, 2003.
Between the Sun and the Moon, Dome Records, 2004.

Singles

"So Good, So Right," 1979.
"Way Back When," 1980.
"Get Here," 1988.
"Gravity," 1988.
"Piano in the Dark," 1988.
"Le Restaurant," 1989.
"Stop Running Away," 1990.

Sources

On-line

"Brenda Russell," *Diva Station.com,* www.divastation. com/brenda_russell/brussell_bio.html (April 15, 2005).

"Brenda Russell Returns with Her New Album, *Paris Rain*, and Top Writing Collaborations," *Songwriter Universe Magazine,* www.songwritersuniverse.com/russell.html, (April 12, 2005).

"Brenda Russell," *VH1.com,* www.vh1.com/artists/az/russell_brenda/bio.jhtml (April 12, 2005).

Other

Additional information for this profile was obtained through an interview with Brenda Russell on April 22, 2005, and through publicity material supplied by Seth Keller of SKM Artist Management.

—Sharon Melson Fletcher

Bobby Short

1924-2005

Singer

Short, Bobby, photograph. Frank Micelotta/Getty Images.

After he took up residence in the lounge of New York's elegant Hotel Carlyle in the late 1960s, vocalist and pianist Bobby Short became an icon of New York and American cultural life. Short called himself a saloon singer, but actually he roosted at the top of the hierarchy of entertainers who perform in cocktail lounges, and indeed he did much to define the modern categories of lounge singer and cabaret singer. New York visitors stopped in at the Café Carlyle for decades to hear Bobby Short, to glimpse the lifestyles of the city's well-heeled residents, and to take a tour through the classics of American popular song with one of its most knowledgeable curators for a guide.

Robert Waltrip Short, the ninth of ten children, was born in the small town Danville, Illinois, on September 15, 1924. His father was a coal miner from Kentucky who sometimes landed higher-paying jobs, and the family had a piano and a radio tuned to jazz. At age four, Short taught himself to play the piano. The resourcefulness that put Short on the road to performing in posh nightclubs was inherited in part from his mother. She "taught survival. I think she had a framework of cast iron," Short told CNN. The young musi-

cian had a childhood remarkably free of racial discrimination. "There was a total absence of any kind of overt racial prejudice in those years, and it was kept that way by our teachers—which I was not aware of then," he wrote in his autobiography, *Black and White Baby.*

Began Performing at Age Nine

But survival instincts were necessary after the Great Depression of the 1930s hit the Short family hard. When he was nine, Short began to supplement the household's income by playing and singing in taverns. His skills developed quickly, and he turned into something of a teenage sensation. Agents who heard of his talent booked him into clubs and hotels in Chicago and New York. Short developed a taste for fine clothes, and later in life he would frequently appear on lists of best-dressed men. But his father's death in 1936 interrupted his high-flying career; he went back to Illinois to be with his family.

Short launched his adult career in 1942, performing at Chicago's Capitol Lounge. His reputation spread, and he landed nightclub slots in other large cities. Some-

At a Glance . . .

Born Robert Waltrip Short on September 15, 1924 in Danville, IL; died on March 21, 2005 in New York; ninth of ten children; children: one adopted son.

Career: Capitol Lounge, Chicago, singing debut, 1942; toured United States, 1940s; Cafe Gala, Los Angeles, singer, 1948-51; England and France, toured, early 1950s; Atlantic label, recording artist, 1955-90(?); Hotel Carlyle, New York, singer, 1968; Telarc label, recording artist, 1993-(?); nine-piece band, co-founder, 1997.

Selected awards: Two Grammy awards; New York Landmarks Conservancy, Living Landmark honor, 1994.

times he shared a bill with singer Nat "King" Cole, a friend who influenced his expressive vocal style. By 1948, Short was a regular at the Cafe Gala in Los Angeles, staying there for three years and leaving only when he felt that he had become stuck in a "velvet-lined rut," as he was quoted as saying in the *Times* of England.

Indeed, Short constantly tried to expand his musical horizons. In the early 1950s he traveled to Paris, finding club jobs there and adding a layer of sophistication to his stage personality. Short also spent time in England, and his speaking voice took on a British accent. His clear diction became one of his trademarks; gradually, he gained the ability to lead listeners through the complicated lyrics of classic Broadway songs by Cole Porter and other composers.

Landed Carlyle Engagement

Short returned to the United States in the mid-1950s and recorded about a dozen albums for the Atlantic label, owned by jazz- and blues-loving Turkish-American brothers Ahmet and Nesuhi Ertegun. Working at the height of the rock and roll era, Short was never a chart-topping artist on the order of Atlantic labelmate Ray Charles. But other musicians admired them; trumpeter Miles Davis named Short as an influence on his own "cool jazz" style. Today, Bobby Short's Atlantic albums are valuable collector's items.

The second flowering of rock music in the 1960s also slowed Short's career. Rather than bemoaning his bad fortune, however, Short spent hours honing his craft, following the inspiration of classical musicians like

African-American opera singer Shirley Verrett, a good friend. In 1968 the Ertegun brothers recommended Short for a fill-in slot at the Cafe Carlyle, located in a durably elegant Central Park-area hotel. Short won the approval of both the hotel's old-money patrons and the tourists who came to the Carlyle to rub elbows with them. In the late 1960s he cemented his reputation by giving two well-received concerts with nightclub vocalist Mabel Mercer at New York's Town Hall.

Short fulfilled the two key requirements of high-end cabaret singing: he brought the established classics of popular song alive, yet his own style was distinctive and personal. Short knew thousands of songs, and Broadway connoisseurs could count on hearing an unknown gem by Cole Porter or George and Ira Gershwin over the course of an evening at the Carlyle. Even though he performed twice a night, five nights a week, for six months a year, Short rarely repeated himself.

As a vocal stylist, Short was quite unusual. *New Yorker* jazz writer Whitney Balliett wrote that Short had "a searching down sound": a versatile baritone that could unexpectedly drop into a gruff tone or emphasize psychologically significant points in a song's lyrics. Short could bring out the sexy qualities that lay behind the conventional rhymes of Broadway pop, and he could find an elegant quality in more raucous old jazz and blues songs. He often performed blues diva Bessie Smith's "Gimme a Pigfoot (And a Bottle of Beer)." Short tried to uncover African-American roots of the classic Broadway sound, and he often revived little-known pieces by the likes of Thomas "Fats" Waller and his Madagascarian-American lyricist, Andy Razaf.

Friendship with Gloria Vanderbilt Caused Controversy

Although Short had no taste for controversy, he did become involved in one well-publicized dispute with racial overtones. The situation arose as a result of Short's long friendship with heiress Gloria Vanderbilt, who was turned down by the board of the posh River House condominiums when she tried to buy a unit there—because, she alleged in a lawsuit, the board feared that she and Short would marry. The dispute eventually simmered down, and Short became one of the few African Americans included on New York's Social Register of prominent citizens. He never married, but he adopted a son, Ronald Bell.

Short made nationally prominent film and television appearances, and his face became well known after it appeared on the billboards of the Gap clothing-store chain. He won two Grammy awards, one for a recording of romantic songs and the other for a Cole Porter disc. Both appeared on the Telarc label. Short appeared as himself in Woody Allen's film "Hannah and Her Sisters," and in 1994 he garnered an honor of a different kind: was named a living landmark by the New

York Landmarks Conservancy. Short spent vacation time at a villa in the south of France.

In 1997, well over 70 years old, Short rethought his backing band at the Carlyle, expanding it from a trio to a nine-piece band. He tried to retire in 2004, but popular demand induced him to sign a contract to appear for another year. He continued to work even after receiving a leukemia diagnosis, and he worked on a new CD of Fred Astaire songs until just before his death. He never finished it, but he left a sturdy legacy nonetheless: the younger cabaret performers that revived the art in the 1990s and 2000s all looked to Bobby Short as an inspiration. "Bobby Short," singer and pianist Michael Feinstein told the *Chicago Tribune*, "was the inventor of what all of us do."

Selected discography

Albums

Songs by Bobby Short, Atlantic, 1955.
Bobby Short, Atlantic, 1956.
Speaking of Love, Atlantic, 1957.
Sing Me a Swing Song, Atlantic, 1957.
Nobody Else But Me, Atlantic, 1958.
The Mad Twenties, Atlantic, 1959.
Bobby Short on the East Side, Atlantic, 1963.
My Personal Property, Atlantic, 1971.
Bobby Short Loves Cole Porter, Atlantic, 1973.
Bobby Short Live at the Cafe Carlyle, Mobile Fidelity, 1975.
Bobby Short Celebrates Rodgers & Hart, Atlantic, 1982.
Moments Like This, Atlantic, 1986.
Guess Who's in Town: Bobby Short Performs the Songs of Andy Razaf, Atlantic, 1991.

Late Night at the Cafe Carlyle, Telarc, 1993.
Swing That Music, Telarc. 1995.
Songs of New York, Telarc , 1999.
How's Your Romance, Telarc, 1999.
You're the Top: The Love Songs of Cole Porter, Telarc, 2001.

Sources

Books

Short, Bobby, *Black and White Baby*, Dodd, Mead, 1971.
Short, Bobby (with Robert Mackintosh), *Bobby Short: The Life and Times of a Saloon Singer*, C. Potter, 1995.

Periodicals

Back Stage, March 24, 2005, p. 6.
Chicago Tribune, March 22, 2005.
New Yorker, December 26, 1970, reprinted March 22, 2005.
New York Observer, March 28, 2005, p. 20.
New York Times, March 21, 2005.
Times (London, England), March 23, 2005.
Washington Times, March 25, 2005, p. A19.

On-line

"Bobby Short," *All Music Guide*, www.allmusic.com (April 1, 2005).
"Impeccable Singer Bobby Short Dead," *CNN.com*, www.cnn.com/2005/SHOWBIZ/Muisc/03/21/obit.short.ap (April 1, 2005).

—James M. Manheim

N'kenge Simpson-Hoffman

1975(?)—

Singer

Among the most versatile new performers in the world of opera in the late 1990s and early 2000s has been N'kenge Simpson-Hoffman, whose talents encompass musical theater, jazz, and popular song as well as traditional operatic repertory. She has performed at the White House and the United Nations, has taken lead roles in operas by composers ranging from Mozart to Puccini, and has given over 100 solo recitals in such varied locales as Israel, France, England, Italy, and Germany in addition to the United States. A former beauty queen, she entranced audiences in lead romantic roles in both operas and musicals. Simpson-Hoffman found perhaps an ideal forum for her varied talents when she became a member of the "Three Mo' Divas" trio created by Three Mo' Tenors mastermind Marion J. Caffey in 2003.

A native of New York City, N'kenge Simpson was born around 1975. She was a product of the strong arts education programs in New York's public schools, graduating from the Fiorello H. LaGuardia High School for the Performing Arts. She also studied at the Harlem School of the Arts. She began to stand out from the crowd in 1992 when she was named one of the first two winners of the ASCAP Leiber & Stoller Foundation Award, a new $10,000 performing arts scholarship established by the songwriting team of Jerry Leiber and Mike Stoller, the composers of "Hound Dog" and "Jailhouse Rock" among other rock-and-roll classics. The 17-year-old student performed a vocal piece by Mozart and an African-American spiritual before an audience of music-industry dignitaries at the awards ceremony at New York's swank Russian Tea Room.

Took Home Pageant Crowns

Simpson-Hoffman enrolled at the Manhattan School of Music, and that year she also took home the title of Miss New York State Talented Teen. She followed up that pageant victory with the Miss Manhattan crown in the Miss America competition two years later. Simpson-Hoffman's operatic career began shortly after she earned her bachelor of music degree in 1994, when she appeared as Clara in George Gershwin's opera *Porgy & Bess* at Colorado's Aspen Opera Theater and also offered a rendition of "Summertime" in a one-hour concert of highlights from the opera. She also appeared that year at Harlem's famed Apollo Theater in a guest slot with the Hal Jackson Talented Teens troupe.

Returning to Aspen in 1995 and 1996, Simpson-Hoffman became better known as a young talent. She appeared at the White House Christmas ceremony in 1995, and the following year she performed two vocal selections from Beethoven's rarely heard music for the play *Egmont* with the New Jersey Symphony Orchestra; a reviewer from the *New Jersey Star-Ledger* (quoted in her press materials) noted that although she "looks like the cute teen-aged kid next door" she "has a big bright voice that could easily fill any of the world's largest houses." Simpson-Hoffman also appeared on ABC television's *Good Morning America* that year.

At a Glance . . .

Born in 1975(?) in New York, NY. *Education:* Attended Fiorello H. LaGuardia High School for the Performing Arts and Harlem School for the Arts; Manhattan School of Music, BA, music, 1994; Israel Vocal Arts Program, student and performer, 1998; Julliard School, MA, music, 1999.

Career: Professional singer, 1990s–; Three Mo' Divas, member, 2003–.

Memberships: none.

Selected awards: ASCAP Leiber & Stoller Award, one of first two recipients, 1994; Five Towns Classical Competition, winner, 1996; Lola Wilson Hayes Vocal Competition, 1997; Liederkranz Foundation competition, award winner, 2003.

Addresses: *Agent*—c/o Thea Dispeker, Inc., Artists Management, 59 East 54th St., Suite 81, New York, NY 10022.

In the mid-1990s, Simpson-Hoffman worked toward a master's degree in music at New York's Julliard School, graduating in 1999. She began to enter vocal competitions, winning the Five Towns Classical Competition (in 1996) and the Lola Wilson Hayes Vocal Competition (in 1997), and placing second in several others. By 1998 she was ready for more substantial roles in operas and sacred vocal works. She traveled to Israel as a member of the Israel Vocal Arts Program and appeared in two operatic productions there, and she sang the soprano part in Johann Sebastian Bach's *St. John Passion* in a performance at the Manhattan School of Music.

Performed in Opera by Famed Composer

Simpson-Hoffman began to build the foundations of an independent career between 1999 and 2002. She issued her first CD, *Red Souvenir,* in 1999 and won praise from the tastemaking magazine *Opera News* that year for her performance in an opera by *Godfather* score composer Nino Rota, *Il cappello di paglia di Firenze.* On a trip to Rome, Italy, she sang the role of Despina in Mozart's opera *Così fan tutte.* She

began to appear in concerts with regional American orchestras, performing the soprano part in Handel's *Messiah* with the Billings Symphony in Montana in 2000.

That year marked Simpson-Hoffman's emergence in high-profile situations. As the *Washington Post* put it, she "lent soulful, lustrously sung advocacy" to two of Aaron Copland's *All-American Songs* in a performance at the Library of Congress in Washington, accompanied by the U.S. Marine Band and nationally broadcast on National Public Radio's *Performance Today* series. She sang in the Zulu language while performing in a new opera about South African leader Nelson Mandela, *No Easy Walk to Freedom,* performed at Hofstra University on Long Island, and she took the lead role of Juliet in a newly rediscovered *Romeo und Julia* (Romeo and Juliet) opera by German composer Boris Blacher. She was part of the cast for the world premiere recording of that work on the Albany label in 2002.

Simpson-Hoffman had continued to perform the ever-popular songs of George Gershwin in appearances with orchestras, and in 2001 she demonstrated her talents in musical theater with the lead role of Luisa in a Lyric Opera of Cleveland production of *The Fantasticks.* The Cleveland *Plain Dealer* praised her as "a natural stage presence" who "beautifully conveys Luisa's romantic yearning and her journey to maturity." Simpson-Hoffman made another European trip in 2002, performing as a soloist in Mozart's *Requiem* mass at Italy's Saluzzo Music Festival and appearing in the large role of Susanna in Mozart's *The Marriage of Figaro* in a Czech Republic touring production. Back in New York, she sang at a United Nations ceremony honoring Secretary-General Kofi Annan.

Toured in Germany

The years 2003 and 2004 brought Simpson-Hoffman to the edge of operatic stardom with two more major roles: she sang the role of Musetta in Puccini's *La bohème* with the Virginia Opera and that of Despina once again in *Così fan tutte* with the Seattle Opera, the latter in a special Young Artist slot designed to introduce new performers to operatic audiences. She traveled to Germany, giving a solo recital and appearing at an Olympus trade show and a concert honoring Secretary of State Colin Powell. She also released an album of German classical songs, known as lieder.

Simpson-Hoffman also performed jazz, performing in concerts at New York's Lincoln Center with jazz giants Wynton Marsalis and Ornette Coleman and appearing in New York City nightclubs. With all these arrows in her performing quiver, she was a natural for the Three Mo' Divas, with whom she appeared several times in 2003 and 2004; like the more famous Three Mo' Tenors, they performed opera, blues, jazz, soul, gospel, and show tunes. "Simpson-Hoffman, the most physical of the group, gets an abundance of showy numbers, such as 'Fascinating Rhythm,' and an audience-participation 'Minnie the Moocher,'" observed Don Braunagel of the *Los Angeles Times* after a 2004 performance.

Continuing to live in New York, Simpson-Hoffman taught music to schoolchildren in Harlem, hoping to create for them some of the same opportunities that she herself had taken advantage of. She held a day job as regional operations manager at her mother's company, Simpson Personnel Services. But with another major award, the 2003 Liederkranz Foundation top prize, under her belt, and more national visibility with the Three Mo' Divas on the way, Simpson-Hoffman's star was still on the rise as of early 2005.

Selected discography

Red Souvenir, LBTV, 1999.
Romeo and Julia, Albany Records, 2002.
A Tribute to German Lieder, CRS, 2003.

Sources

Periodicals

Daily News (New York), August 27, 2003, p. Suburban-7.
Los Angeles Times, March 23, 2004, p. E3.
New York Times, July 24, 1992, p. B6.
Newsday (Long Island, NY), November 20, 2000, p. B9.
Plain Dealer (Cleveland, OH), June 29, 2001, p. E8.
San Diego Union-Tribune, July 17, 2000, p. E3.
Sun (Baltimore, MD), June 13, 2000, p. F3.
Washington Post, November 16, 2000, p. C5.

On-line

N'Kenge Simpson-Hoffman, www.nkenge.net (March 5, 2005).
"N'kenge Simpson-Hoffman," *Thea Dispeker Inc.,* www.dispeker.com (March 5, 2005).

—James M. Manheim

Jonathan Slocumb

19??—

Comedian

Slocumb, Jonathan, photograph. Chris Graythen/Getty Images.

In an era when it is common for comics to use four-letter words and make sexual innuendos, Jonathan Slocumb is known as "Mr. Clean." "Mixing comedy with gospel messages and music is certainly a unique approach," wrote Janine Coveney in *Billboard*, "and that's the road taken by newcomer Jonathan Slocumb." The difference for Slocumb is his Christian outlook. "My greatest challenge," he told the *Atlanta Journal-Constitution*, "is to show people that you can enjoy life, laugh and be a Christian. Besides, your health is better when you laugh." In one routine, Slocumb asks all of the Christians in the audience to raise their hands. Once identified, he asks them to perform the Christian slap test: slap your neighbor and see if they turn the other cheek. "I am gifted with the gift of laughter," Slocumb was quoted on Jewel Diamond Taylor's Web site. "I also have a commitment to the Lord and to myself to always entertain without vulgarities."

Even in grade school, Slocumb possessed a natural talent for comedy, and was voted "Most Humorous" by his classmates. He received the same honor in high school. At home, he entertained his parents and siblings in the family living room. Slocumb also had a talent for music and began serving as a choir director at the age of 12 in a Seventh Day Adventist church. Slocumb credited the church as a positive force in his early life. "Being raised in the Seventh Day Adventist denomination offered one of the most disciplined way[s] of growing up," he told Taylor. "There were many different ministers and other balanced individuals that impacted my life."

Slocumb attended Oakville College in Huntsville, Alabama, but nearly dropped out of the broadcast journalism program because of financial difficulties. During the last day of the term of his junior year, however, his friends presented him with a basket filled with money. Because Slocumb had the ability to make them laugh, they had raised enough money to keep him at Oakville for the next year and a half.

Slocumb started performing as a comic in his late twenties after working as an account representative for AT&T. He was discovered when Gail Hamilton of Choice Management saw him serve as the master of ceremonies for a gospel concert. Hamilton asked him if

At a Glance . . .

Born Jonathan Slocumb in Atlanta, GA. *Education*: B.S. in Broadcast Journalism, Oakville College, Huntsville, Alabama.

Career: Christian comedian, late 1980s–.

Addresses: *Office*—Life Entertainment, Inc., 3717 S. Labrea Ave., Suite 525, Los Angeles, CA 90016. *Web*— www.jonathanslocumb.net.

he had any more material, and soon he was touring as the opening act for Take 6. Later, Slocumb would open concerts for performers like Natalie Cole, Vanessa Bell, and Shirley Caesar, and co-host the Stellar Awards and Lou Rawls' Parade of Stars. His comic work was influenced by other "clean" comics like Bill Cosby, Sinbad, and Arsenio Hall. He admitted to Taylor that a number of comedians make him laugh. "But no one does it like Bill Cosby!!! He and Sinbad are the ones making my life as wonderful as it is."

Slocumb attended and performed at Kingfest in Montgomery in 1989, and appeared on a syndicated radio program, "Inspirations Across America," in 1990. He also made a habit of appearing in churches, including the Atlanta Metropolitan Christian Center, and the Antioch North Baptist and Ben Hill United Methodist churches. Once at a Redd Foxx Talent Search audition, Slocumb used profanity in his routine. The experience, however, left him feeling dishonest: he was attempting to be somebody he wasn't. "One of my ultimate goals is to find more Christian comics and form a Blessed Pack—not a Black Pack or a Brat Pack," Slocumb told the *Atlanta Journal-Constitution*. "We're living in the age of Eddie Murphy where any black comedian is expected to be like him. I don't have to be that way."

Many have insisted on seeing Christian comedy as no more than a novelty act. Slocumb and his peers, however, have found their niche in a quickly growing Christian entertainment empire. "Christian comedy, a growing segment of the $4 billion Christian entertainment market, has established itself as a viable genre," noted David Hiltbrand in the *Philadelphia Inquirer*. As Christians, comedians like Slocumb also emphasize their ability to offer a healthier style of family friendly comedy. "I have some strong moral spiritual standards," he told *Jet*. "I'm trying to keep the Cosby tradition alive. If it wasn't for Sinbad clean comedy would be dead." Slocumb likewise notes that the use of profanity and racial slurs by many black comedians also negatively impacts the African-American community. "White people love to promote and give as much

negativism to our people as possible. That's why they are willing to back all of these people," he told *Jet*.

In 1997 Slocumb released *Laugh Yo' Self 2 Life!* on Warner Brothers. The album included the retelling of Biblical stories ("Noah 'Jackson' / David 'Holyfield' & Goliath / Job's Blues"), church humor ("Preachers" and "People in the Pews") and growing up ("Childhood"). "Recording artist Jonathan Slocumb carves out his own recording genre, Gospel/Comedy, with *Laugh Yourself 2 Life!*," wrote Teresa Graham in the *Times Union*, "providing observation humor on a portion of African-American life often overlooked by comedians—the church." *Billboard* concurred: "Slocumb professes his faith and love for African-American women," wrote Janine Coveney, "pokes gentle fun at some of the church's stock characters, and skewers the family.... Nothing too heavy or satirical, just lighthearted fun."

Through live appearances, TV work, and radio programs, Slocumb's career continues to expand to new audiences. "Everyone says that it is refreshing to know that comedy is making a clean comeback," he told the *Atlanta Journal-Constitution*. "And adding a spiritual message makes it a rewarding experience." Besides touring regularly, he has made television appearances on HBO's *DefComedy Jam*, BET's *Bobby Jones Gospel,* and PAX's *Gospel Fire*. He frequently opens for Bill Cosby, and has toured with Sinbad. Slocumb has also gained exposure from his role of "Clyde the Slide" on *The Steve Harvey Show*, and appeared on the popular *The Tavis Smiley Show* on National Public Radio (NPR). "This is a new age of Christianity," Slocumb told the *Atlanta Journal-Constitution*. "The traditional means of witnessing are being replaced by contemporary music, drama and other forces. People should be open-minded."

Selected discography

Laugh Yo' Self 2 Life!, Warner, 1997.

Sources

Periodicals

Atlanta Journal-Constitution, June 30, 1990.
Billboard, November 1, 1997, p. 20.
Jet, January 19, 1998, p. 30.
Philadelphia Inquirer, July 22, 2004, p. D1.
Times Union, May 14, 1998, p. 27.

On-line

Jonathan Slocumb, www.jonathanslocumb.net/ home.htm (May 18, 2005).
"Jonathan Slocumb," *LoneOak Entertainment,* www. loneoakentertainment.com/indexA.htm (May 18, 2005).

"Jonathan Slocumb Interview," *Jewel Diamond Taylor*, www.donotgiveup.net/ (February 3, 2005).

—Ronnie D. Lankford, Jr.

Warren Spears

1954-2005

Choreographer, dancer, master teacher

A highly regarded dancer, choreographer, and teacher, Warren Spears created a variety of modern ballets. After spending his early years with the Alvin Ailey American Dance Theater, Spears went on to dance and choreograph for numerous companies in the United States and Europe. He settled in Copenhagen where he helped establish the New Danish Dance Theatre (NDDT), introducing modern dance to the people of Denmark. As a dancer he was strong and athletic with a soft and pliable technique. Real people, including artists, writers, and his grandfather, often served as the theme from which his ballets evolved. Audiences and critics loved his fast-paced and imaginative staging and use of space. He choreographed to music ranging from that of Henry Purcell and J. S. Bach to Igor Stravinsky, John Adams, Philip Glass, Keith Jarrett, Steve Reich, and contemporary jazz and rock.

Spears, Warren, photograph. Courtesy www.warrenspears.com. Reproduced by permission.

Began Dancing as a Teenager

Born on May 2, 1954, Warren Spears grew up in Detroit, Michigan, the son of Walter and Theresa Wilma (Davis) Spears. No one in his family was inclined toward music or dance and as a teenager Spears planned to become an architect. However he took up dance after being mesmerized during a matinee performance by the Alvin Ailey American Dance Theater. Spears's first teacher had danced with Isadora Duncan and his second teacher was a member of the Katherine Dunham Dance Company. While still in high school Spears began dancing with a small professional group, the Clifford Fears Dance Company, and choreographing for the Michigan Opera Company.

In 1972 Spears moved to New York City with a full scholarship to study in the Dance Division of the Juilliard School. Working with some of the greatest dancers of the day, Spears studied modern, classical, and contemporary dance, composition and choreography, music, and dance and music history. On evenings and weekends he explored the dance studios of New York. At the Clark Center for the Performing Arts, Spears studied the Lester Horton technique with Thelma Hill. At the Alvin Ailey American Dance Center, Spears studied jazz forms with Fred Benjamin. He spent his summers at the American Dance Festival in

New London, Connecticut, working with Louis Falco and Walter Nicks.

Choreographer Joyce Trisler urged Spears to audition for Alvin Ailey. When he was invited to join Ailey's company in 1974, Spears had to call his mother first, since he had promised her that he would graduate from Juilliard. For the next four years he performed and toured the world with the Alvin Ailey American Dance Theater.

Spears left Alvin Ailey in 1978 to devote more time to choreography and to dance with other companies. He choreographed for the Alvin Ailey Repertory Ensemble—the junior Ailey troupe—and, between 1972 and 1982, he choreographed 15 ballets for his own dance company, the Spears Collection. Between 1978 and 1981 Spears danced with the Joyce Trisler Dance

Company, the Pearl Lang Dance Company, the Kazuko Hirabayashi Dance Theater, and the Walter Nicks Dance Company, among others. He also performed in the musical films *The Wiz* and *Hair*.

Brought Modern Dance to Denmark

Spears was with Joyce Trisler's company when she died in 1979. The following year he traveled to Copenhagen to perform as a soloist in her "Dance for Six," on Denmark's national television. Spears moved to Denmark in 1984, along with other dancers and choreographers who were set on introducing the country to modern dance. In 1987 he created "Rowing in Eden" for the Royal Danish Ballet, with music by John Adams and stage design by Spears's frequent collaborator, Danish artist Lin Utzon, a designer for Royal Copenhagen porcelain.

Spears served as artistic director and resident choreographer at the NDDT from 1987 until 1999, choreographing more than 20 ballets for the company. Some were longer abstract pieces whereas others were one-act themed ballets. However he was best known for his full-evening themed productions. The NDDT grew into the largest and most international of Denmark's modern dance companies. Spears led the NDDT through twice-yearly Copenhagen premieres, tours of Denmark, and guest performances throughout Europe and Australia.

In 1989 Spears created "Black." On a summer's night in Detroit in 1968, with the sounds of rioting in the streets, three men and three women move around each other in a party room. Although rock music takes over for a while, the gunshots and sirens return. It was performed by the nationally acclaimed Dayton Contemporary Dance Company (DCDC) at the Joyce Theater in New York in 2000. Critic Jennifer Dunning of the *New York Times* wrote that "the greatest fascination of 'Black' is the ways he [Spears] uses cliches of recent modern dance by black American choreographers with a knowing affection and respect that makes them fresh."

Critics and Audiences Praised his Ballets

"Skagen," first performed in 1990, became one of Spears's most popular works, with subsequent performances in Denmark, Norway, Germany, and Spain. Named for a cape at the northern tip of Denmark, it focused on the painter P.S. Krøyer and Danish impressionistic paintings of the late nineteenth century. The figures in the paintings danced out of their frames to the music of Puccini.

In 1993 Spears created his own version of "Sacre du Printemps"—"The Rites of Spring." Later he choreographed "Dex," based on the expatriate jazz saxophonist Dexter Gordon, and "Milne," based on A. A. Milne, author of the *Winnie-the-Pooh* stories.

One of Spears's best-known works—"Tanne"—was inspired by the life of the Danish writer and storyteller Karen Blixen. Tanne was the family's nickname for Blixen, better known as Isak Dinesen, author of *Out of Africa*, a memoir of her life in Kenya. Spears told Anne Flindt Christensen of *Dance Magazine*: "I wasn't born in Denmark and raised in the Danish culture, so [I] hope I'll be able to portray Blixen with the fresh curiosity of a foreigner. My intention with Tanne is not to show all her literary achievements but to focus on the feminine part of the myth that she has become. Her fights against the old-fashioned view of women and her struggle against a deadly illness [syphilis] must have been of major importance to her life as a woman and as an artist. I think that the audience of today will see the parallels to our huge problem with AIDS and also to the constant attempt of every artist to improve." Blixen's lives as a young woman, as a lover, and as a creative artist were portrayed by three different dancers. The NDDT premiered the work on April 8, 1994.

Continued to Grow as an Artist

Between 1982 and 2003 Spears was a guest choreographer with various groups including the Philadelphia Dance Company, the Impulse Dance Company of Boston, the Dallas Black Dance Theater, Kaleidoscope Dance Company in Indiana, and the Djazzez Dance Company in Holland. He also choreographed for theater and musical productions in the United States, France, and Denmark. A master teacher of contemporary modern dance based on the techniques of Lester Horton and José Limon, Spears guest taught at universities, private schools, dance companies, and international workshops in the United States and Europe, including Copenhagen's Dancers House, Copenhagen University, Poitiers University in France, the University of New Mexico, Wright State University in Ohio, Michigan State University, Western and Central Michigan Universities, and the New Orleans Center for Creative Arts.

Spears left the NDDT in 1999 to pursue a freelance career of dancing and choreography. He appeared in the film *Dancer in the Dark* by the Danish filmmaker Lars von Trier, along with Catherine Deneuve and the Icelandic pop star Bj&oumlaut;rk. In 2001 Spears choreographed and danced in a Web-based interactive production called "The Room," based on James Baldwin's novel *Giovanni's Room*. With funding from a variety of Danish sources, Spears made his premiere as a solo dancer in "Eugene," a ballet based on the life of his grandfather Eugene Davies. He performed the work, with music by pianist and composer Keith Jarrett, in Copenhagen and on a tour of Denmark in 2001 and 2002. He then received Danish funding to produce

"Kiss Me, I Love You" in Copenhagen in 2003. In addition to choreographing and directing this ballet, for the first time Spears designed the costumes and sets himself. In 2003 he produced "Without Sanctuary," a theater-ballet based on the book and gallery exhibition of the same name by James Allen.

Knighted by Queen Margrethe

Spears had a long-term relationship with the DCDC in Ohio, a dance company dedicated to promoting the work of black dancers and choreographers. He created several pieces for DCDC and his work has remained in the their repertoire. "On the Wings of Angels," with music by John Adams, was included in DCDC's "The Flight Project," a 2003 tribute to the Wright Brothers on the 100th anniversary of their maiden flight. Spears's piece was a tribute to the Tuskegee Airmen, a courageous group of black World War II fighter pilots. "The Flight Project" toured the United States on DCDC's 35th anniversary.

In 2003 Spears was knighted by Queen Margrethe of Denmark with the Cross of the Order of Dannebrog, in recognition of his contributions to Danish dance. "Random Cruelties," choreographed and designed by Spears—who also performed as the solo dancer—premiered in 2004 with music by Henry Purcell and John Adams and a performance by Spears's partner, the singer Karsten Mach.

Warren Spears died in Copenhagen on January 8, 2005, at the age of 50, from the effects of treatment for a recurrence of multiple myeloma. In "Danish Modern Dance's Relevance Today," published on his Web site in October of 2003, Spears wrote: " Maybe we should both remember our historic past look forward to the future, and once again ask ourselves, why do we dance? The answers are because we have something in our hearts, in our muscles and because we must express it through our bodies!"

Selected works

Choreography

"The Spears Collection," 1972-82.
"Knutsen Variations," 1982.
"Sculpture Park," 1982.
"The Exiles," 1983.
"Dream of the Gods," 1985.
"Drum Suite," 1985.
"Scenes of Death," 1985.
"Blue, Red Green and Yellow," 1986.
"When Giants Learn to Dance," 1986.
"Again," 1987.
"Carmina Burana," 1987.
"Carmina Variations," 1987.
"Four Movements," 1987.

"Rowing in Eden," 1987.
"Songs of My Youth," 1987.
"The Last Waltz," 1988.
"Black," 1989.
"The Firebird," 1989.
"Skagen," 1990.
"The Power of the Harp," 1991.
"Stravinsky—The Rites of Spring," 1993.
"Tanne," 1994.
"1995—An Installation Ballet," 1995.
"Brandenburg Concerto No. 5," 1995.
"Short Pieces," 1995.
"Worshiping Icons," 1995.
"Dex—A Jazz Odyssey," 1996.
"On the Wings of Angels," 1996.
"Milne," 1999.
"Aretha," 2001.
"Eugene," 2001.
"Orange," 2001.
"The Room," 2001.
"Colors," 2003.
"Kiss Me, I Love You," 2003.
"Without Sanctuary," 2003.

"Extravagantly Dressed on a Strange Planet," 2004.
"Random Cruelties," 2004.

Films

The Wiz, 1978.
Hair, 1979.
Dancer in the Dark, 2000.

Sources

Periodicals

Dance Magazine, April 1994, pp. 30-1.
Detroit News, January 13, 2005.
New York Times, October 16, 2000, p. E5; January 23, 2005, p. 26.

On-line

Warren Spears, www.warrenspears.com (May 1, 2005).

—Margaret Alic

Arthur Ray Thomas

1951—

International fraternity president, attorney, activist

Arthur Ray Thomas, Esq. is the thirty-first International President of the Phi Beta Sigma Fraternity, a 125,000 member black fraternity with chapters in the United States, St. Thomas, Japan, Germany, and the Bahamas. He is an accomplished attorney who has worked tirelessly on behalf of political and social issues affecting young African Americans, seniors and the disadvantaged. His work to provide assistance in securing affordable housing has helped many gain a foothold on the path to a better life. With an eye towards better health care, Thomas has been instrumental in gaining support from Phi Beta Sigma members. By adopting national initiatives that enhance the lives of many, his life's work establishes the fraternity as a serious player in the effort to create greater opportunities for blacks. Thomas has also served as a staff member for U.S. Congressman Gillis Long and is a past president of the Southern University Law Center Alumni Association and the Louis A. Martinet Legal Society.

Thomas was born in the small Louisiana town of Ville Platte, on August 17, 1951, the fourth of 12 children born to Artellus Jr. and Ernestine Thomas. In school Thomas ran track, captained the basketball team, and was considered an all-around athlete. He excelled academically, graduating third in his class at James Stephens High School in 1969, and played the saxophone. Thomas was a member of his high school ROTC program and considered entering the military after graduation. Later the death of a friend killed in Vietnam would cause him to reconsider.

Developed Interest in Activism

Thomas entered Southern University in Baton Rouge and after his junior year in 1971 joined the Phi Beta Sigma Fraternity. Motivated by the prejudice he experienced growing up in a small town, he decided to pursue a law degree. "In a place like Ville Platte it's obvious," he said in an interview with *Contemporary Black Biography* (*CBB*). "Blacks lived on one side of the tracks, whites on the other. Doctors' offices had separate doors for the races and blacks had difficulty securing employment. All this was in the back of my mind. I wanted to go back and help."

His college years were a time of major social and political change in America; many colleges were experiencing campus unrest. Thomas worked along side fellow members of the Black Stone Society, a group of political science students seeking to improve conditions on campus. During Thomas' last year there activists seized the administration building to protest conditions. National guardsmen were called in and two students were killed. This early exposure to political activism and a desire to improve the lives of young people would become a persistent theme of Thomas' work during law school and in the coming decades. In 1972 Thomas received a bachelor's degree in political science and in 1976 he graduated from the Southern University Law Center. "My mother was particularly happy about it," he told *CBB*. "I'll never forget the smile on her face the day I graduated." After his parents had

At a Glance . . .

Born Arthur Ray Thomas on August 17 1951, in Ville Platte, LA; married Dr. Veronica Mitchell, 1978; children: Raven Denaye, Shannon. *Education:* Southern University, BA, political science, 1972; Southern University Law Center, JD, 1976. *Religion:* Baptist.

Career: Louisiana House of Representatives, Baton Rouge, LA, committee clerk, 1978-79; Louisiana House of Representatives, Baton Rouge, LA, staff member of U.S. Congressman Gillis Long, 1980-81; Johnson, Taylor & Thomas Law Firm, Baton Rouge, LA, partner, 1980-90; Louisiana Attorney General's Office, Baton Rouge, LA, staff attorney, 1981-84; Arthur R. Thomas and Associates, 1990–; Renaissance Development Corporation, 1993–; Phi Beta Sigma Fraternity, Inc., Washington, DC, 31st International President, 2001-05.

Memberships: Capital Area Legal Services Corporation; Phi Beta Sigma Fraternity; National Pan-Hellenic Council; Louisiana Capital Fund, Inc.; Louis A. Martinet Legal Society; Southern University Law Center Alumni Association.

Awards: Capitol High School CEO Employer of the Year Award, 1995; Baton Rouge Association Real Estate Brokers Community Service Award, 1996; Martin Luther King Foundation Award, 1997; Sigma Man of the Year Award, 1992; *Ebony* Magazine, 100 Most Influential Black Americans Award, 2002, 2003, 2004 and 2005.

Addresses: *Office*—Phi Beta Sigma Fraternity, Inc., International Headquarters, 145 Kennedy Street, NW, Washington, DC 20011-5294.

Program, geared towards geriatrics, advising seniors on matters such as Social Security. "We were very entrepreneurial and saw an opportunity for law students to get some clinical experience," Thomas said. "There were lots of administrative hearings and we advised seniors of their rights. I enjoyed speaking with seniors; it taught me stability, patience, and listening skills."

Thomas opened the law firm of Johnson, Taylor & Thomas in 1980 and later in 1990 started the firm of Arthur R. Thomas and Associates. Much of his legal work involved personal injury and civil rights litigation, with one case being the longest-running school board desegregation case in the country. His firm also worked as lead attorneys on *Clark v. Edwards*, an important case in Louisiana aimed at increasing the number of black judges in the state.

Community Programs Influenced Fraternity Work

In 1993 Thomas started the Renaissance Development Corporation to serve Baton Rouge Parish, building 85 affordable homes in blighted areas. The company qualifies first-time homebuyers, provides training and credit counseling, and funds for purchasing. Thomas took the project a step further with his Renaissance Youth Build Program. Providing opportunities for at-risk youth to get their GED and job skills, the program offers on-the-job training in housing construction and bi-monthly stipends. "My passion is helping young kids especially black males," Thomas told *CBB*. Although real estate development is not his main focus, a lot of these activities "flowed into his fraternity work prior to becoming president of Phi Beta Sigma," Thomas said.

The Phi Beta Sigma initiative he is most proud of is the youth component. The program started in 1950, but its true potential had not been tapped until Thomas got involved. "I took a centrist program and divided it, incorporating a three part program: First, the job shadowing program to offer job training; second, the tutorial program working directly with youth offering educational opportunities and scholarships, and third, a teen pregnancy program named SATAPP (Sigma Against Teenage Pregnancy Plus)," Thomas explained.

Under Thomas local alumni chapters appreciated the focus and structure he brought to the project; he won their support. Previously it had limited recognition nationally and is now constitutionally recognized as the Sigma Beta Club Foundation. He feels this will be one of his greatest contribution to the organization followed by the establishment of the Thurgood Marshall Scholarship fund Sigma Beta Club Scholarship Endowment, which will benefit Sigma Beta Club and Collegiate members of the organization. "When someone looks at us as an organization they see us involved with young black males across the country and an organization

divorced years before, Ernestine's years of raising 12 children had not been without difficulty. She was indeed very proud of her son's accomplishments.

Thomas then went to work as a clerk for the Louisiana State Legislature Health and Welfare Committee and as an assistant law librarian. Later, along with a law partner Thomas started the Southern University Aging

involved in community service with a greater amount of financial stability and fiscal responsibility," he said.

"Membership has increased under my administration, the largest in the fraternity's history," Thomas said. "I was able to accomplish this because I learned when I was very young that people become interested because you are doing positive things. If you focus on helping young black men there are many Fraternity members who want to help. They see themselves in these young Black males and they want to be part of it. Our members are informed of what we are doing, the grant opportunities we are seeking, we're making our national programs much more structured, and we are providing the necessary ingredients to fulfill the dreams of our Founders. Also, to keep our brothers interested we have provided a greater amount of efficiency in member services and those services that members expect."

Worked For Better Health Care

Thomas has met with Bush Administration policy advisors to secure major grants for health care and spoke with the first lady regarding her initiatives for at-risk kids. "My task is to make this a component of all Greek letter organizations," Thomas said. "I think it's important that we partner to make a greater impact on our youth and health-related issues." Thomas is the chairman of the Council of Presidents of the Pan-Hellenic Organization, a decision-making body comprising all national fraternity presidents.

A tireless and effective administrator and attorney, Thomas works for many causes. One important program that continues under Thomas is Sigmas Waging War Against Cancer (SWWAC). Partnering with the American Cancer Society, it focuses on early screening and detection for colorectal cancer. The National Marrow Donor Program began under Thomas to urge fraternity members' involvement with donor registration. Phi Beta Sigma's St. Jude's Children's Hospital Project raises funds and advocates for children's health.

So what does Thomas see as the key to success for these young people he spends his life leading and mentoring? "Starting out things are tough for African-American males; the odds are against us and opportunities are not always there," he told *CBB*. It is important to recognize that education is a critical part of preparation. Be focused, set goals, and know you can do it. These things will allow you to put together a plan of action. With this you can achieve great heights. I am a prime example of someone who came from a very small rural area during an era when there was not a lot of help. I became focused." Focused and relentless, giving back and making a difference, Thomas has paved the way for many.

Sources

On-line

Phi Beta Sigma Fraternity, Inc., www.pbs1914.org/ (February 01, 2005).

Other

Additional information for this profile was obtained through an interview with Attorney Arthur R. Thomas on February 21, 2005, and through biographical information supplied by Attorney Thomas.

—Sharon Melson Fletcher

Kenan Thompson

1978—

Actor

Kenan Thompson has been making people laugh ever since he was a school boy impersonating Bill Cosby. Since then he has spent nearly half his life entertaining people—from wacky sitcom antics on Nickelodeon to grown up gags on *Saturday Night Live* to a real-life portrayal of cartoon biggie Fat Albert. Is there a secret to his hilarious success? "I'm a happy person, and I want everybody else to be happy," he told *People Weekly*. "Nothing wrong with that."

Got Laughs from Early Age

Kenan Thompson was born on May 10, 1978, into an Atlanta, Georgia, household steeped in Southern traditions of manners and cordiality. Thompson told *People Weekly* that his mother Elizabeth Ann, a nurse, "raised me to be a Southern gentleman. To this day she keeps me in line." Thompson first got a taste of the spotlight at the age of five when he won the role of the Gingerbread Man in a school play. Soon after he discovered that he was funny. "It came from being so much younger than my brother, I was often entertaining myself," he told the *Bay State Banner*. "People would laugh at what I did. Later on I figured out how to format that but I really wanted to be an actor."

Thompson kept acting all the way through high school, where he met teacher Freddie Hendricks. "[He was] the person who made a difference for me," Thompson told the *PBS* Web site. "[He] taught me drama in high school and got me involved in his theater group." A self-proclaimed good student—"I didn't want to be the

class clown and get in trouble," he told a *PBS* interviewer—Thompson juggled his school work with auditions. "I tried out for like a million and one commercials before I got my first one," he told *PBS*.

At the age of 15 Thompson made his film debut with the role of Russ Tyler in *D2: The Mighty Ducks,* the story of an underdog pee-wee hockey team making it big. The following year he had a small role in *Heavyweights*, and in 1996 he reprised the role of Russ in *D3: The Mighty Ducks.* He also had a stint as a movie reviewer for the CNN program "Real News for Kids."

Found Fame and All That

While he earned sporadic small credits on the big screen, Thompson was rapidly becoming a star on the small screen. In 1995 he auditioned for Nickelodeon's *All That,* a comedy skit show featuring an all-child cast. Thompson landed a spot on the show after auditioning with a routine he had done since his playground days: a dead-on Bill Cosby impression. "His timing and ability to mimic were amazing," director Brian Robbins told *People Weekly.*

All That soon became Nickelodeon's top-rated show and Thompson learned to adjust to life as a teenaged celebrity. "It was great," he told *New York Daily News.* "We couldn't go certain places. We would go to the mall and see how long it would take before we would get attacked by little girls." He added, "we had middle-school stalkers."

At a Glance . . .

Born on May 10, 1978, in Atlanta, GA. *Education*: Attended Santa Monica College.

Career: Actor, 1994–.

Memberships: none.

Awards: Cable ACE Award, Best Children's Series, 7 Years Old and Older, *Kenan and Kel*, 1997; Kid's Choice Award, Favorite Television Show, *Kenan and Kel*, 1998.

Addresses: *Agent*—The Endeavor Agency, 9601 Wilshire Blvd., Tenth Floor, Beverly Hills, CA 90212.

On the *All That* set Thompson met his comedic soul brother, Kel Mitchell. "The chemistry between me and him happened when they put us together in an *All That* sketch called 'Mavis and Clavis,'" Thompson told *Daily News*. In the bit, the teens played a pair of cranky senior citizens heckling the show. Midway through the first rehearsal Thompson and Mitchell began improvising and soon had the entire cast and crew in stitches. "They had us dying on the first run-through," Robbins recalled to *Daily News*. "They had these brain waves. It was magic. After we did the first season of *All That* we all knew that these guys had to have their own show."

Earned His Own Comedy Show

In 1996 Thompson and Mitchell became the first African-American actors to headline a primetime show on Nickelodeon. *Kenan and Kel* followed the comic misadventures of the always-scheming Kenan Rockmore and his dim-witted best friend Kel Kimble. "We could have just played characters from *All That* on the new show, but this is more of a challenge," Mitchell told *USA Today*. "And besides, these guys are more like us." The show became a hit for Nickelodeon and cemented the duo's fame.

With child-aged fame came adult-sized responsibility. "I know kids look up to us—little kids," Thompson told the *Virginian Pilot*. With that in mind, the teens kept a clean image and promoted education on shows such as BET's discussion forum, *Teen Summit*. *Kenan and Kel* garnered several award nominations and won the 1998 Kid's Choice Award for Favorite Television Show.

Thompson and Mitchell also starred in the 1997 feature film *Good Burger* as a couple of bumbling fast food workers trying to save their mom-and-pop employer from ending up in the deep fryer at the hands of a competing burger giant. Though not a box office smash, Nickelodeon fans ate it up. Parents also appreciated the good intentions the film served on the side. "There are lots of lessons to learn like not to lie, don't judge a book by its cover and whatever you sow, you reap," the then-19 year-old Thompson told *Jet*.

Grew Up to Saturday Night Live

Kenan and Kel finished its four-year run in 1999. The following year, *All That* signed off the air. Thompson teamed up once more with Mitchell in 2000 for a 90-minute *Kenan and Kel* television movie called *Two Heads Are Better Than One*. Meanwhile Thompson took up residency all over teen TV. He had recurring roles on *Felicity* and *The Steve Harvey Show*. He also appeared on *Sabrina the Teenage Witch*, *The Parkers*, and *Sister, Sister*. He made it back to the big screen with bit parts in the feature films *Big Fat Liar* and *Love Don't Cost a Thing*.

By 2003 Thompson had been starring in shows for young people for over eight years. Though still baby-faced, he was 25. It was time to grow up. To do so, he auditioned for and landed a spot on the cast of *Saturday Night Live (SNL)*, late-night television's grand-daddy of adult sketch comedy. "In *SNL*, we are free to do edgy-type stuff. On Nickelodeon, we couldn't touch certain stuff," Thompson told the *Boston Herald*. "The clean stuff doesn't really work at night. No one wants to see that stuff."

SNL also pushed him creatively. "We're responsible for coming up with new characters," he told the *About Hollywood Movies* Web site. "It's like a new experience for me. And it's challenging too because if I don't write my own stuff, then I'll be playing somebody's daughter…. I'll be a victim of somebody else's sketch." In addition to a handful of characters, Thompson has expanded his impressions repertoire to include dozens of celebrities from Gary Coleman to Serena Williams to Chaka Khan.

Hit the Big Time with Fat Role

In 2004 Thompson landed a bit part in *Barbershop 2: Back in Business*, the sequel to the wildly popular, all-black ensemble feature about life in an African American barbershop in inner-city Chicago. However it was life in inner-city Philadelphia that gave Thompson his first leading role. Bill Cosby's cartoon *Fat Albert*, based on his childhood in the projects of Philadelphia, was a staple of Saturday morning television in the 1970s. After years of trying, Cosby finally got a film version of *Fat Albert* into production by 2004. Rumor has it that Cosby watched Thompson's audition tape for less than 15 seconds before choosing him for the title role. When asked why he thought Cosby chose him, Thompson told the *Philadelphia Tribune,* "Because the character had to be charming and compassionate and whatnot. I just believed in my likeability!"

Despite nearly a decade in front of the cameras, Thompson was terrified to meet Cosby. When the pair finally met up on the first day of filming, Thompson hid his nerves by launching into his now-famous Bill Cosby impression. Cosby didn't react. He later told *People Weekly,* "It was not the time to fool around." Despite the chilly introduction, the two men became friends, and Cosby admitted to being a great fan of Thompson's impression. Thompson told the *Bay State Banner* about a visit to a Philadelphia club where Cosby was performing. "He insisted I get up on the stage and do my imitation of him. He loved it!"

Though critical reaction to *Fat Albert* was uniformly dismal, Thompson's characteristic good humor would not be dampened. "I think right now I'm seasoned enough to handle whatever's gonna happen, whether I become a huge star or whatever," he told NPR's Tony Cox. With parts in the 2005 films *Candy Paint* and *Peter Cottontail: The Movie,* plus his continued laugh tracks on *SNL,* "huge star" seemed a much more likely prospect than "whatever."

Selected works

Films

D2: The Mighty Ducks, 1994.
D3: The Mighty Ducks, 1996.
Good Burger, 1997.
Two Heads Are Better Than None (TV), 2000.
Big Fat Liar, 2002.
Barbershop 2: Back in Business, 2004.

Fat Albert, 2004.
Peter Cottontail: The Movie, 2005.

Television

All That, 1995-1999.
Kenan and Kel, 1996-99.
Saturday Night Live, NBC, 2003–.

Sources

Periodicals

Bay State Banner (Boston), December 9, 2004.
Boston Herald, December 19, 2004.
Daily News (Los Angeles), July 22, 1997.
Jet, August 11, 1997.
People Weekly, January 10, 2005.
Philadelphia Tribune, December 24, 2004.
USA Today, August 15, 1996.
Virginian Pilot, July 25, 1997.

On-line

"Kenan: 'All' the Better," *New York Daily News,* www.nydailynews.com/entertainment/story/302608p-259066c.html (April 5, 2005).
"It's My Life: Kenan Thompson," *PBS Kids,* http://pbskids.org/itsmylife/celebs/interviews/kenan.html (April 5, 2005).
"Kenan Thompson Joins the Crew of Barbershop 2," *About Hollywood Movies,* http://movies.about.com/cs/barbershop2/a/bb2kt013104.htm (April 5, 2005).

Other

"Interview: Kenan Thompson," NPR Special with Tony Cox, December 24, 2004.

—Candace LaBalle

Gina Torres

1969—

Actress

Learning her craft through appearances in high-quality live theater, New York City-born actress Gina Torres became known for the well-crafted characterizations she brought to a series of television and film roles in the late 1990s and early 2000s. Those roles brought Torres before the public in some of the most stylish and widely publicized productions of the day, including two of the *Matrix* films and the *Alias* and *24* television series. Torres specialized in action parts, and she needed no stunt doubles to do her fight scenes–scenes in which she drew on the feelings generated by her own experiences as an artist. "You have to have a spirit of warrior in you," she explained to Robert Bianco of *USA Today.* "You're going to be facing battles as a woman in this industry and a woman of color. You have to be prepared to face battles of respect and pride and sexuality, and you can't tire of fighting."

The youngest of three children, Gina Torres was born on April 25, 1969, in Manhattan, New York, but her family soon moved to the Bronx borough of the city. Her father was a newspaper typesetter. Both her parents were natives of Cuba and Latin jazz enthusi-

Torres, Gina, photograph. Vince Bucci/Getty Images.

asts. Torres attended the elite High School of Music and Art in New York's public school system, gravitating toward music and pursuing a vocal curriculum. She sang opera, jazz, and gospel, finding special inspiration in the classes of a jazz percussion teacher. Torres applied to several colleges and was admitted, but her family finances didn't permit her to enroll.

Attracted Notice While Answering Phones

Torres took that setback in stride, resolving instead to win a place on stage as quickly as she could. She landed a clerical job at New York's Lincoln Center, hoping to get noticed. A casting director for a Cole Porter musical asked her whether she could dance, and Torres (according to her Web site) replied, "Nope. But I move well." That comeback led to a role in a different musical, a Bridgeport, Connecticut, production of *Dreamgirls.* Back in New York, Torres appeared in a series of classic plays including the ancient Greek classic *Antigone* and Federico Garcia Lorca's Spanish tragedy *Blood Wedding,* the latter at the prestigious Public Theatre.

At a Glance . . .

Born on April 25, 1969 in New York, NY; raised in the Bronx; married Laurence Fishburne September 29, 2002. *Education:* Attended High School of Music and Art, New York.

Career: Actor, 1990s–.

Awards: American Latin Media Arts (ALMA) award for Outstanding Lead Actress in a Syndicated Drama Series, 2001.

Addresses: *Agent*—c/o Badgley Connor King, 9229 Sunset Blvd., Suite 311, Los Angeles, CA 90069.

Building on this solid foundation, Torres began to audition for television roles. She showed up in small parts–a different one each time–on the durable daytime soap opera *One Life to Live,* and in 1992 she broke into prime time with an appearance on the NBC show *Law & Order.* A part in the British Broadcasting Company mini-series *Unnatural Pursuits* followed, and then, in 1994, a more prominent appearance in the much-discussed pilot of *M.A.N.T.I.S.,* a science-fiction detective drama featuring future *Alias* star Carl Lumbly.

Torres returned to Broadway in *The Best Little Whorehouse Goes Public* and continued to seek out television parts. After a slow start, she scored recurring roles in 1997 and 1998 on the syndicated action series *Xena: Warrior Princess* and *Hercules.* The producers of those shows then cast Torres in the lead role of Hel, one of a trio of female fighters, in their futuristic action series *Cleopatra 2525.* The series lasted only one season, but Torres threw herself into the conditioning regime required by the highly physical part and got high marks for her performance. To Jefferson Graham of the *Chicago Sun-Times* she described the concept of the series as "three great-looking chicks keeping the world safe from evil."

Studied Martial Arts

The actress was conscious of the subtler effects of these entertainment vehicles. "There's a degree of responsibility to it, of course," Torres noted while discussing her *Xena* and *Cleopatra* roles with *Xena Magazine.* "I think that these characters can't help but be empowering to women because of their strengths and convic-

tions. In Cleo, for instance, it's a community supporting each other, watching each other's backs and pulling each other up when the time is right." Prior to taking on the *Cleopatra 2525* part, Torres took martial arts classes and sought out instruction in stunt fighting.

These roles raised Torres's profile among network casting personnel, and her parts became more substantial. On *Alias,* one of the most fashion forward of 2001's new shows, Torres played Russian intelligence agent Anna Espinosa, who emerged as an ongoing thorn in the side of series heroine Sydney Bristow (Jennifer Garner) and returned to the series in later subplots. In 2002, she had another one-season starring role in the *Firefly* series, helmed by hot producer Joss Whedon. *USA Today* named Torres one of "five prime-time faces to watch" that year. She was also cast in *The Matrix: Revolutions* and *The Matrix: Reloaded,* blockbuster sequels to the inventive science-fiction film *The Matrix.*

Married Laurence Fishburne

The big news in Torres's life that year, however, was personal: she married *Matrix* star Laurence Fishburne on September 29, 2002. Their relationship had begun long before *The Matrix,* however, getting underway with a few dates in 1995. One of those occurred during a blizzard, when the pair went to New York's Fort Tryon Park for a walk that turned into a snowball fight. After that, Torres told *InStyle,* "we sat on a bench, knee-deep in snow, overlooking the Hudson River. Laurence pulled out his harmonica and serenaded me. At that moment I knew he was a good candidate." The wedding at Fort Tryon Park was a lavish affair featuring a range of music from classical to Afro-Cuban jazz to "Dream a Little Dream of Me" by the Mamas and the Papas. "When Laurence is away on location, I sing that to him at night to tuck him in long distance," Torres told *InStyle.*

In 2003 Torres had a recurring role on *24* and was cast several times in Whedon's *Angel* series. The following year she had her first film starring role opposite comedienne Mo'Nique in the hair-styling comedy-drama *Hair Show.* In 2005, Torres's Anna Espinosa character was revived on *Alias,* and she had two new films, *Serenity* (another futuristic Western directed by Whedon) and *Fair Game,* ready to open. Several more projects were in the works. Torres broke into the popular animation genre with a voice part in the Cartoon Network series *Justice League.* And her role as a terrorist opposite Fishburne in the thriller *Five Fingers* promised to bring together her action-series experience with her natural chemistry with Fishburne. With solid training, good looks, and an instinct for fitting in to hot new entertainment genres, Gina Torres was definitely a star on the rise.

Selected works

Films

Bed of Roses, 1996.
The Substance of Fire, 1996.
The Matrix: Reloaded, 2002.
The Matrix: Revolutions, 2003.
Hair Show, 2004.
Serenity, 2005.

Plays

Dreamgirls (musical), Bridgeport, CT.
The Best Little Whorehouse Goes Public, Lunt-Fontanne Theatre, New York City, 1994.
Face Value, 1997.

Television

Law & Order, 1992 and 1995.
M.A.N.T.I.S. (pilot), 1994.
NYPD Blue, 1995.
Dark Angel (television movie), 1996.
Xena: Warrior Princess, 1997.
Hercules: The Legendary Journeys, 1997-99.
La Femme Nikita, 1998.
Cleopatra 2525, 2000.
Alias, 2001 and 2005.

Firefly, 2002.
Angel, 2003.
24, 2003.

Sources

Periodicals

Atlanta Journal-Constitution, October 15, 2004, p. H5.
Chicago Sun-Times, January 28, 2000, p. 18.
InStyle, February 2003, p. 256.
Jet, May 14, 2001, p. 45.
Knight Ridder Tribune News Service, December 8, 2003, p. 1.
USA Today, September 18, 2002, p. D1; February 23, 2005, p. D8.

On-line

"Biography," *Gina Torres,* www.gina-torres.com (March 13, 2005).
"Gina Torres," *All Movie Guide,* www.allmovie.com (March 13, 2005).
"Gina Torres Interviewed," *Xena Magazine #16,* www.xenaville.com/articles/titan_torres.html (March 13, 2005).

—James M. Manheim

Reggie Watts

1972(?)—

Vocalist, instrumentalist, comedian

The musical activities of Seattle, Washington's Reggie Watts are so diverse that they are difficult to classify. His lyrical and wide-ranging baritone voice has drawn comparisons with those of various classic soul stylists of the 1970s, most often Al Green. As lead singer of the Seattle band Maktub, Watts has partnered with musicians from the rock, hip-hop, and electronic fields, and he brings influences from his own classical and jazz backgrounds to bear on his musical creations. A performer with a tireless drive toward improvement, Watts has regularly participated in freeform musical improvisations, done comic revues and standup comedy, and been active as a dancer. All that seemed to hold him and his band back from mass success was the tendency of the music industry to pigeonhole artists for the benefit of format-driven radio programmers and retailers.

Watts was born in Germany around 1972, the son of a French mother and an African-American father who was an officer in the United States Air Force. He is a second cousin of the writer Alice Walker, and his full name was Reginald Lucien Frank Roger Watts. "My mother's French. It's a European thing to have three middle names," he explained to the *Seattle Times*. Watts began classical piano lessons at age five and also studied the violin for eight years, with the result that, as his friend Heather Duby told *Seattle Weekly*, he "can play circles around a lot of people." Watts benefited from strong parental involvement. "My mother supported every aspect of my creativity, ranging from

violin and piano lessons to after-school theater," he told the *Seattle Times*. Later, he and the rest of the members of Maktub would reflect on how unusual it was that all their parents remained married.

Staged Play in Elementary School

By the time he was in fourth grade, Watts and his family had moved to Great Falls, Montana. He wrote a play that was put on that year at Chief Joseph Elementary in Great Falls. The play had an anti-drug theme. "I wasn't anti-drug at all," he told the *Times*. "I just figured it was the best way to get them to let me put on a show." (He later said, however, that the strongest drug he had ever used was Robitussin cough syrup.) After winning several dramatic competitions in high school he and a friend lit out for New York City, where they auditioned for a play. The friend was hired, but Watts was not. After returning home, he took off in the other direction, attracted by Seattle's booming music scene. The year was 1990, and he was 18.

Watts quickly fell in with the city's vibrant musical community. He sang and played in upwards of 20 different bands in the early 1990s, ranging from jazz to rock and R&B to a cover band called Hit Explosion. He also performed in several dance and theater pieces. And he studied jazz singing at Seattle's Cornish College of the Arts. In 1996 he joined with bassist and electronics specialist Kevin Goldman and drummer Davis

Born Reginald Lucien Frank Roger Watts in 1972(?) in Germany; raised in Great Falls, MT; son of an Air Force officer father and a French mother. *Education:* Attended Cornish College of the Arts, Seattle, studying jazz vocals.

Career: Seattle, WA, dancer and band member of various dance productions and numerous bands in various genres, 1990–; Maktub, founder with Kevin Goldman and Davis Martin, 1996-1999; comedy and musical improvisation performer, 2000-01; re-formed Maktub with new members, 2001.

Selected awards: (With Maktub) Best R&B Album, Northwest Music Awards, 1999, for *Subtle Ways.*

Addresses: *Label*—c/o nonLinear Productions, 305 NW 42nd St, Seattle, WA 98107; *Group Web site*—http://www.maktub.com.

Martin to form Maktub (pronounced mock-TUBE); the name was an Arabic word, drawn from the novel *The Alchemist* by Paulo Coelho and meaning roughly "it is written." The band later took on keyboardist Alex Veley and began to build a strong following in Seattle clubs and on the progressive radio station KCMU. Watts's trademark 1970s-style Afro, once called the largest in the Northwest, provided Maktub with an instantly identifiable visual trademark.

Maktub spent several years honing the material for its debut album, *Subtle Ways,* which was released in 1999. The release garnered a Best R&B Album award at the Northwest Music Awards and won the band fans from as far afield as England after it was made available on the MP3.com Web site. With radio support and a strong local buzz, Maktub seemed to be headed for national exposure–but things didn't work out that way. "There was a period of time when we were getting called by every record label you can imagine, then it just kind of fell off," Watts told the *Seattle Times.*

Pioneered "Ambient Comedy"

The problem was that Maktub's music fit neither the mold of the neo-soul sound cultivated by vocalists such as D'Angelo nor the Seattle rock of Pearl Jam and its cohorts, although it bore traces of both. The band took an 18-month break as Veley departed for Brazil, while Watts kept busy with other bands and with improvisation sessions several times a week. Some of those sessions involved spoken-word elements. "It's some-

thing I call 'ambient comedy,'" Watts told the *Times.* "Three DJs [spinning] records, and me as the vocalist, telling stories—comedic things." He even headlined a comic revue called "A Very Reggie Xmas" in 2001.

Maktub re-formed in 2001 with keyboardist Daniel Spils and guitarist Thaddeus Turner. The following year they released their album *Khronos,* which featured Watts's reflections on the passage of time. "I want to see so many things in this world...I'm in hyperactive mode," he told the *Times.* Musically, the album dipped into classic soul and rock sounds, highlighting Watts's vocal versatility. Critics nationally began to raise the Al Green comparisons, but, noted the *Boston Globe*'s Renee Graham, "Watts can also coax his easy-like-Sunday-morning vocals into a full-throttle howl, as with Maktub's cover of Led Zeppelin's 'No Quarter.'"

Once again, audiences in the Northwest reacted enthusiastically to the album, and a run of 20,000 copies quickly sold out. Major labels again showed interest in the group, but Maktub elected to sign with the New York-based independent label Velour, and sales stalled out at 30,000 copies. Watts continued to gain critical raves, and the group was lumped in with other artists sometimes referred to collectively as the black fringe.

Pressured to Conform to Radio Formats

"I've had so many conversations with [industry] people about how Reggie needs to look like D'Angelo," lamented Maktub manager Dave Meinert, to the *Seattle Times.* "But Reggie is really more of a modern rock artist than he is an urban radio artist. What happens with black artists is that people don't necessarily judge them on what they're doing as artists, but they judge them on being black artists. It's gotten worse, with consolidation of the formats on the radio. Where would Prince get played on radio today?"

Undiscouraged, Watts released *Simplified,* a debut solo album of his own in 2003, on Seattle's small nonLinear label. The album merged soul with 1980s New Wave rock sounds and was called by *Seattle Times* reviewer Tom Scanlon "a very strong starting point for Watts's solo career." Maktub showed no sign of losing its strong ability to draw a crowd, and Watts added live onstage sampling to his instrumental repertoire.

Maktub returned to the studio to assemble its third album, *Say What You Mean,* which was due for release in the spring of 2005. The album was produced by Bob Power, who had helmed recordings by other unclassifiable bands like the international Los Angeles-based group Ozomatli. Watts headed for Europe in January of that year for a month-long tour as a standup comedian. "He's a true entertainer," Seattle DJ Rebecca "Misskick" West told the *Times.* "Always on the go."

Selected discography

Albums

(With Maktub) *Subtle Ways,* Jasiri Media Group, 1999.
(With Maktub) *Khronos,* Velour, 2002.
Simplified, nonLinear, 2003.
(With Maktub) *Say What You Mean,* Velour, 2005.

Sources

Periodicals

Boston Globe, April 22, 2003, p. E1; August 9, 2003, p. C5.
Oregonian (Portland), May 10, 2002, p. 38.

Seattle Times, April 15, 1999, p. G14; May 19, 2000, p. TK15; December 4, 2001, p. E8; April 19, 2002, p. H15; August 31, 2003, p. K4; February 15, 2004, p. G3; August 3, 2004, p. E1; December 19, 2004, p. RZ8.
Seattle Weekly, November 3, 1998.
Washington Post, August 1, 2003, p. T7; August 6, 2003, p. C5.

On-line

"Maktub," *Vermillion Media Group,* www.vermillion mediagroup.com/maktub (March 13, 2005).
"More Music at the Moore: Reggie Watts, MC," www.theparamount.com/education/mm-2003.asp (March 13, 2005).
"Reggie Watts: Simplified," *nonLinear Productions,* www.nonlinear.com (March 13, 2005).

—James M. Manheim

Elisabeth Welch

1908-2003

Singer

Elisabeth Welch enjoyed a long and esteemed career as a cabaret singer and London stage star over several decades of the mid-twentieth century. A New York City native, Welch had her earliest successes in the all-black musical revues on Broadway in the 1920s. After a hiatus of nearly fifty years, she returned to perform in her hometown in a 1980 jazz festival tribute to that earlier era. Later that decade, she had a one-woman show in New York, but retired to London once again, where she died in 2003 at the age of 99. "She belonged to an elite group of singers who gave definitive shape to the works of the Gershwins, Cole Porter, Jerome Kern, Noel Coward, and the other songwriters of the golden age," asserted the writer of her *Daily Telegraph* obituary. "Her style was poised, her voice mellow and dignified…. Her art was classic."

For many years, Welch gave her birthdate as February 27, 1908, but her brother later revealed she was actually born in 1904. She was born at home near 63rd St. and Amsterdam Avenue, in an area of Manhattan known as San Juan Hill at the time and later cleared to make way for the performing-arts landmark

Welch, Elisabeth, photograph. AP/Wide World Photos.

of Lincoln Center. Her mother, Elizabeth, was from Edinburgh, Scotland, and of mixed Scottish and Irish ancestry. Welch's father, John, was part African American and part Native American, with roots going back to the Lenape tribe in Delaware. Several years older than Welch's mother, John Welch worked as a gardener on an estate in Englewood, New Jersey, where he met his future wife when she came from Scotland to work as an aide to the family's nanny. The couple would have three children in all, with one of Welch's brothers also proving musically inclined and becoming a classical musician as an adult.

Though her mother often played records from such popular Scottish crooners of the day as Harry Lauder and Will Fyffe, Welch was also the daughter of a strict Baptist father, who disapproved even of her habit of whistling. He did have a taste for the musicals of Gilbert and Sullivan, and it was in a production of their classic *HMS Pinafore* that Welch made her stage debut at the age of eight. As a youngster, she attended Public School 69, and sang in the choir of St. Cyprian's Episcopal Church, where her booming notes earned

At a Glance . . .

Born Elisabeth Margaret Welch on February 27, 1904 (some sources say 1908), in New York, NY; died on July 15, 2003, in London, England; daughter of John Wesley (a gardener) and Elizabeth (Key) Welch; married Luke Smith (a musician), 1928 (divorced).

Career: Singer, 1922-03; Broadway cabaret performer, 1920s.

Awards: Obie Award, 1986, for *Time to Start Living.*

her the tag, "the loud alto." Her mixed-race heritage seemed to present few challenges for her during World War I-era New York City, and she later noted there were many other such families in her neighborhood. She attended Julia Richards High School and planned to become a social worker, but was cast in a 1921-22 musical titled *Liza,* with a score by Maceo Pinkard, who had a later hit with "Sweet Georgia Brown." In the show, which ran for five months, Welch debuted the Charleston—a massive dance craze later that decade-before New York audiences, but *Liza* closed in April of 1922 and the fad failed to catch on at the time.

Father Walked Out on Family

When Welch's father learned of her new job, he strenuously objected, especially when he realized that his wife had known of it and kept it from him. Using the nickname for their daughter, as well as the slang term for dancing on the stage, he reportedly exclaimed, "'Girlie's on the boards. She's lost!'" Welch's *Times* of London obituary reported, for a stage career was considered somewhat disreputable for a young woman of the era. Her father abandoned his family not long afterward. Welch held herself personally responsible for the loss, once telling an interviewer, "He associated show business with low life, and he thought I would become a whore," according to the *Daily Telegraph.* She made the financial support of her mother a priority for many years thereafter.

Liza was part of a new wave of black-oriented musicals to hit Broadway, spurred by the success of *Shuffle Along* in 1921, the creation of ragtime pianist Eubie Blake and a musical that featured Broadway's first all-black cast. Welch found work in another early black Broadway show, *Runnin' Wild,* as a chorus dancer in 1923, and this one also featured the Charleston dance. She was also tapped to sing the accompanying tune, "The Charleston," which she later dismissed as a throwaway composed merely to help popularize the

dance, which it did. She went on to appear in another Eubie Blake show, *Chocolate Dandies,* in 1924, alongside Josephine Baker.

Still in school for her social-worker's certification, Welch abandoned that plan altogether when she was cast in the revue *Blackbirds of 1928,* a tremendous success on Broadway and one in which she earned good reviews for her bit in a comedy sketch. The show went on to Paris in 1929, and Welch went with it. She stayed in the Montmartre section, the less-affluent artists' quarter of the city, and found singing jobs in nightclubs there. She returned to New York City in 1930 when she was invited to open a new nightclub, the Royal Box, as its headliner.

For her repertoire, Welch included a new song from sophisticated hit songwriter Cole Porter, "Love for Sale." The tune had been written for a Broadway revue, *The New Yorkers,* and its veiled reference to the world's oldest profession caused it to be banned from radio airplay for a number of years. Not surprisingly, *The New Yorkers* caused somewhat of a scandal when it opened on Broadway, for the young blonde actress who performed that song was dressed as a schoolgirl and sang it on a set built to resemble Park Avenue. The conservative newspaper columnists had a field day, and Porter was so miffed by the puritanical hysteria that he left the country. But the show's producers knew that Welch also sang the song in her nightclub routine, and offered her the chance to do double-duty and sing it in *The New Yorkers.* The stage props were changed to look like Harlem, with Welch dressed in a more soignée costume, and her performance regularly brought down the house during her run in the first months of 1931.

Moved to London

Porter invited Welch to England to appear in a London show, *Dark Doings,* which marked her London stage debut. In this one, she sang another showstopper, "Stormy Weather," from songwriter Harold Arlen, who would later pen "Somewhere over the Rainbow," the theme song to *The Wizard of Oz. Dark Doings* ran in London during the summer of 1933, during an unusual London heat wave that served to boost the haunting song's popularity. For Welch, Porter wrote the song "Solomon" specifically for her, and she sang it in his *Nymph Errant* onstage in a Turkish harem setting during the show's 1933 run. "It is a blackly humorous piece with a tortuously difficult line," noted Welch's *Daily Telegraph* obituary writer. "No one ever sang it better, and it was firmly associated with her for the rest of her life."

Welch's star continued to rise in London, and in 1934 she shared billing alongside scat singer Cab Calloway and his band in an engagement at the London Palladium. Another leading figure of the London musical stage was Ivan Novello, and he penned "Shanty Town" for Welch, which she sang in his new musical, *Glamorous Night,* in the spring of 1935. She also had a regular radio engagement by then as well, and began taking roles in British films, beginning with *Murder at Broadcasting House* in 1934. She also appeared with noted actor Paul Robeson in *Song of Freedom,* from 1937 and 1938's *Big Fella,* both of which were also British-made movies. She and Robeson "broke new ground for black actors, who hitherto had been cast for the most part as comic servants," noted her *Daily Telegraph* obituary, which had been done "to please distributors in the southern states who threatened to boycott anything featuring a black person in a non-servile role."

Welch went on to make a few more films in England, but was usually cast as the featured cabaret act. She stayed in England and entertained British troops during World War II on wartime-service missions with a roster of top British stars. After the war's end, she appeared in several more London stage musicals, scoring another hit with her interpretation of the Edith Piaf classic, "La Vie en Rose," in *Tuppence Colored* in 1947. Her star faded a bit as musical tastes changed in the 1950s and 1960s, but she had her first one-woman show, *A Marvelous Party,* in 1969, in which she reprised all her classics.

Still Brought Down the House

In her later years, Welch was debilitated by arthritis, but Broadway director and choreographer Bob Fosse cast her in his musical 1973 *Pippin* for its London premiere, and she took the one-song job just to earn enough money to pay for double hip-replacement surgery. She could barely walk at the time, but Fosse worked with her to get her on stage easily for her show-stopping number for this musical story of Charlemagne's son. The operation helped immensely, and Welch was able to return to the stage. Another noted director, Derek Jarman, cast her in his 1979 adaptation of the Shakespeare classic *The Tempest,* and as "the Goddess" she delivered yet another show-stopping moment, this one with her signature tune, "Stormy Weather" at the finale, surrounded by dancing sailors.

A year later, Welch finally returned to the American stage when she was invited to take part in the "Newport in New York" jazz festival in its tribute segment to black Broadway musicals of the 1920s. She had not performed before an American audience in 49 years at that point, but earned excellent reviews. Back in London, she had another one-woman show, and continued to appear in theaters and supper clubs; one night in 1985, she was mugged on a London street and assaulted to the point of unconsciousness, but still performed the next day. In early 1986, she returned to New York City again, this time to appear in the Broadway revue, *Jerome Kern Goes to Hollywood,* for which she earned her first Antoinette Perry (Tony) Award nomination. She stayed in town for another solo show, this one titled *Time to Start Living,* which also ran in 1986. Reviewing it for the *New York Times,* journalist Stephen Holden called her "a one-of-a-kind cultural hybrid. While her singing contains elements of the blues, her style is more that of an expatriate bohemian in the parlor tradition of Mabel Mercer." For that show she won an Obie Award, the honor for shows that are staged "off Broadway."

Welch's inimitable voice survives in a handful of recordings she made during the 1980s and 1990s, which include *Elisabeth Welch Sings Irving Berlin* and *Live in New York.* She lived in the same elegant flat she had moved into in the 1930s, near the London landmark of Harrod's department store, but spent her last four years in a west London retirement home. She died on July 15, 2003, at the age of 99. She once told an interviewer that her only regret was that her career seemed to have prevented her from becoming a mother. She was married just once, to a musician, when she was eighteen years old, but the union lasted less than a year. Her lengthy career, she once reflected, had occurred entirely by accident, not by design, nor ambition. "I've never made any effort to do anything," she joked with *New York Times* writer John S. Wilson in 1980. "It's disgraceful."

Selected works

Albums

Where Have You Been, DRG, 1986.
Elisabeth Welch Sings Irving Berlin, Verve, 1988.
This Thing Called Love, That's Entertainment!, 1989.
Elisabeth Welch Sings Jerome Kern, RCA, 1990.
Irving Berlin Songbook, That's Entertainment!, 1995.
Live in New York, That's Entertainment!, 1995.

Films

Murder at Broadcasting House, 1934.
Song of Freedom, 1937.
Big Fella, 1938.

Sources

Periodicals

Daily Telegraph (London, England), July 16, 2003, p. 1.
Independent (London, England), July 16, 2003, p. 16.
New York Times, May 16, 1980, p. C5; March 21, 1986, p. C5; July 18, 2003, p. C11.
Times (London, England), May 2, 1996, p. 21; December 17, 1987; July 16, 2003, p. 27.

On-line

"Elisabeth Welch," *Contemporary Musicians Online,*
http://galenet.galegroup.com/servlet/BioRC
(March 17, 2005).

—Carol Brennan

Kanye West

1977—

Rapper, producer

The double-platinum, triple-Grammy award success of Kanye West's debut album, *The College Dropout,* was a surprise to many in the industry, but not to West himself. The young rapper and producer had confidently touted the classic status of his work, shaped creatively during a harrowing period of recovery from an auto accident. Some charged him with arrogance, but West, as he put it in his autobiographical track "Last Call," used "arrogance as the steam to power my dreams." "I always say you have to be a little postal to push the envelope," he pointed out to Margena A. Christian of *Jet.* And push the envelope he did: *The College Dropout* was a brilliantly innovative 21-track production that diverged sharply from the gangster stereotypes of the hip-hop music of its day and, in its hit single "Jesus Walks," merged hip-hop and gospel musical languages in an entirely new way.

Born to Be a Star

Born June 8, 1977 in Atlanta, Kanye West (whose first name is Swahili and has been translated as "only one") was raised on Chicago's South Side. His father Ray

West, Kanye, photograph. Paul Hawthorne/Getty Images.

West was a former Black Panther who earned two master's degrees, becoming an award-winning photojournalist and later a counselor. West's paternal grandfather, West told Chris Campion of England's *Daily Telegraph* newspaper, was "the original hustler. He shined shoes and did whatever he had to do to send all his kids to college." His mother Donda West was an English professor at Chicago State University. A strong thread of activism ran through both sides of the family. West's parents divorced when he was three, but both remained involved in his upbringing. As a child, West often spent summers with his father in Maryland.

"I was really raised in the church, and raised as a good Black man," West told Kimberly Davis of *Ebony.* That said, his background was an unusually varied one; when he was ten, his mother landed a one-year teaching job in Nanjing, China, and West became proficient enough in the Chinese language to be an interpreter for his mother in restaurants. "I think that got me ready to be a celeb because, at that time, a lot of Chinese had never seen a black person," he told Campion. "They would come up and stare at me, rub my skin, fishbowl me." West became fascinated by hip-hop music at a young age, successfully badgered his mother into buying him a sophisticated electronic keyboard, and wrote his first raps by the time he was ten. His abilities first became apparent at school talent shows. "I would help the others because I just knew I was going to win anyway," West told Campion. "The teachers used to say, 'This ain't meant to be the Kanye West show.'"

Soon West had his eye on bigger and better things. "I thought I was going to get signed back when I was 13 years old," he explained to Associated Press writer Nekesa Mumbi Moody, "and come out with a record and take [youthful rap group] Kriss Kross out." These ambitions had to take a back seat to West's education for a while, though. He graduated from Chicago's Polaris High School, and, having shown skills as a visual artist as well as a verbal one, enrolled at Chicago's American Academy of Art on a scholarship. He then transferred to Chicago State, declaring an English major but spending most of his time, he told Campion, "in music class or in the lunch room talking to girls."

Made Misstep in Meeting at Columbia

An initial brush with the big time helped to divert West's interests away from higher education. The Columbia label made noises about offering him a recording contract, and he was shuttled to Columbia's offices in a limousine. But West mishandled his meeting with Columbia executive Michael Mauldin, claiming confidently that he would be bigger than superstar Michael Jackson or Atlanta producer and rapper Jermaine Dupri—not knowing at the time that Mauldin was Dupri's father. Whether or not it was because of that faux pas, West's promised contract did not materialize. But the experience only strengthened his determination.

West left Chicago State, becoming the college dropout later referred to in the title of his debut album. After *The College Dropout* became a hit, West took criticism from some who believed he was encouraging young African Americans to abandon their schooling. In response, he drew a distinction between high school and college. "I feel like high school is a necessity, but college is a choice…," he explained to Davis. "[Some people] have no idea what they're even going to college for, other than they believe that's what you're supposed to do." West backed up his commitment to education by forming the Kanye West Foundation, whose "Loop Dreams" initiative helped finance production equipment for school music programs.

Initially, it was West's production skills that helped him break into the music business. In 1997 he co-produced some cuts on rapper Mase's album *Harlem World;* Mase later returned the favor by making a guest appearance on a remix of "Jesus Walks." He notched other successes as a writer and producer in the late 1990s, but his music-business profile spiked sharply upward after he began working with rapper Jay-Z, one of the top hip-hop hitmakers of the day. He produced Jay-Z's "This Can't Be Life" and composed such Jay-Z cuts as "Izzo H.O.V.A.," "Encore," and "'03 Bonnie and Clyde." Soon West found himself in demand as a producer, working with rappers Twista and Ludacris and with R&B chanteuse and pianist Alicia Keys ("You Don't Know My Name").

West's production style was distinctive, and he succeeded in transferring it to his own music after being signed to entrepreneur Damon Dash's Roc-a-Fella label in 2002. He favored samples from classic soul and R&B pieces, with the vocals often sped up so that they turned into rhythmic high-pitched squeaks but were not distorted to a point where they were totally unrecognizable. This technique, the *All Music Guide* pointed out in its analysis of West's "peerless" beatmaking skills, was matched by "a likewise trademark stutter-step drum-programming touch—a simple yet potent combination." West's eclectic tastes brought him in contact with new sounds that showed up in his own music; he was known as a fan of the alternative rock band Franz Ferdinand.

Sampled Vandross Hit

A good example of West's characteristic sound was provided by his composition "Slow Jamz," based on a sample from the Luther Vandross hit "A House Is Not a Home" (originally composed by Burt Bacharach and Hal David) and first recorded in a version featuring fellow Chicago rapper Twista before West added new text on a single released at the beginning of 2004. Samples from the Vandross song are heard at various speeds, while West's rap likewise manipulates the listener's perception of time, accelerating to a blistering pace in one extended passage. On top of this virtuoso mastery of the ebb and flow of musical time, West delivers a rap that deftly satirizes the seduction clichés of urban contemporary music.

By the time "Slow Jamz" appeared, West had gone through a near-death experience: he fell asleep at the wheel of his Lexus after a late-night production session in October of 2002. He later recalled little of the episode except for intense pain and the sensation of the steering wheel hitting his face. His jaw was broken in three places, and he underwent reconstructive surgery. "Being that I was so close to dying, I realized that nothing in life is promised *except* death," West told Davis. "So, while I'm here, I have to make the most of it."

During his rehabilitation, West continued working on the album that became *The College Dropout*—not just thinking about it, but actually rapping through his wired jaw about his own predicament on "Through the Wire," a piece that cleverly samples a song by R&B vocal diva Chaka Khan called "Through the Fire." "Through the Wire" was also released at the beginning of 2004 and became a hit along with "Slow Jamz," setting the stage for the debut of the long-delayed but much-anticipated *The College Dropout*. West's skill as a producer was unquestioned, but whether he could put together an album's worth of original raps and concepts was in doubt.

Remixed Album to Foil Pirates

Any doubts were dispelled when advance tracks of the album leaked out. The hyperactive West stayed one step ahead of the pirates by remixing much of the album's contents and adding several tracks. What finally emerged in February of 2004 was a complex group of 21 pieces that touched on many different themes but completely avoided the violence of many of West's hip-hop contemporaries. Much of the album was marked by West's pointed sense of humor, rooted in everyday situations; "Workout Plan" satirized aerobics programs and their music, while "Spaceship" depicted the frustrations of a token black employee at a mall clothing store. "All Falls Down" took aim at materialism with its jab at a "single black female addicted to retail." New versions of "Slow Jamz" and "Through the Wire" were also included.

The most successful track from *The College Dropout* was "Jesus Walks," which West, clad in white, performed at the 2005 Grammy awards ceremony. Three separate videos of the song were aired. Religiously oriented hip-hop had been attempted almost since the genre's beginnings, but "Jesus Walks," with its serious marching-band rhythms and rhythmically complex gospel vocal-group backing, sounded completely new. The song referred to police abuse and included a long passage in which West listed "hustlers, killers, murder-ers, drug dealers, even the strippers" and had his backing vocal group affirm that "Jesus walks for them." *Ebony*'s Davis praised West for his "amalgamation of the street hustler's credo and the Black Protestant ethos." With his mother Donda serving as his manager (and experiencing what she described to Christian as "a huge learning curve" in moving from her professorial duties to the music industry), West went on tour with R&B superstar Usher.

West's frequent assertions of the value of his work ("It's something completely different.... It's definitely a classic," he told Moody) gained support when he garnered ten 2004 Grammy nominations, eight of them for *The College Dropout* and two for his work on the album *The Diary of Alicia Keys*. He won three (for best rap album, best rap song for "Jesus Walks," and best R&B song for Keys's "You Don't Know My Name"), losing the best new artist award to rock group Maroon 5—who seemed surprised to win and praised West from the podium as they accepted the award. Sales of *The College Dropout,* even in a depressed music market, rose toward the three-million mark.

By early 2005, Kanye West was riding high. He had founded his own record label, G.O.O.D. (Getting Out Our Dreams), and it had already delivered a major hit album, balladeer John Legend's *Get Lifted.* He was preparing to launch a line of sneakers, and his preppy look, which he himself compared to that of the character Carlton on the television series *The Fresh Prince of Bel-Air,* seemed to offer potential big dividends in its total divergence from the bling-bling trends of the day. Unattached after several years in a committed relationship, he inspired speculation about his romantic future. The only question mark was his sophomore CD, *Late Registration,* whose release date was pushed back several times and was finally slated for the summer of 2005. At first West seemed daunted by the idea of following up what was widely considered a hip-hop masterpiece, but by 2005 he had warmed to the task. "The best thing [about success] is being able to get my creative ideas out," he told Davis. "That's why I rap in the first place–so my voice can be heard."

Selected discography

The College Dropout, Roc-a-Fella, 2004.

Sources

Periodicals

Associated Press, August 4, 2004.
Daily Telegraph (London, England), September 11, 2004, Arts section, p. 8.
Ebony, June 2004, p. 90; April 2005, p. 156.
Jet, January 31, 2005, p. 54.
London Free Press (London, ON, Canada), February 14, 2005, p. D1.

On-line

Kanye West, www.kanyewest.com (May 18, 2005).
"Kanye West," *All Music Guide,* http://www.allmusic.
  com (May 7, 2005).
"Kanye West," *AskMen,* www.askmen.com/men/en
  tertainment_150/155_kanye_west.html   (May   7,
  2005).

Other

"Rising Career of Kanye West," *Day to Day,* National
  Public Radio (transcript), December 7, 2004.

—James M. Manheim

Josh White, Jr.

1940—

Blues vocalist, guitarist, actor

The son of one of the most famous performers the blues tradition ever produced, Josh White Jr. has patterned his music after his father's and has devoted part of his musical life to carrying on his father's legacy. Yet he has never been simply a Josh White imitator. He has used various media to communicate his message, appearing on television, in films, in clubs, and on stage, making recordings, and very often appearing at schools and local festivals. In all these situations, White's aim has been not to replicate his father's music but rather to explore his unique approach to the blues.

White, Josh Jr., photograph. John Fraser/Toronto Winterfolk III. Reproduced by permission.

Josh White Sr. was born in 1915 and grew up like many of the other Southern pioneers of the blues. He played blues guitar himself, but he also served as a guide for several famous blind blues musicians, including Blind Lemon Jefferson. Recuperating from a hand injury, he learned to sing and act, and in the 1930s he became one of the first musicians to take the blues north and east to an urban and racially integrated audience. He popularized such American standards as "House of the Rising Sun," and, appearing at the White House before President Franklin Roosevelt and his wife Eleanor, he used his music to speak out against racial discrimination when few other black musicians were doing so. It was into this milieu that Josh White Jr. was born on November 30, 1940, in New York.

Made Debut at Age Four

The youngster was immediately initiated into the performing world, taking the stage with his father at New York's Café Society nightclub in a miniature version of his father's onstage wardrobe. He was four years old. "I just went along with the program," White told the Allentown, Pennsylvania, *Morning Call.* "It was just the thing to do, to wear the suits and put my foot up on the stool like he did—people thought it was cute." For five years, this father-and-son show toured theaters around the northeast. By the time nine-year-old Josh Jr. won a role in a Broadway play called *How Long til Summer?,* he was a seasoned theatrical veteran. He won a special Tony award for Best Child Actor in 1949.

Attending the Professional Children's School in New York, White continued his theatrical career. He appeared in a half-dozen different plays between 1949

At a Glance . . .

Born on November 30, 1940, in New York City; son of Joshua Daniel White, a blues singer, and Carol Carr White; married Jackie Harris, 1963 (died 1971); married Sara, 1978; children: Joshua III, Jason. *Education:* Attended Professional Children's School, New York.

Career: Broadway and television actor, 1950s–; recording artist, 1956–; folk performer, 1960s–.

Selected awards: U.S. government, "Voice of the Peace Corps" and "Voice of VISTA," 1980; Michigan Man of the Year, 1984; National Association of Campus Activities, Harry Chapin Humanitarian Award, first recipient, 1984; honorary doctoral degrees, University of Maine, University of West Florida.

Addresses: *Agent*—Music Tree Artist Management, 1414 Pennsylvania Ave., Pittsburgh, PA 19233-1419. *Web*—www.joshwhitejr.com.

and 1960 and added more than 50 television guest-star slots to his resume during that period. His recording career began with the *See Saw* album on the Decca label in 1956.

By the early 1960s, White's child-star novelty had begun to wear off, and the general lack of opportunity for African-American actors was staring him in the face. At the same time, however, the 1960s boom in folk music was getting underway with huge outdoor festivals at which surviving members of the early Southern blues scene were invited to perform. White began to focus more on music. He recorded albums for the major Mercury and United Artists labels in the 1960s, mixing blues with pop fare. "I am so fortunate to have the sort of apprenticeship that I did," he told the *Lincoln Journal Star.* "I learned from [my father] what it is to be a good solo performer. When you're a solo performer, it's all on you." Unlike other show-business families, father and son remained close until the death of Josh White Sr. in 1969.

Became Known for Campus Appearances

White lived in New York with his first wife, Jackie, in the 1960s. They had two children, Joshua "Buddah" White III, born in 1963, and Jason, born six years later (neither became a musician). White performed in major concert venues, but after the death of his wife in 1971

he cut back on touring. He continued to appear at college and university events, however, topping more than 2,000 campus concert bills between 1963 and the early 1980s. In many ways, Josh White Jr. was the African-American voice of the campus folk-music revival.

Moving to Detroit in 1976, White remarried two years later; he and his wife Sara would eventually preside over a combined total of 13 grandchildren. He continued to record, and he became a staple of the late-night television talk show circuit. In 1979 he starred in the first of several Public Broadcasting System concert specials, "Ramblin' with Josh White Jr." He sometimes toured with 1960s folk icon Tom Paxton, appearing with him and blues singer Odetta in the *Soundstage: Just Folks* PBS special in 1980.

In the early 1980s, White became interested in exploring his father's career artistically. Although the senior White had been one of the best-known blues musicians in the country in the 1930s, his fame had declined somewhat as white rock and roll listeners became interested in hard-core country blues musicians who had spent their entire lives in the rural South. White decided to return to the theatrical stage, this time as both performer and author. He and his friend Mayon Weeks warmed up with a small show called *One for Me, One for You,* and in 1983 he teamed up with another friend, Peter Link, to create the one-man show *Josh: The Man and His Music,* which dramatized his father's career and revived some of his best-known songs and performances.

Highlighted Father's Civil Rights Role

That show proved a roaring success, and White revived it in national tours every few years after its creation. The senior White, he told the Allentown *Morning Call,* was "someone our whole country should know about." He stressed his father's pioneering role in the struggle for racial equality. "Very few black performers in the '30s and '40s spoke about racial injustice for fear of reprisal," he told the Peoria, Illinois, *Journal Star.* "My dad and [actor] Paul Robeson, they both felt, 'If not us, who? If not now, when?'"

By the late 1990s, his efforts to ensure the recognition of his father's legacy bore fruit as the United States Postal Service included Josh White Sr. along with Leadbelly, Woody Guthrie, and Sonny Terry in a stamp series honoring folk and blues pioneers. In 2000, blues author and musician Elijah Wald wrote a biography of the elder White, entitled *Josh White: Society Blues.* White and Wald toured together to promote the book's release.

Yet White continued to maintain an independent musical identity. His concerts included a variety of material ranging on occasion from Frank Sinatra's romantic ballad "One for My Baby" to the Garth Brooks country anthem "We Shall Be Free." He began writing songs for what his Web site terms "single-digit people" and developed a flourishing career giving concerts for children in the 1990s and early 2000s. His concerts for all ages reflected the idealistic values of the folk revival that had nurtured his music in the 1960s, and he told the *Columbus Dispatch* that he performed "songs that help people take pride in themselves." In 2002 he became the first artist asked and allowed to sing at the Ground Zero site that commemorated the terrorist attacks of September 11, 2001 in his hometown of New York.

Selected discography

Albums

See Saw, Decca, 1956.
Do You Close Your Eyes, Mercury, 1962.
(with Beverly White) *Good & Drunk & Goozey,* Sonnet, 1963.
I'm on My Own Way, Mercury, 1964.
The Josh White Jr. Album, United Artists, 1967.
One Step Further, United Artists, 1968.
Josh White Jr., Vanguard, 1978.
Delia's Gone, FFMM, 1983.
Jazz, Ballads & Blues, Rykodisc, 1986.

In Tribute to Josh White: House of the Rising Son, Silverwolf, 1999.
Cortelia Clark, Silverwolf, 2000.
Live, Silverwolf, 2003.

Other

The Guitar of Josh White (instructional video), 1998.
It Starts with a Book...AND YOU (instructional video for children), Vince Deur Productions.

Sources

Periodicals

Boston Herald, November 18, 2000, p. 25.
Columbus Dispatch, February 27, 1992, p. 11.
Journal Star (Peoria, IL), February 23, 2001, p. B6.
Lincoln (NE) *Journal Star,* October 3, 2003, p. 17.
Morning Call (Allentown, PA), June 19, 1987, p. D1.
Reader (Chicago, IL), February 16, 2001, p. S3.
Washington Post, April 18, 1982, p. H3.

On-line

"Josh White Jr.," *All Music Guide,* www.allmusic.com (March 13, 2005).
"Josh White Jr.: Biography," *Josh White Jr.,* www.joshwhitejr.com/bio.html (March 13, 2005).

—James M. Manheim

Jacqueline Woods

1962—

Corporate executive

Woods, Jacqueline, photograph. AP/Wide World Photos.

As vice president for global marketing and pricing at software giant Oracle, Jacqueline Woods has been responsible for guiding the company through a rapidly changing market for database sales and licensing. Database licensing is considered by IT industry executives to be one of the most complex and challenging areas because it involves responding to changes in the way companies hire staff, and to technological advances, both of which undermine previous licensing policies and affect the software provider's bottom line. Woods arrived at Oracle from Ameritech where she was a director of product management overseeing a $600 million portfolio. In 2002 she was named by *Fortune* magazine as one of the top 50 most powerful black executives.

Jacqueline Woods holds a bachelor's degree from the University of California, Davis, and an M.B.A. from the University of Southern California, where she focused on marketing and venture management. After graduation she worked in the marketing division of GTE, the telecommunications company that merged with Bell Atlantic to form Verizon Communications. Her interest in sales and marketing strategies emerged at GTE where she held responsibility for managing some of the

company's largest accounts. Woods moved to Ameritech where she developed and implemented pricing and licensing strategies for the company's customer premise equipment business. She joined Oracle at director level in the worldwide strategic marketing division and later became a senior director.

Woods became vice president for global marketing and pricing at Oracle just at a time when licensing issues were becoming a hot topic in the IT business. In 2002 outsourcing was beginning to make licenses based on the number of "seats" in a company much more difficult to manage, while new multi-core processing chips meant that licenses based on the number of processors owned by a company also changed. On the latter topic Woods made it quite clear that, for example, dual core chips would be regarded as two central processing units (CPUs) for licensing purposes. Under Woods's direction in January 2004 Oracle responded to the problem of outsourcing by introducing user-based licensing alongside its per-processor licensing. This enabled the company to charge per named user (rather than per computer terminal), or per processor where the number of users was not easy to calculate. It is believed that by 2010 this "subscription-based" model will be adopted across the industry. Woods has strongly rejected the licensing model in which users pay only when they are using the software, known as a "lights on-lights off" model, on the basis that it elevates costs.

Oracle Corporation's business was in decline from the late 1990s and by 2002 radical changes were required to ensure the company's survival. As part of her strategy Woods oversaw a revision in the way Oracle applied its pricing, including the production of a 40-page guide that marked a shift away from the piece-meal approach to deal making typical of the industry. But while such a document might have been seen as an inflexible rule book, Woods understood that existing customers would not want to suffer an increase in cost simply because Oracle had established a new policy. In particular many feared that along with IBM, Oracle was exploiting the new multi-core processors to increase the number of licenses they could sell. When existing customers complained about rising costs and accused the company of profiteering Woods responded by grandfathering their license deals; she allowed their existing deals to run their course under the old structures.

Further evidence of Woods' flexibility and pragmatism can be found in her attitude to licensing infringements. Oracle claims 200,000 mostly corporate customers around the world but is able to audit only 300-400 companies per year. This means that many of Oracle's customers are using Oracle databases on systems for which they are not licensed. Rather than cracking down on licensing violations, Woods is realistic about how and why corporate customers use unlicensed software, understanding that the majority do so because business needs change faster than license deals. She told *Linux-world*: "Some have been inadvertent users of software, some are cheaters. You can't do anything about people who cheat because those are people who cheat and we're not going to sniff those people out." Woods's answer to the problem of businesses being out of compliance with their software licenses is to simplify the licensing in the first place. Her aim is to make sure companies have systems in place for monitoring and updating their software licenses, but she has told several interviewers that "switching off" the software used by non-compliant companies is not part of her plan. Allowing a proportion of customers to run unlicensed software has long been used by software companies to maintain and extend market share.

Woods's revisions to Oracle's licensing strategy since 2002 have sometimes been controversial, but she has shown clear vision and a willingness to defend her position in the face of an industry under heavy pressure to cut costs. In 2005 Oracle's position in the market was being challenged on several fronts, but the company remains a significant force and Woods holds an influential position within it. She is arguably even more influential than in 2002 when she was named one of *Fortune* magazine's top 50 most powerful black executives.

Sources

Periodicals

Associated Press, August 29, 2002.
Fortune, July 22, 2002.

On-line

"Q&A: Oracle VP on Asset Management and Vendor Consolidation," *Computerworld*, www.computer world.com/printthis/2003/0%2C4814%2C83 514 %2C00.html (March 7, 2005).
"Jacqueline Woods," *Oracle Corporation*, www.ora cle.com/corporate/pressroom/html/jwoods.html (March 7, 2005).
"Interview with Jacqueline Woods," *Oracle Corporation*, www.oracle.com/corporate/pressroom/j woods_multicore.html (March 7, 2005).
"Software Licensing Issues Debated," *Linuxworld. com Australia*, www.linuxworld.com.au/index.php? id=1366175332 (March 7, 2005).
"An Answer to the Software Licensing Maze," *ZDNet Australia*, www.zdnet.com.au/insight/toolkit/itman agement/asset/0,39023878,39143580,00.htm (March 7, 2005).

—Chris Routledge

Bruce McMarion Wright

1918-2005

New York State Supreme Court justice, writer

"Black judges in this country are a very lonely caucus," New York State Supreme Court justice Bruce Mc-Marion Wright told Les Payne in a 1991 interview for *Essence*. A highly controversial figure dubbed "Turn-Em-Loose Bruce" during his career on the bench of New York City's criminal court, Wright devoted his life to delineating the two systems of justice he believed existed in the United States—one for the white and privileged, and another for people of color and the poor. His best-selling book *Black Robes, White Justice* addresses this issue. Payne described Wright—who was also a poet and decorated war veteran—as "both praised and damned as a keen analyzer of judicial practices, especially as they touch the lives of African-Americans who come before the bar."

Wright was born December 19, 1918, in Princeton, New Jersey. A bright student, he entered Virginia State University in 1936. But when he devised a pun that read "Religion Weak," instead of "Religion Week," for a headline in the school newspaper—the editorial adjustment an early indication of his maverick nature—Wright was expelled from school. He applied to Princeton University, from which he won a scholarship in 1939. But, according to Wright, he was discouraged from attending by a note from the dean of admissions. Wright says the note acknowledged that the school did not practice any form of discrimination but stipulated that Wright might feel uncomfortable at Princeton, where there were no black students.

Eventually enrolled at Lincoln University, Wright chose to become a doctor. He was unable, however, to make an incision on an anesthetized rabbit during a premedical course and thus decided to study law. He graduated from college in 1942 and promptly entered the U.S. Army. Serving as a private in the 26th infantry regiment, Wright was awarded several medals for valor in World War II, including the Purple Heart with Oak Leaf Cluster and Bronze Star with Oak Leaf Cluster. He left the service in 1946. According to Wright, he met poet and future first president of Senegal Leopold Senghor while AWOL from the army in Paris in the months following World War II. "I was introduced to him as an American poet," Wright recounted to Payne; Wright's book of poems *From the Shaken Tower* had been edited by acclaimed African-American writer Langston Hughes and published in 1944. Wright told Payne: "All I ever wanted to be in life was a poet."

Upon his return to the United States in 1946, Wright enrolled at New York University to continue his law studies. For four years he worked during the day and took courses at night. During his last year of law school, Wright accepted a legal clerkship at the prestigious New York City law firm Proskauer, Rose, Goetz & Mendelsohn. When Wright passed the bar examination in 1950, he consulted the managing partner about his future with the company. According to Wright, he was apologetically dissuaded from considering further prospects with the firm. Wright went on to work in estates, appeals, and some civil rights cases at several black law firms in the years that followed. In 1967 he began working for New York City's Human Resources Administration.

At a Glance . . .

Born on December 19, 1918, in Princeton, NJ; died on March 24, 2005, in Old Saybrook, CT; son of Bruce Alleyne Summers (a baker) and A. Louise (Thigpen) Wright; married Elizabeth Davidson (sixth marriage); children: Geoffrey D. S., Keith L. T., Alexis, Bruce C. T., Patrick, Tiffany. *Education*: Lincoln University, BA, 1942; New York University Law School, LLB, 1950.

Career: Judge, author, and poet. Proskauer, Rose, Goetz & Mendelsohn (law firm), New York City, clerk, c. 1950; Human Resources Administration, New York City, general counsel, 1967-1970; New York City criminal court judge, 1970-1974 and 1978-1979, civil court judge, 1974-1978 and 1980-1982; Supreme Court of New York, justice, 1983-94. Cofounder, National Conference of Black Lawyers.

Memberships: Fortune Society, advisory board member; Urban League of Greater New York, member of the board, 1952-56; Inner City Round Table for Youth, member of the board, 1976.

Awards: Purple Heart with Oak Leaf Cluster, Bronze Star with Oak Leaf Cluster, Conspicuous Service Cross, all from World War II; honorary LL.D., Lincoln University, 1973; named judge of the year, National Bar Association, 1975.

Wright was appointed to New York City's criminal court in 1970 by then-Mayor John V. Lindsay. In that post, Wright was markedly outspoken on civil rights issues. And in numerous public speeches, he defended his belief that bail should not be a means of detaining the accused until trial, but a way to ensure the accused's appearance in court. His position was unpopular with the New York City police department; when in the early 1970s Wright set bail at $5,000 for a man accused of shooting a policeman, a former head of the Patrolman's Benevolent Association called Wright one of the best friends criminals ever had. Wright stated in *People*: "The Eighth Amendment says bail should not be excessive. So what is excessive? If you come into my court and you have one penny, and my bail is two cents, that's excessive…. If [the accused] has roots in the community, there is no high bail…. Their families and friends live in the community, and they stay for that reason."

Wright's position brought consequences and he was reassigned to civil court in 1974. But by 1978 he was reinstated to the criminal courtroom. Investigated by the New York City Appellate Division's Judiciary Relations Committee several times, allegations of misconduct over the years failed to deter him. Little official censure had actually taken place, though in 1975 Wright was admonished for treating a policeman too roughly for having drawn his gun on a man accused of a traffic violation. In fact, studies by the New York Bar Association revealed that Wright's low bail pronouncements resulted in no fewer appearances of defendants in court than had the higher bails posted by his fellow judges. "Despite the fact that I'm known as a bleeding heart," Wright told *People*, "I look with horror on burglaries, assaults, and the like. I've been burglarized seven times myself. One day I came home and the entire wall was broken down—it looked like a bomb had hit the place."

Wright was appointed to the New York State Supreme Court in 1983. Four years later he penned his book *Black Robes, White Justice. New York Review of Books* contributor Andrew Hacker was critical of Wright's premise, stating: "Wright does not explain just how he came to conclude that resentment against white society accounts for blacks' crimes against whites; and he wholly ignores crimes committed within black communities." Wright stated in his book, as reported by Hacker, that "black defendants often [receive] much harsher sentences than whites convicted of identical crimes." Though Hacker saw truth in Wright's contention, admitting, "There is such a double standard," he found fault with the justice for merely relying on his observations while on the bench and not presenting statistical evidence to support his claim. Despite this critic's challenge, *Black Robes, White Justice* became a best-seller.

Appraising the American judicial system, Wright disclosed in *Essence*, "We have to change the thinking of white America. In my view, Black Americans have been heroic in trying to civilize white Americans. And we've tried to do it with their own Constitution, and its amendments…. We've tried to explain to white people the true meaning of the Constitution." Wright spent his career trying to do just that, standing up to critics and other opponents his entire career. John Sheehan, who worked as a clerk for Wright during the 1970s, admired Wright's ability to weather his critics' complaints. Sheehan told the *Daily Princetonian* that Wright received hate mail daily "from police offices, from other people who disliked him…. This went on every day for all of the two years I worked for him and probably continued until he retired." Attorney Robert Van Lierop related in the *Amsterdam News* that "For him to challenge the system and to uphold the Constitution was very courageous."

Wright retired from his 25-year judicial career on the State Supreme Court in 1994. His health failed him in

2000, when he suffered a heart attack. At the age of 86, he died in his sleep on March 24, 2005. Sheehan remembered his friend to the *Daily Princetonian* as "a giant" who was "not given enough credit for the work that he did in his community and for being the symbol that he was." Former New York Mayor David Dinkins recalled Wright to the *Amsterdam News* as "one of my heroes, a legal scholar, and probably a genius," adding: "He will be sorely missed."

Selected writings

Books

From the Shaken Tower (poetry), edited by Langston Hughes, [England], 1944.
(With Hughes and others) *Lincoln University Poets* (poetry anthology), 1954.
Repetitions (poetry), 1980.
Black Robes, White Justice, Lyle Stuart, 1987.

Sources

Periodicals

Amsterdam News, March 31, 2005.
Essence, November 1981; November 1991.
New York Review of Books, March 3, 1988.
New York Times, March 26, 2005.
New York Times Biographical Service, April 1979.
People, April 17, 1978.

On-line

"Activist Judge Wright Dies," *Daily Princetonian,* www.dailyprincetonian.com/archives/2005/03/28 /news/12456.shtml (June 6, 2005).

—Marjorie Burgess and Sara Pendergast

Cumulative Nationality Index

*Volume numbers appear in **bold***

American

Aaliyah **30**
Aaron, Hank **5**
Abbott, Robert Sengstacke **27**
Abdul-Jabbar, Kareem **8**
Abdur-Rahim, Shareef **28**
Abernathy, Ralph David **1**
Abu-Jamal, Mumia **15**
Ace, Johnny **36**
Adams Earley, Charity **13, 34**
Adams, Eula L. **39**
Adams, Floyd, Jr. **12**
Adams, Johnny **39**
Adams, Leslie **39**
Adams, Oleta **18**
Adams, Osceola Macarthy **31**
Adams, Sheila J. **25**
Adams, Yolanda **17**
Adams-Ender, Clara **40**
Adderley, Julian "Cannonball" **30**
Adderley, Nat **29**
Adkins, Rod **41**
Adkins, Rutherford H. **21**
Agyeman, Jaramogi Abebe **10**
Ailey, Alvin **8**
Al-Amin, Jamil Abdullah **6**
Albright, Gerald **23**
Alert, Kool DJ Red **33**
Alexander, Archie Alphonso **14**
Alexander, Clifford **26**
Alexander, Joyce London **18**
Alexander, Khandi **43**
Alexander, Margaret Walker **22**
Alexander, Sadie Tanner Mossell **22**
Ali, Hana Yasmeen **52**
Ali, Laila **27**
Ali, Muhammad **2, 16, 52**
Allain, Stephanie **49**
Allen, Byron **3, 24**
Allen, Debbie **13, 42**
Allen, Ethel D. **13**
Allen, Marcus **20**
Allen, Robert L. **38**
Allen, Samuel W. **38**
Allen, Tina **22**
Alston, Charles **33**
Amerie **52**
Ames, Wilmer **27**
Amos, John **8**
Amos, Wally **9**
Anderson, Anthony **51**
Anderson, Carl **48**
Anderson, Charles Edward **37**

Anderson, Eddie "Rochester" **30**
Anderson, Elmer **25**
Anderson, Jamal **22**
Anderson, Marian **2, 33**
Anderson, Michael P. **40**
Anderson, Norman B. **45**
Andrews, Benny **22**
Andrews, Bert **13**
Andrews, Raymond **4**
Angelou, Maya **1, 15**
Ansa, Tina McElroy **14**
Anthony, Carmelo **46**
Anthony, Wendell **25**
Archer, Dennis **7, 36**
Archie-Hudson, Marguerite **44**
Arkadie, Kevin **17**
Armstrong, Louis **2**
Armstrong, Robb **15**
Armstrong, Vanessa Bell **24**
Arnwine, Barbara **28**
Arrington, Richard **24**
Arroyo, Martina **30**
Artest, Ron **52**
Asante, Molefi Kete **3**
Ashanti **37**
Ashe, Arthur **1, 18**
Ashford, Emmett **22**
Ashford, Nickolas **21**
Ashley-Ward, Amelia **23**
Atkins, Cholly **40**
Atkins, Erica **34**
Atkins, Juan **50**
Atkins, Russell **45**
Atkins, Tina **34**
Aubert, Alvin **41**
Auguste, Donna **29**
Austin, Junius C. **44**
Austin, Lovie **40**
Austin, Patti **24**
Avant, Clarence **19**
Ayers, Roy **16**
Babatunde, Obba **35**
Bacon-Bercey, June **38**
Badu, Erykah **22**
Bailey, Buster **38**
Bailey, Clyde **45**
Bailey, DeFord **33**
Bailey, Radcliffe **19**
Bailey, Xenobia **11**
Baines, Harold **32**
Baiocchi, Regina Harris **41**
Baisden, Michael **25**
Baker, Anita **21, 48**
Baker, Augusta **38**

Baker, Dusty **8, 43**
Baker, Ella **5**
Baker, Gwendolyn Calvert **9**
Baker, Houston A., Jr. **6**
Baker, Josephine **3**
Baker, LaVern **26**
Baker, Maxine B. **28**
Baker, Thurbert **22**
Baldwin, James **1**
Ballance, Frank W. **41**
Ballard, Allen Butler, Jr. **40**
Ballard, Hank **41**
Bambaataa, Afrika **34**
Bambara, Toni Cade **10**
Bandele, Asha **36**
Banks, Ernie **33**
Banks, Jeffrey **17**
Banks, Tyra **11, 50**
Banks, William **11**
Baraka, Amiri **1, 38**
Barber, Ronde **41**
Barboza, Anthony **10**
Barclay, Paris **37**
Barden, Don H. **9, 20**
Barker, Danny **32**
Barkley, Charles **5**
Barlow, Roosevelt **49**
Barnes, Roosevelt "Booba" **33**
Barnett, Amy Du Bois **46**
Barnett, Marguerite **46**
Barney, Lem **26**
Barnhill, David **30**
Barrax, Gerald William **45**
Barrett, Andrew C. **12**
Barrett, Jacquelyn **28**
Barry, Marion S(hepilov, Jr.) **7, 44**
Barthe, Richmond **15**
Basie, Count **23**
Basquiat, Jean-Michel **5**
Bass, Charlotta Spears **40**
Bassett, Angela **6, 23**
Bates, Daisy **13**
Bates, Karen Grigsby **40**
Bates, Peg Leg **14**
Bath, Patricia E. **37**
Baugh, David **23**
Baylor, Don **6**
Baylor, Helen **36**
Beach, Michael **26**
Beal, Bernard B. **46**
Beals, Jennifer **12**
Beals, Melba Patillo **15**
Bearden, Romare **2, 50**
Beasley, Jamar **29**

Beasley, Phoebe **34**
Beatty, Talley **35**
Bechet, Sidney **18**
Beckford, Tyson **11**
Beckham, Barry **41**
Belafonte, Harry **4**
Bell, Derrick **6**
Bell, James "Cool Papa" **36**
Bell, James A. **50**
Bell, James Madison **40**
Bell, Michael **40**
Bell, Robert Mack **22**
Bellamy, Bill **12**
Belle, Albert **10**
Belle, Regina **1, 51**
Belton, Sharon Sayles **9, 16**
Benét, Eric **28**
Ben-Israel, Ben Ami **11**
Benjamin, Andre **45**
Benjamin, Regina **20**
Bennett, George Harold "Hal" **45**
Bennett, Lerone, Jr. **5**
Benson, Angela **34**
Berry, Bertice **8**
Berry, Chuck **29**
Berry, Fred "Rerun" **48**
Berry, Halle **4, 19**
Berry, Mary Frances **7**
Berry, Theodore **31**
Berrysmith, Don Reginald **49**
Bethune, Mary McLeod **4**
Betsch, MaVynee **28**
Beverly, Frankie **25**
Bibb, Eric **49**
Bickerstaff, Bernie **21**
Biggers, John **20, 33**
Bing, Dave **3**
Bishop, Sanford D. Jr. **24**
Black, Albert **51**
Black, Barry C. **47**
Black, Keith Lanier **18**
Blackburn, Robert **28**
Blackshear, Leonard **52**
Blackwell Sr., Robert D. **52**
Blackwell, Unita **17**
Blair, Jayson **50**
Blair, Paul **36**
Blake, Asha **26**
Blake, Eubie **29**
Blake, James **43**
Blakey, Art **37**
Blanchard, Terence **43**
Bland, Bobby "Blue" **36**
Bland, Eleanor Taylor **39**

185

Cumulative Occupation Index

Volume numbers appear in **bold**

Cumulative Subject Index

Volume numbers appear in **bold**

Cumulative Name Index

Volume numbers appear in **bold**